Fire

upon the

Earth

BISHOP MICHAEL ANTHONY FLEMING, O.S.F.

Vicar Apostolic of Newfoundland 1830-1847
Bishop of Newfoundland 1847-1850

Fire

upon the

Earth

The Life and Times of
Bishop Michael Anthony Fleming, O.S.F.

by

Brother J.B. Darcy C.F.C.

St. John's, Newfoundland and Labrador
2003

Le Conseil des Arts | The Canada Council
du Canada | for the Arts

We acknowledge the support of The Canada Council for the Arts for our
publishing program.

We acknowledge the financial support of the Government of Canada through the
Book Publishing Industry Development Program (BPIDP) for our
publishing program.

∞ Printed on acid-free paper

Published by
CREATIVE PUBLISHERS
an imprint of CREATIVE BOOK PUBLISHING
a division of Creative Printers and Publishers Limited
a Print Atlantic associated company
P.O. Box 8660, St. John's, Newfoundland and Labrador A1B 3T7

First Edition
Typeset in 11 point Century Schoolbook

Printed in Canada by:
PRINT ATLANTIC

National Library of Canada Cataloguing in Publication

Darcy, J. B., 1920-
Fire upon the earth : the life and times of Bishop Michael Anthony
Fleming O.S.F. / by J.B. Darcy.

Includes bibliographical references.
ISBN 1-894294-59-9

1. Fleming, Michael Anthony, 1792-1850. 2. Catholic Church—
Newfoundland—Bishops—Biography. 3. Newfoundland—Church history. I. Title.

BX4705.F53D37 2003   282'.092   C2003-900973-4

Royalties from this book will be donated to the restoration of the Basilica of Saint John the Baptist, to the construction of which Bishop Fleming devoted so much of his life and energies.

*"I have come to cast fire upon the earth;
and how I wish it were already kindled."*

- Luke 12:49

*"He is, to my mind, cast in the very type of a
primitive Bishop."*

*- (Bishop Fleming as depicted by his contemporary,
the Anglican Bishop Edward Feild)*

ACKNOWLEDGMENTS

Acknowledgments are due to many people for their assistance in the preparation of this book. First to Doctor John FitzGerald for providing the initial sources on which this work is based. To Brother John G. Shea, C.F.C., and the late Brother Michael A. Connolly, C.F.C., for obtaining additional and essential documentation from the Archives of Propaganda Fide in Rome, for their generous assistance in the translation of documents from Latin and Italian, and for many other services. To Father Thomas Fennessy, O.F.M., librarian of the Franciscan Library in Kilkenny, Ireland, for his gracious assistance with the Irish background of Bishop Fleming. To Doctor Alison Feder and to Brother Gordon R. Bellows, C.F.C., Ph.D., for their many incisive comments on the manuscript while this work was in progress. To Mr. Edward Kavanagh and Brother P. J. Batterton for their very careful proofreading of the manuscript in its final stages. To the staffs of the Archives of Propaganda Fide in Rome, of the Archives of the Dublin Archdiocese, of the Centre for Newfoundland Studies of Memorial University, of the Archives of the Province of Newfoundland and Labrador, of the Newfoundland Centre of the Hunter Library. To Sister Perpetua Kennedy of the Presentation Congregation and to Sisters Marie Michael and Kathrine Bellamy of the Sisters of Mercy. A special thank you to Monsignor Francis Coady and Mr. Larry Dohey, archivists of the Archdiocese of St. John's. All the above contributed greatly to the information on which this book is based. Grateful thanks also to Mr. Jim Fleming of Seattle, Washington, for his constant encouragement and for the financial assistance which made the hard cover edition of this book possible.

Special thanks to Creative Book Publishing, in particular Ms. Dawn Roche and Mr. Dwayne LaFitte, for making possible the publication of this work. The author, of course, is solely responsible for the opinions expressed therein.

Included in this volume is a short biography of the principal characters. Readers may find this helpful in keeping track of the developing narrative. On the first appearance of these characters, their names are printed in **bold font** followed by an asterisk to indicate that this information is available, starting on page 274.

Table of Contents

PROLOGUE

". . .a naked rock, . . . a drying ground in mid-ocean for
fishing nets"
- Ezekiel, 26:4,5.

When the prophet Ezekiel wrote these lines, Newfoundland
was not to be discovered for another 2,000 years, yet these
words are an uncannily accurate description of that island
as it must have appeared to the young cleric who stood peer-
ing eagerly through the mist at the rocky crags before him
from the prow of the cramped sailing vessel. He was bone
weary from the continual buffeting he had undergone as the
vessel plowed its way through the spring gales of the North
Atlantic week after week since he had embarked from a west
England port. The year was 1823, but the means of trans-
portation across the Atlantic had not greatly improved since
Cabot had first reached Newfoundland in 1497. The vessel
was crammed with supplies for the fishermen of that island,
its deck continually awash with icy waves which searched
out the uncomfortable passenger quarters, leaving in their
wake repellent dampness, their food cold and tasting of salt
water.

But all this was forgotten as he contemplated the forbid-
ding line of apparently unbroken cliffs that guarded his
future home, constantly attacked by waves dashing angrily
against their bases in a vain attempt to break through their
defences and conquer the defiant land beyond. Just when it
seemed that the captain was steering the boat to its destruc-
tion, the cliffs opened themselves grudgingly before it, and
revealed a passage hardly wide enough to permit two vessels

to pass at once. The entrance was guarded below by menacing rocks lurking just under the surface to ensnare the unwary, and above by even more menacing artillery ready to train on any enemy ship that should dare to attempt entrance. A little farther on, the passage took a sharp left turn and revealed a deep harbour about a mile in length and 300 yards in width. On the left this harbour was protected from even the worst Atlantic gales by towering cliffs until it reached its southern limits where it met relatively level ground broadening out into a sheltered valley bisected by a wide river rushing to empty itself into the harbour. On the right the ground rose less precipitously but equally determinedly till at its summit it encountered a barren plateau devoid of any vegetation but the occasional embattled shrub and stunted tree. On this plateau could be vaguely glimpsed through the clinging fog the outlines of a considerable military fort and nearby a "plain somber house resembling something between the characters of a prison and a private lunatic asylum," as he himself was to describe it many years later. From this fort, he could trace a road running along the side of the hill and dipping gradually until it met fairly level ground at the spot where he had just entered the harbour. Here the road encountered another military fort and stopped, having completed its mission of connecting the two establishments and having no reason to proceed further.

His fellow travellers crowded around him to get their first sight of land. Turning to them, he inquired about the house he had noticed before. Great was his shock to learn that it was the home of the governor of the island. His expectations of the quality of the other houses of the settlement dropped sharply and, as his glance moved downward again towards the harbour, those expectations were realized. Not a building of any pretensions whatsoever revealed itself, though some were indeed more solid than the mass of squalid hovels which housed the majority of the population of about 15,000 persons. These buildings, if they may be called such, were scattered along two streets which stretched the length of the harbour like two sides of a surrealistic ladder. The main street nearest the harbour staggered along like a drunken sailor, ducking under and between casually erected fishing flakes—wooden platforms covered with boughs, on which were spread the salt cod to be cured for the European market. He was not surprised to hear that it was named Water Street. Its companion, more sedate, wider and straighter, was of more recent vintage. He was informed that it was named Duckworth Street after the governor who undertook its construction. Those two streets were connected, as by the rungs of a ladder, by narrow meandering lanes, not according to any plan, but simply where it was convenient to place them.

The harbour itself was lined with wharves jutting out into the water to welcome the arriving ships. These wharves were busy with the bustle of the fishery and landing of goods. Here and there could be seen, besides the regular workers, swarms of young barefooted boys darting in and out of the wharves hoping to earn a penny by getting some odd job and, even more important, to collect their own "noggin of rum" which, through immemorial custom, was doled out to the sailors three times a day.

This was the scene that met the eyes of the youthful Father Michael Anthony Fleming as, in the spring of 1823, he arrived at St. John's, the capital of the island of Newfoundland, to assist his fellow Franciscan, Bishop Thomas Scallan, in caring for the Catholic people of the island. As he stood on the prow of the vessel while it cautiously felt its way through the "Narrows" and gazed at the scene before him, his heart must have filled with mingled emotions of anticipation and of apprehension. Nor could he help but wonder at the unexpected series of events which had led him to this day.

How different were these rugged shores from the tranquil scenes of his childhood—their placid valleys, gentle streams and verdant fields where meandered ruminating cows and timid sheep. Born just thirty years before in 1792 near Carrick-on-Suir, a small country town nine miles from the bustling seaport of Waterford in southern Ireland, the youthful Michael Fleming had worked and played with his five younger brothers and sisters on his father's extensive farm. As a lad, he had earned a few pennies by selling buttermilk along the main street of this prosperous town. Not that he really needed these pennies, for he had the good fortune to be born into a family which was reasonably well off for a Catholic family of the time, prosperous enough to send him to school. Since the Penal Laws prohibited any Catholic school from being established, he was sent first to a school run by a Protestant clergyman named Parson Foley and then to the Protestant Grammar School at Clonmel a few miles away. At these schools he had received, as was customary at the time, a thorough grounding in the Latin and Greek classics. After completing these studies when just sixteen years of age, Michael had expressed to his uncle, Father Martin Anthony Fleming, his desire to join him in the Franciscan Order. The latter had arranged for his acceptance into the seminary of the Order in Wexford, and in his honour Michael had taken Anthony as his religious name. As if to foreshadow his future career, the Superior who received him into the seminary and clothed him in the Franciscan habit was Father Thomas Scallan, later to become the third Vicar Apostolic[1] of Newfoundland. After his ordination on October 15, 1815, Father Fleming was, to his delight, assigned to his home town of Carrick as assistant to his uncle now about seventy years of age. He set to work there with that mixture of spiritual zeal and youthful enthusiasm which was to characterize him all his life.

One incident must have stuck in his memory. The church at Carrickbeg, a village just outside Carrick, was an ugly, thatched chapel in a dilapidated condition, but to build another elsewhere was illegal. One day in 1820, when both priests were away, the local people gathered and simply knocked the chapel down, leaving just enough standing to give partial protection to the sanctuary. The next day they started to collect for the new chapel. On returning to town, the Flemings were simply told, "Oh, Father, sure the storm blew it down on Thursday night. It was a poor affair anyway for the Mass to be offered up in and so we are going to build a new one." In this unusual manner, Father Fleming received his first experience in both church building and in fund raising, possibly also in learning to deal with unjust laws.

He was happy in his mission but still longed for greater sacrifice. There was in the town of Carrick, a free school established in 1806 by a former merchant, Brother Ignatius Rice, for the poverty-stricken boys of the area to enable them to rise above their seemingly hopeless condition. Brother Rice had just received formal approval from Rome for his Society—the first lay religious Congregation of men to be founded in Ireland. Realizing the enormous good the Brothers were doing and attracted by the saintly nature of Brother Rice, Father Fleming asked to join him. Reluctantly Brother Rice had to refuse—the Rule of his Society specified that only lay Catholics could become members. Still this missionary zeal and interest in education were not quenched and now, as his vessel edged into the harbour of St. John's, far greater opportunities to fulfill them lay before him.

How drastically his life had changed from the quiet life he had led at Carrick. In 1816, his former superior, Father Scallan, had been appointed coadjutor to his own uncle, Bishop Lambert, O.S.F., the second Vicar Apostolic of Newfoundland. He found a great shortage of priests to minister to the Catholic population there. Having succeeded Bishop Lambert in the following year, Bishop Scallan was not long in turning to his confreres in Ireland for help, and his stirring appeal made a deep impression on Father Fleming. By 1822 he had obtained permission from his Provincial Superior to join the Newfoundland mission, had said farewell to Father Martin and his parishioners and had booked passage on a vessel sailing from Waterford to Newfoundland. Great must have been his confusion when, having set off on foot for Waterford to catch the boat, he found himself pursued by a crowd of parishioners who surrounded him and refused to let him proceed, urging that his uncle was too old to run the parish unaided and that the new chapel wasn't yet finished nor paid for. He had to turn back, frustrated but yet grateful for the appreciation his parishioners showed for him. The call of this far off mission, however, continued to haunt him. In the following autumn, a St. John's businessman, Henry Shea, a native of Carrick, visited the town. From him, Father Fleming learned that a vessel was to leave Waterford for Newfoundland in a few days. On the appointed day, he stole out of the town without a word to anyone, not even his uncle, with little more than the clothes on his back, and even without official permission from his superiors. This time, to the dismay of his people, he succeeded in making his escape across the ocean to his new apostolate which was now spreading its challenging vista before him.

INTRODUCTION

"If it should ever be thought right again to apply to the Court of Rome (a humiliating necessity) on the subject, the enclosure might be added to the proof against that incendiary priest."

- Sir John Stephen, Colonial Office 194/100 1838
January 4, 1838

ire was the constant companion of Michael Anthony Fleming, O.S.F., fourth Vicar Apostolic and first Bishop of Newfoundland. A disastrous fire in 1846 destroyed most of the capital city of St. John's and, with it, much of his hopes. His own fiery temperament led him, at times, into impulsive and sometimes imprudent actions. To many of his contemporaries, particularly those in positions of authority, this "incendiary priest" was a political firebrand igniting the flames of discord throughout the island of Newfoundland. To others—by far the majority of those who knew him—he was a prelate on fire with the love of God and neighbour, driving himself to incredible lengths for the sake of the spiritual and material welfare of his flock. Which picture is correct?

Throughout the history of the Church, there has been a long stream of heroic Bishops, from the Apostles to our own times, who, in exercising their responsibilities, have battled with both civil and religious enemies who were determined to destroy them. St. John Chrysostom in the fourth century is a classic example of such a bishop. Pope John Paul II, Cardinal Mindzenty in Hungary and Archbishop Romero in San Salvador are similar examples in the twentieth century.

In the case of the early bishops, history has, in most cases, given the lie to the attempts of their enemies to discredit them, and has revealed the true stature of those majestic figures. In the case of bishops of our own times, the truth is emerging only gradually against the aggressive efforts of their opponents to prevent this from happening.

Bishop Fleming, however, falls between both stools. He is not far enough in the past for history to judge him impartially—the prejudices which bedeviled him during his lifetime are still very much alive today. He is not close enough to the present for his defenders to be able to give their own living witness. There is, indeed, a massive amount of documentation dealing with him and his era, but most of this, particularly that available from official Government sources, was produced by his political and religious enemies. From the earliest years of his episcopacy, a few alienated Catholics poured a constant stream of vituperation into the ears of the civil authorities in Newfoundland. The latter, who had their own reasons for detesting Bishop Fleming, conveyed these condemnations to the authorities in London, and added their own. Accepting such censures as factual, the English authorities not only protested to Rome, but, at one stage, convened a Select Committee of Parliament, composed of such weighty personalities as William Gladstone, Lord Grey and the like, to investigate him, surely the only case in history of such an august committee being convened to investigate the doings of an obscure colonial bishop. Consequently from his day to this, historians, uncritically relying on these sources, have consistently depicted him as an uncaring, ignorant person using his spiritual authority for his personal political advantage, or, as an official of the Colonial Office termed him: "that incendiary priest."

Owen Chadwick has claimed that "Historians have often experienced this truism, that an early, one-sided, clever and popular treatment of a large subject takes the field and thereafter hampers, often for many years, subsequent saner treatment by historians." The present writer has not found it easy to unearth the nuggets of truth from beneath this mountain of misinformation. Gradually, however, there has emerged the conviction that such an unfavourable account is far from justified. Instead, Bishop Fleming fits into the pattern of these heroic defenders of the faith whom St. John Chrysostom typified. As our story proceeds, I hope to be able to show that this belief is justified.

When Michael Anthony Fleming became Vicar Apostolic of Newfoundland in 1830, Newfoundland was a very different place from the rather minor province it has since become. St. John's was a bustling port where hundreds of ships arrived each summer. It was a hub of England's empire, the source, through the teeming waters which surrounded it, of much of England's wealth, a major source also of many of the experienced sailors who manned its fleet and through whom it maintained its domination of the seas. McGregor in his *British America* claimed that "it is doubtful if the British Empire could have risen to its great and superior rank among the nations of the earth, if any other power had held the possession of Newfoundland."

But the Irish Catholics of that island, who constituted much of its population, were barely tolerated, and only because their labour was essential to the fishery. As a group they were illiterate, living in squalor and immorality. Even though the Penal Laws had recently been removed from their mother country, these laws were still in force in Newfoundland, and Irish Catholics there were treated like the subject people they were.

Into this scene Bishop Fleming burst like an earlier Martin Luther King. Without a penny to his name and without any influence beyond his own integrity, he challenged the Establishment, both civil and religious, and summarily defeated it. When it tried to have him removed from office, he confronted the English government and became the centre of a conflict between that government and the Holy See.

At one stage the English government threatened to withhold the salaries of all the Catholic bishops in all the colonies unless he was removed. Even Prince Metternich of Congress of Vienna fame was dragged into the combat, and still Bishop Fleming prevailed.

Called by his Anglican contemporary, Bishop Feild, the very type of a primitive Bishop, he was filled with zeal for his poverty-stricken, neglected flock, a neglect exemplified by there being only three active priests in the Vicariate at the time of his installation. To provide the spiritual nourishment his people needed, he undertook hazardous journeys by land through uncharted territories, and by sea in fragile fishing boats in treacherous waters, journeys that rivaled those of the great apostle Paul.

Though impoverished, he built numerous churches and commuted back and forth across the Atlantic, usually in the depth of winter, to obtain the wherewithal to finance them as well as to gather zealous missionary priests to staff them. To provide for the education of his people, he introduced two Orders of Teaching Sisters and one of Teaching Brothers from Ireland, providing for them out of his own limited purse. The result was that, at his death in 1850, the Catholic population was well educated, morally upright, and were taking their full and rightful share in the political, social and economic life of the town.

When he arrived in St. John's there was not a respectable building in the town except for Government House which, as he described it, was "a cross between a penitentiary and an asylum." Before his death, he had dotted the town with fine stone buildings which still ornament it, and had done the same to many of the outlying settlements. His greatest building achievement was the massive Cathedral of St. John the Baptist, in its time probably the largest church in North America, and even now one which the wealthiest diocese of North America would hesitate to attempt to erect. To obtain the land for this venture, he travelled many times across the Atlantic and overcame the determined opposition of the Governor and the leading citizens of Newfoundland. He began this gigantic work without money and with only the pick and shovel and wheelbarrow of his workers as mechanical aids. As Archbishop Hughes of New York exclaimed at the consecration of this cathedral, his achievement rivaled that of the building of the pyramids in Egypt. He used the same means, huge teams of men and women, who were, however, not slaves, as their prototypes had been, but eager volunteers. He worked beside them in the quarries and in the foundations of the building, most of the time being his own architect. Little wonder that this church is one of the few throughout the world honoured with the title of Basilica.

With all this he was a voluminous writer, pouring out his aspirations, his frustrations and his hopes as he reported his progress and the needs of his Vicariate to the Roman authorities or, a common device of his for raising money, sending long letters to priest friends in Ireland or Italy who were then expected to have them published in the local papers. These letters make fascinating reading. It would be difficult to find another Bishop who has depicted so thoroughly the religious, social and political nature of his times. His account, for example, of the great fire which destroyed St. John's in 1846 is a masterpiece of tragic writing. These writings bear comparison with the Relations of the North American Jesuits of the seventeenth century, and, as history records, they may be equally valuable.

In spite of these achievements, Bishop Fleming is virtually unknown to all except a few scholars in Newfoundland. Yet he was undoubtedly one of the greatest figures of the first half of the nineteenth century. Fortunately, many original documents in various languages about and by him are still extant in the Archives of Propaganda in Rome, in the Colonial Office records in England, in the National Library in Ireland, in the Provincial Archives of Newfoundland and particularly in the Roman Catholic Archdiocesan Archives of St. John's. His story is now presented here to all those interested in the history of Newfoundland and Labrador and in its relation to England in the early nineteenth century with the hope of vindicating the name and achievements of "that incendiary priest."

CHAPTER ONE
PAST AND PRESENT

The number of Papists at St. John's this past year was 600 men, women and children but I could get no exact account of the number in the other ports but it is generally computed that 1/4 part of the inhabitants are Irish Papists.

- D'Alberti Transcripts, 1748-1752

iven the turmoil which beset Bishop Fleming during his entire episcopacy, it is perhaps appropriate that the Ireland into which he was born in the year 1792 was such a turbulent one. Ireland, seething under the age-old yoke of its oppressors, was girding itself once more for a desperate effort to throw off its servitude to its British overlords. The example of the successful, if savage, revolution in France in 1789 gave renewed hope to the Irish militants. A Society of United Irishmen was formed, and in 1898 when Michael was just six years of age, agitation erupted into rebellion. Unlike the result in France, however, this revolt was brutally stamped out, a French army under General Humbert having arrived too late to be of assistance. England seized the opportunity to dissolve the Irish Parliament and, by the Act of Union of 1801, placed the country under the direct rule of the British Crown. Many of the participants in this rebellion were executed but some escaped to other countries, particularly the United States, Canada and Newfoundland where, to the discomfort of the local authorities, many continued their rebellious activities.

County Waterford, where Michael was born in the little town of Carrick-on-Suir, was adjacent to County Wexford where the most ferocious fighting took place. As a boy he must have heard many tales of the horrors of the conflict and, perhaps, witnessed some of its tragedies himself. Waterford County, however, remained relatively peaceful, and we can assume that Michael's father was not involved in the rebellion since we have no evidence that he suffered any loss of property because of it. Again, the fact that he sent Michael to a Protestant teacher and later to a Protestant school for instruction implies that he remained loyal to the established government or at least neutral towards it. In the light of Michael's future career, we may even assume that his father pointed out to his young son the futility of armed rebellion against a vastly superior armed force.

However, if the road of armed rebellion was proving to be an impasse, the right to vote by the small landowner was opening a more favourable avenue for progress. This opportunity was seized by a prominent Irish lawyer, Daniel O'Connell, later to become a friend and advisor of Bishop Fleming. In 1823, the year in which Father Fleming left for Newfoundland, O'Connell, with a group of fellow lawyers and other sympathizers, formed a Catholic association to campaign for emancipation. The people flocked to his standard and the world's first mass political party was born. By 1829, the pressure of this movement forced the British Government to grant Catholic emancipation for Ireland so that henceforth Irish Catholics were eligible for all offices and employments except those of the very highest rank. O'Connell was given the title of the "Great Liberator" by his grateful countrymen.

Although Father Fleming had to follow these developments from afar, there is no doubt that he had a tremendous admiration for O'Connell and believed in his approach to the emancipation of the Irish people. There is extant a letter from him to an unknown person in Ireland which says in part:

> That I should take the liberty of troubling you with the parcel that accompanies this needs I am sure only one word of explanation to win its excuse from one so devotedly attached to Irish Liberty and consequently to Mr. O'Connell.

What baggage, therefore, did Father Fleming carry with him as he left the port of Waterford to enter on his new career in Newfoundland? Materially, he had almost nothing; spiritually and intellectually, he had developed several fundamental convictions. While maintaining his loyalty to the established government, he was one of the new breed of Irishmen who, rejecting the subservient attitude of their predecessors and believing in the fundamental equality of all men, were not prepared to accept the denial of this dignity and its accompanying rights. He had learned to reject violence as a means of acquiring these rights. Instead, he had realized the possibilities that the new type of mass political action offered to obtain them. On the other hand, as a loyal churchman, he rejected the application of the new democracy to the Church and its discipline and gave his fealty to its hierarchical structure as divinely constituted. It was now his opportunity to apply these principles to his adopted mission of Newfoundland, so alike in some ways and so different in others from the country of his birth.

Newfoundland, as it appeared to Father Fleming when he arrived at the harbour of St. John's in 1823, was a phenomenon for which nothing in his previous experience could have prepared him. Many centuries previously, the Island, particularly its eastern section, had been scoured by the last Ice Age and largely bereft of its soil. As the ice-pack receded, it had left behind a barren land strewn with huge boulders scattered helter-skelter like the debris from a pre-historic

battle of giants. Father Fleming was exchanging the fertile
meadows, the lowing cattle and the sweet smell of new-
mown hay of his native Ireland, for the brooding cliffs, the
raucous squeals of sea gulls and the pungent odours of rotting seaweed and drying fish typical of his adopted homeland. He was exchanging also the rich brogue of his native
Waterford for the hodgepodge of the many Irish, English
and Scottish accents typical of this sea-port town.

Still another difference was the climate. In its approach
to the two islands, the Atlantic Ocean had shown flagrant
favouritism. To Ireland it presented the warming caress of
the Gulf Stream, thus making the climate of that island
much more temperate than its latitude, on a parallel with
Labrador, would normally have warranted. Newfoundland,
on the other hand, though on the same latitude as France,
was confronted with the frigid assault of the Labrador
Current which not only numbed it in winter, but with its
flotilla of icebergs, blocked the coming of spring until the
rising heat of the sun belatedly forced it to release its chill-
ing grip and permit the onset of summer.

Fortunately, while thus disadvantaging Newfoundland,
the ocean also presented the Island with compensating
advantages. The ice-age, in its death throes, had ejected its
burden of soil into the ocean just south east of the island and
thus created, for the denizens of the sea, a fertile, shallow
breeding ground known as the Grand Banks. Through the
centuries too, the fleets of icebergs, sailing past the Island
on their way to melt into the enticing embrace of the Gulf
Stream as it turned eastward towards Europe, deposited
their purloined soil and thus further enriched this "home of
the cod," an area so profitable for the fishing industry that
the nations have been squabbling over it from the day it was
first discovered until now. So important did the British
Government consider this, its first colony, that Pitt the
Elder categorically stated that "one point was of such
moment, as not to be surrendered, though the enemy was

master of the Tower of London;—the Newfoundland fisheries."

Politically and socially, however, Father Fleming found Newfoundland largely a continuation of the Irish situation. Both were governed by a solitary individual responsible only to the government of England. In Ireland, the Lord Lieutenant presided at Dublin Castle and was responsible to the British Home Secretary. In Newfoundland, the Governor resided in the recently erected Government House in St. John's and was responsible to the British Colonial Secretary. Both had Advisory Councils whose advice could be rejected. In both countries, the extension of the right to political representation was being increasing pressed. Daniel O'Connell, the leader of this movement in Ireland, had his counterpart in Newfoundland in the person of the fiery **Doctor William Carson,*** the initatator of the campaign for Representative Government. Where the aristocracy in Ireland kept the national wealth jealously in their own hands, in Newfoundland, it was the merchants who hoarded it avariciously for themselves. Whereas in other developing countries, settlement was encouraged and financial inducements offered to entice people to migrate; in Newfoundland, the English merchants did everything in their power to prevent such settlement and to discourage agriculture. Sadly, in this they were strongly supported by the British Government. Gradually and reluctantly these restrictions were relaxed, but still the attitude of the merchants remained that Newfoundland belonged to them and that settlers were a necessary evil. As Joseph Smallwood, Newfoundland's first Premier after Confederation, stated in his own picturesque fashion: "Newfoundland was their orange, and they sucked it."

The position of the Roman Catholics in both countries was almost identical. To understand the hostility with which Father Fleming had to contend particularly when he became Bishop, it is essential to realize the humiliating sit-

uation of the Roman Catholics in Ireland. It is difficult for
us now to appreciate the contempt, and even hatred, which
the upper classes in England and Ireland at the time had
towards the Irish Catholic peasants. But Alexis de
Tocqueville, writing in the 1830s, observed that "All the
Irish Protestants whom I saw . . . speak of the Catholics with
extraordinary hatred or scorn. The latter, they say, are sav-
ages . . . and fanatics led into all sorts of disorder by their
priests." In Newfoundland, the same vitriolic contempt for
Catholics existed among many of the merchant class and the
governing elite. As in Ireland, Catholics in Newfoundland
could hold no official positions and were simply tolerated
according to the whims and prejudices of their masters.

One last, rather surprising point will be of interest.
Given the centuries of oppression and grinding poverty they
had experienced, it might naturally have been expected that
the Irish Catholic peasants would be physically weak and
unsuited to any demanding physical activity. But the opposite was the case. According to the Irish historian, William
Leckie, they were physically robust, hospitable to strangers,
earthy and vital. Their diet of potatoes, milk and eggs was
probably more nourishing than the "fast foods" which are
the staple diet of many of their present-day descendants.
Arthur Young, touring Ireland in the 1770s noted this:

> When I see the people of a country, in spite of
> political oppression, with well formed vigorous
> bodies, and their cottages swarming with chil-
> dren; when I see their men athletic, and their
> women beautiful, I know not how to believe them
> subsisting on an unwholesome food. . . .

Possessing such brawny health and vitality, the Irish
emigrants to Newfoundland were thus ready to withstand
the rigours of the climate and the hardships of the fishing
industry. Such a strong constitution may also explain the

extraordinary physical stamina of Father Fleming which later served him so well in his exhausting travels by land and sea.

CHAPTER TWO
LEARNING THE ROPES

The Governor acquaints Mr. O'Donel that, so far from being disposed to allow of an increase of places of religious worship for Roman Catholics of the Island, he very seriously intends, next year, to lay those established already under particular restrictions.

- Governor Milbanks to Bishop O'Donel, 1790

he welcome Father Fleming received from Bishop Scallan on his arrival in St. John's more than made up for the hardships of his Atlantic crossing, even for the seasickness which plagued him as it did on all his later voyages. He was happy to be appointed the Bishop's assistant at St. Mary's Chapel, a dilapidated building on Henry Street, totally inadequate for the size of its congregation but still the only Catholic church in the town. He set to work with a will to get to know his people and the conditions under which they lived. As he trod the muddy streets to visit their homes, his senses were assaulted by the unaccustomed sights, sounds and smells of his new abode. The thudding of the horse-driven carts as, laden with barrels of salted fish for export or barrels of molasses for home consumption, they bumped their precarious way along the deeply rutted streets competed with the hubbub of the fishermen and their helpers as they busily loaded and unloaded the hundreds of small vessels ranged along the wharves and the raucous shouts of gangs of carefree urchins racing from one wharf to another in the hope of a few pennies. Heard too was the occasional barked command as a troop of colourfully dressed soldiers tramped through the town on some military exercise.

The smells were equally varied: the pungent odor of the barked twine drying on the fences being readied to be made into nets, the stench of the rotting caplin strewn on the tiny garden patches to bring some fertility to the rocky soil, the pungency of the seal oil stored in the numerous vats, the all-pervasive smell of the salt codfish drying on the fish flakes. All these sights, sounds and smells typified the bustling commercial and military outpost which was St. John's.

When Father Fleming entered the homes of his congregation, he found in most of them little improvement from conditions outside. Usually one storey wooden structures, each crouched against its neighbour for protection from wind and weather, these houses were crowded with numerous children, often ill-fed, ill-clothed and unwashed. With their primitive sanitary arrangements, these hovels were prime material for the deadly epidemics which frequently swept through the town.

He found the people an intriguing mixture of virtue and vice. Courageous to the point of recklessness, the fishermen plied their dangerous trade, equally generous with the fruits of their industry when they had it to give and capable of incredible endurance of hardships. But they succumbed readily to drunkenness, to immorality and to sudden violence during the long winter months which condemned them to idleness. Father Fleming's heart went out to them in their pitiful condition. He saw the results of their being exploited materially by the merchants and oppressed spiritually by the government and he vowed to improve their situation.

It was not long before he began to learn the peculiarities of Newfoundland society. Every restriction against Catholics in Ireland was equally in force in Newfoundland, with other constraints as well. For instance, when he inquired about the possibility of building a more adequate chapel, as he had done in Carrick, he was informed that, when, some thirty years previously, the first Vicar Apostolic, Bishop O'Donel, had applied to the Governor for permission to build other churches, he had received the curt answer quoted at the beginning of this chapter.

Ever since the receipt of that letter, successive Bishops had kept a very low profile, so as not to provoke the Governor to implement this threat. This was one reason why St. John's was hardly a model of Christian piety. Without the Mass or the sacraments, without spiritual instruction, morals were at a low ebb. Soldiers or sailors, even women, performed the marriage ceremony, the people preferring them to government-appointed magistrates. Babies were baptized by mid-wives or nurses. The dead were buried without even a prayer. As the population increased, so did public disorder—drunkenness, debauchery, public disturbances, crimes of violence. In fact, it could be said that anarchy reigned supreme.

All this would seem challenge enough for any missionary, no matter how apostolic, but there was another problem as well, perhaps even more serious since it concerned the better educated members of the Catholic community. As Lewis Anspach asserted in his *History of the Island of Newfoundland* (c.1818), Thomas Paine's *Age of Reason* and his *Rights of Man*, with its rejection of Christianity and established authority, had poisoned the public mind and had more weight than either the Bible or the acts of parliament. Consequently many people, particularly of the better educated, had become indifferent in matters of religion, and many Catholics, while still attending Sunday Mass in the morning, took part in the Anglican services in the evening, and often lived lives at variance with their faith. This was particularly true of those few ambitious Catholics who strove to ingratiate themselves with the Protestant establishment. We can imagine how disconcerted Father Fleming must have been when, soon after his arrival in St. John's, he discovered that Bishop Scallan was himself infected by these tendencies, attended Anglican services "in his pontifical robes"[1] and had permitted these "liberal" Catholics, the Chapel Committee, as they called themselves, to take almost complete control of the church in St. John's, even of its finances. Later, the now Bishop Fleming was to describe them as a self-appointed Committee of the principal Catholics who took into their hands the proceeds of every collection raised for the improvement of the Church. A pane of glass could not be put in a window by the Bishop without their consent. They were accustomed, he claimed, to buying the needed materials from one another at highly inflated rates. The situation was made much worse, according to the Bishop, by the fact that "not one of that self-constituted Body . . . frequented the Sacraments, some of them lived in open adultery, and several of the most wealthy & influential members were Freemasons professed & walked in public Masonic Processions."

This last custom provided another instance of the power of this Committee. One Saturday, a Masonic procession, in which the members of the Chapel Committee took a prominent part, marched through the streets of St. John's. Next day, Father Whitty, one of the curates, preached a powerful sermon against this practice. No sooner was the Mass over than the Committee went to the Bishop in a body and lodged a formal complaint. Notwithstanding that membership in the Masonic Order entailed automatic excommunication, Bishop Scallan, in the presence of the Committee and of Father Fleming, forbade Father Whitty, under pain of suspension, to broach the subject ever again.

Father Fleming several times suffered a similar humiliation. Once, a member of the Committee complained that he had refused to enter the Protestant church in a funeral procession (then forbidden to Catholics by Canon Law). He was reproved by the Bishop for his behaviour. On another occasion, he had, with the Bishop's permission, collected £760 sterling for the repair of the Church. When the Committee learned this, they demanded that he hand the money over to them, saying that he was too young to be entrusted with such a large sum. Father Fleming refused their demand. They referred the matter to the Bishop who ordered him to comply. The result was that the money was squandered with not a shadow of improvement to the church.

These were particular occurrences which, when finished, were over and done with. The next incident, however, was far more serious. It was the beginning of a battle which was to occupy him for several years. The battleground was a school conducted by the Benevolent Irish Society, a non-sectarian philanthropic organization composed of many of the leading Irishmen of the town, now controlled by the same persons who formed the Chapel Committee. In 1826, the BIS, as it is still commonly known, had established a school for poor children. The teacher and all the students were Catholics, but when Father Fleming tried to prepare these children for the reception of the Sacraments, even after school hours, he was refused admittance. He complained to Bishop Scallan. To his surprise, the Bishop sided with the Society and forbade him under pain of suspension to enter the school for this purpose. He had to find other places and times for this instruction. When the time came for the First Communion of those children, the Committee learned that he intended to parade the children, dressed in white dresses and clean clothes, through the streets to the Church for the ceremony. They complained that this public display would upset the Protestant community, and once more the Bishop threatened him with suspension. He was obliged to abandon his plan, but bided his time.

Nevertheless, in spite of Father Fleming's many frustrations, for six years he found ample work and satisfaction in the Newfoundland apostolate. He was blessed with excellent health and stamina, and he reveled in the challenge involved in visiting the outlying settlements, particularly along

Conception Bay, which could only be reached by small boat or on foot. He learned at first hand to appreciate the poverty of the people and their exploitation by the merchants. He became more and more immersed in the country and its people, while they, in turn, learned to admire his zeal and self-sacrifice on their behalf.

In 1828, he returned to Ireland for a visit. It is worth noting that he had not yet achieved that degree of self-forgetfulness which he was later to display. Arranging his passage back to Newfoundland, he wrote that he "wants exclusive use of the "State Room" or some other comfortable apartment off from the cabin."

In spite of the differences in outlook between himself and Bishop Scallan, the latter appreciated his zeal, having discovered that his assistant lived up to the claim of "most useful indefatigable Missioner" which his uncle Father Martin Fleming, O.S.F, had made for him. A year after Father Fleming's arrival in St. John's, the Bishop, when writing to Father Richard Walsh, O.S.F., the Guardian of the Wexford monastery, had declared: "Father Fleming is a real treasure to me. In fact he is so good, that, in confidence I tell you, I have been seriously thinking of him as my successor at a future period."

Bishop Scallan's health was delicate. He seems to have suffered a series of strokes and spent long periods in Europe for the sake of his health. By 1827, his health was rapidly deteriorating. He asked **Propaganda Fide*** for a coadjutor, but without success. In September of the following year, he wrote again, suggesting Father Fleming for the position. This time, he was more successful and on July 10, 1829, Father Fleming was consecrated **Bishop of Carpasia*** and coadjutor to Bishop Scallan with the right of succession.

There was a frantic fuss over the preparations for his consecration. The whole town caught the spirit of the event. With no time to send to Europe for his episcopal robes and accouterments, a Miss Margaret Meehan, who was a skilled

artist, set to work in haste. When she needed spangles for
grapes which formed part of the design, everyone in town
who owned an article with spangles on it hastened to offer
it. The Carter family possessed a court dress and even this
was sacrificed. A mitre of Bishop Scallan's was taken apart
and the pattern cut from it. The shoes were ornamented and
sent to the shoemaker to be made up. Father Fleming gilded his own crosier. All was ready in time. It was impossible
to obtain the presence of two other Bishops as normally
required, so, on October 28, 1829, with Fathers Thomas
Ewer, O.S.F., Nicholas Devereux and Nicholas Heron as
assistants, Bishop Scallan consecrated Father Fleming
Bishop of Carpasia. The day after the ceremony, in appreciation for Margaret's efforts, Bishop Fleming sent her a
beautiful alabaster clock.

With his new dignity, he was not long in challenging the
liberal Catholics. He approached Bishop Scallan again and
this time obtained his permission to renew his application to
give religious instruction at the BIS school. The BIS executive surrendered, and he prepared over 400 of the children
for their First Communion. Over renewed protests, he
marched these children in their festive robes through the
streets to the Chapel for the ceremony. A few days later, he
called a meeting of all Catholic supporters, had the "Council
of liberals" as he called it, dissolved and "from that day to
this" he later wrote triumphantly to Propaganda Fide, "the
school has been placed under my immediate direction."[2]
Although he thus defeated those Catholics (whom, he
claimed, numbered only six or seven people), he earned their
undying hatred. They were influential citizens, and from
that time on, they carried on an unrelenting warfare to discredit him and even to get him deposed. In this latter
attempt, as we shall see, they very nearly succeeded.

It was not long before the Bishop felt the sting of prejudice. He had sent to Europe for more appropriate episcopal
attire than the makeshift robes that had been hurriedly

assembled for his consecration. He had been assured that these goods would be admitted to the country free of duty. But when they finally arrived, the officer in charge of customs insisted that he pay an amount almost equal to the value of the goods themselves. Bishop Fleming complied but was not prepared to accept this injustice. He wrote a strong complaint to the Treasury in London as a result of which the duty was rescinded and the local officials given a severe reprimand.

Bishop Scallan died[3] on May 29, 1830. While he was on his deathbed, a document arrived from Rome reprimanding him severely for attending Protestant services. Bishop Fleming, however, as a last act of kindness to his old mentor, decided not to deliver this admonition to the dying Bishop. Later the rumor spread around the town that Bishop Scallan had died excommunicated. To refute this, when the new Cathedral was built, a marble bas relief was erected there in Bishop Scallan's memory. It depicted the dying Bishop receiving the Last Rites at the hand of Bishop Fleming who had left money in his will for this purpose.

His apprenticeship now over, Bishop Fleming took up the reins of office as Fourth Vicar Apostolic of Newfoundland. As he was to relate later, not yet thirty-three years of age, he felt himself "standing alone, unequal, both in talents and in grace, to the task before him." When he considered the needs of his people, he shuddered at the thought of the spiritual abyss into which they had fallen. When he pondered the challenges that lay before him, he was filled with doubt and foreboding. Nevertheless he set his shoulder to the plow and never turned back.

CHAPTER THREE
THROWING DOWN THE GAUNTLET

A total change was necessary, and from that moment I began.

- Bishop Fleming

he civic authorities of Bishop Fleming's time, and later historians as well, tended to depict him as a despotic commander of his priests and people. The reality, however, was far different. In the previous chapter, we have seen with what uncertainty he faced the future. At thirty-two, he was very young indeed to expect the automatic loyalty of his people. The few ambitious Catholics who previously had run the Church deeply resented his taking that power from them. On the other hand, the great mass of illiterate people were willing enough to obey his spiritual leadership in religious matters but, among them, drunkenness and immorality were widespread. Moreover, accustomed as they were to the hazardous life of the open sea or the perilous ice floes, they were, according to the Bishop, "a wild and hardy race. . . reckless of every consequence when their passions are excited. . . . little removed from a savage State." Aware of how the French peasants had become inflamed during the Revolution of 1792 and of how the Irish peasantry ignored the edicts of their Bishops when political or economic matters were involved, Bishop Fleming knew that he had to tread very cautiously indeed to maintain their loyalty.

His clergy could give him little support. There were seven priests on the island. Of these, one was eighty-two years of age, another suffered from mental disease, a third languished in the last stages of tuberculosis, while a fourth had largely abandoned his priestly duties to ally himself with the Bishop's opponents. So when he claimed to be standing alone, he was not far from the truth.

However, his own determination was never in doubt. He had two main objectives: first, to abolish the serious abuses that had grown up among the Catholic people and to revivify their religious life; second, to ensure that the civic and religious rights of his people were respected. When he pondered why it was that, after the passage of forty-two years from the arrival of Bishop O'Donel on the island, so little had been accomplished for the spiritual betterment of the people, he traced the cause back to the rebuff that Bishop O'Donel had received from Governor Milbanks in 1790, and the fear of offending those in power that this reproof had engendered. He decided, as he said, that "a total change was necessary and from that instant I began."

Whether he intended to or not, his first actions were such as to endear himself to the hearts of the Catholic people. There were two taxes which particularly irked them. One was that for every Catholic marriage a fee of 14 pence had to be paid to the Governor. The other was that for every Catholic burial, 12 shillings and 6 pence had to be paid to the Anglican Rector even though the ceremony was performed by a Catholic priest. This latter tax was a heavy burden, and it was a common spectacle to find the family of a deceased person going from door to door begging for a penny to help them bury their dead. As soon as he was installed, Bishop Fleming protested these taxes. When this produced no effect, he simply refused to pay them, and they were never again demanded. This was hardly a prudent way to begin his episcopacy, but the Bishop was determined to make clear his position from the beginning. Such an independent attitude, so different from that of his predecessors, must have come as a shock to both the Governor and the

Anglican Rector. Though neither found it expedient to make an issue of the matter since both taxes were clearly irregular, still the deterioration of relations between them and Bishop Fleming could, perhaps, be traced from that moment.

No general can wage a war without officers. The actions described above could be taken on his own initiative, but for wider and more long-term projects, he needed more than the three active priests now in the Vicariate. So, having settled his various affairs, on December 26, 1830, he set sail in the *Arno* for Ireland on the first of his many trans-Atlantic voyages to obtain help for his Vicariate. Two of his companions were James and John Kent, young natives of Waterford, who were just setting themselves up in business in Newfoundland and who were to play an important role in the Bishop's life and in that of the country.

In the early nineteenth century, to cross the Atlantic in a small sailing boat when the winter storms were setting in required considerable courage. Many vessels were lost with all on board during these winter passages, and each time that he embarked, Bishop Fleming knew that he was taking his life in his hands and inevitably subjecting himself to the agonies of sea-sickness to which he was susceptible. His parishioners, too, understood the risk he was taking, and attended his departure with the elaborate ceremony which usually accompanied important personages. He was conducted by thousands of his parishioners from his residence to the King's Wharf. Here a six-oared gig waited to conduct him to the *Arno*. As he set out from the shore, deafening cheers rose from the nearby wharves and vessels. The Bishop was deeply moved by this display of affection and acknowledged the crowds by bowing and waving his hand.

With the lifting of the Penal Laws in 1829, various seminaries had sprung up in Ireland and vocations to the priesthood were plentiful. Having arrived safely, Bishop Fleming now made the round of these institutions, and his passionate pleas for the spiritual needs of his adopted country found ready listeners. Nine clerics volunteered for the mission, six of whom were prepared to leave for Newfoundland as soon as passage was available.[1]

Passing through England on his way back to Newfoundland, Bishop Fleming had his first contact with political life. The authorities in Newfoundland had been slow to apply the provisions of the Relief Act to Newfoundland. Various petitions were drawn up by the Catholic people, and Bishop Fleming was asked to present them to Parliament. The request was successful, but the Bishop hardly deserves as much credit as he claims for this since Parliament was quite favorably disposed.

Once back in Newfoundland, the Bishop deployed his officers for the coming campaign. He knew that some of the older priests would object to having their parishes divided, so he shrewdly disarmed their objections by beginning with his own territory, making Bay Bulls a separate parish and putting young Father Patrick Cleary in charge. As a result he was able to divide other districts with little opposition. Three of the young priests he kept with him in St. John's where the bulk of the Catholic population resided.

This done, he attacked his next objective, the merchants. He could do little at the moment about the merchants' despotic power to decide the price the fishermen should receive for their fish and the charge for the provisions and equipment they needed—a power which meant that the fishermen rarely, if ever, saw ready cash, and which left them perpetually in debt to the merchants. But there was one area where religion and business came into conflict, and here he could act. It was the custom for the merchants to insist that their employees should work on Sundays and holidays. Bishop Fleming wrote a series of pastoral letters demanding that the Lord's Day should be kept holy and insisting that no unnecessary servile work be done. Some Catholic workers took him at his word and refused to work on such days. The merchants took them to court and the courts upheld the merchants' claims and imprisoned and fined those who refused to work on holy days. One of the Catholic merchants, after winning his case, turned to the people in the courtroom and mockingly declared: "If I could have exchanged a bill of lading with Saints Peter and Paul, or rather with the Pope, to indemnify me for the loss I suffered on the day that my servants refused to work, I would have been able to observe that feastday." But Bishop Fleming persisted and "after a difficult battle of five years, I reached the point of upholding the inviolability of the holy day of the Lord which had never been observed up to then except by those Catholics who were not dependent on the merchants."

Having obtained the loyalty of his people by standing up for their interests, the Bishop now turned his attention to their spiritual condition. He flatly forbade Catholics to take part in Protestant services. Although he and his priests were showered with abuse for this "intolerance" and for trying to "break the friendship of Catholics with Protestants," once more he persisted and eventually was able to put an end to this practice. His action, however, still further strained his relations with the dissident few.

With equal firmness he and his priests preached against sexual license, drunkenness, and swearing. Some years later, he claimed that his campaign against the first had been totally successful so that "through the course of several years not even a single street in St. John's has been marred by the appearance of a single woman of evil life, nor has the whole island been stained by the existence of a single brothel within the circuit of its shores."

Drunkenness was undoubtedly the major source of the squalor in which so many of his people lived, and the one most difficult to eradicate. It was the custom among his parishioners regularly to "take the pledge"; i.e., to take a solemn oath before a priest to abstain from drink, a pledge that was no sooner taken than broken, taken again and broken again. The Bishop continually condemned these sacrilegious oaths. His enemies seized on this, distorted his intent and spread the report that he was encouraging drunkenness. Not for years did he have much success in combating this vice until, learning from the example of Father Matthew in Ireland, he was able to establish a Temperance Society in which eventually 20,000 people pledged themselves to Total Abstinence. The results, as he reported later, were remarkable: "There is an unwonted air of comfort and happiness amongst our poor people. They are comfortably clothed, and their houses are clean and orderly, but above all things are they improved, greatly improved in virtue and the love and practice of Religion, for now are they, indeed, capable of appreciating the instructions of their respective pastors."

One would expect that, since he exercised his office with such severity, Bishop Fleming would be resented by his Congregation, but, except for the few malcontents mentioned above, they rallied to his support and converts were numerous. His people appreciated the sincerity of his interest in their welfare and the greatness of the sacrifices he was making for them. They saw, for example, the hardships involved on his regular Sunday routine. There were four churches in his district. Besides St. Mary's in St. John's, there were churches at Portugal Cove, Torbay and Petty Harbour, each approximately nine miles from St. John's. There were no roads to these settlements nor was it possible to ride a horse there because of the bogs and almost impenetrable woods. So each Sunday, the Bishop would say Mass in St. John's. Then, still observing the obligatory fast, he would set out on foot for one of these other settlements. After celebrating Mass there, saying his Office and taking some refreshment, he would walk back to St. John's, arriving at St. Mary's in time to preach at evening prayers at 5 p.m. He boasted that, from the first Sunday after his consecration as Bishop, he never omitted this duty when he was at home no matter what the weather or his own physical condition. This was an extraordinary feat, when one considers how difficult these journeys must have been in winter with its deep snow and howling blizzards.

His people saw him impoverish himself for their sake. When he introduced a community of Religious Sisters to take care of the education of the poor girls of St. John's, he took upon himself the obligation of providing personally for their support. To do this, he had to cut back drastically on his own standard of living. He reduced the number of his servants, contenting himself with just a general maid and a livery boy. He had kept a carriage and fine pair of horses; now he sold these and limited himself to one horse. Even his meals were retrenched to such an extent that he was accused of being parsimonious.

In 1841, Captain Geary, who had lived for several years in St. John's as captain of the artillery, stated in his testimony before a **Select Committee of the British Parliament**:*

> I have the highest respect for him in every way....
> He is a most laborious man; he lives like the meanest curate in the place, and devotes every farthing that he has in charity and in building churches and chapels, and so on; in fact, his whole life is spent in going about the country doing good. If the small-pox breaks out in any place, you find that the bishop sets out directly, carrying off a cow or something of that kind for the benefit of the people. He is one of the most laborious and one of the most virtuous men I ever met with.

When asked whether the Bishop was greatly loved by all the people, he answered, "Yes, by the great body of the people. There are only about half a dozen that give him trouble."

Bishop Fleming took practical steps as well to assist his people. He claimed to have begun the practice of building roads to the various communities. Speaking of the road to Portugal Cove which, he said, "was scarcely passable for carts. It was I who first undertook to induce a large number of the people to assemble for the purpose of clearing the wood on this way and to drain the swamps and cover over the rivers with rude bridges." Perhaps it was here that he first experienced his ability to organize and enthuse large groups of people, a talent which he later put to such good use when building his cathedral.

CHAPTER FOUR
ENTANGLED IN POLITICS

I have, I acknowledge, interfered in some respect in politics; but, in reality, how shall the bishop of Newfoundland learn to unmix religion and politics? Where politics are debated there are to be found the strongest denunciations against the religion and priesthood of the people.

- Bishop Fleming

The year 1832 marked a radical change in the social structure of Newfoundland. Until that year there had been relative peace in the island, though a peace based more on oppression and submission than on justice and equality. After that year, there was increasing polarization between the "haves" and the "have nots", and, since the "have nots" were mainly Catholics and the "haves" Anglicans, this division extended to the religious groups as well.

The year did not begin well. The winter of 1831-32 was exceptionally harsh. As late as June, **Governor Cochrane*** reported to the Colonial Office that there had been "terrible weather for three months, bays filled with ice . . . bordering on (if not actual) famine." On one occasion, a pathetic group of starving people assembled in the Chapel yard waiting for the distribution of twenty cwt. of bread and 100 barrels of potatoes which Bishop Fleming had purchased for them from his own funds. In March, he headed a group of leading citizens who were organizing a system of relief.

The merchants likewise were feeling the pinch and decided to take some action to offset their losses. Traditionally, the sealers had been able to dispose of their share of the seal hunt as they saw fit, but at the beginning of 1832, the merchants of Conception Bay decided to impose upon their sealers the truck system used with the fishermen. The truck system was a procedure whereby the merchants outfitted the fishermen at the beginning of the fishing season and received their catch at its close. They placed their own valuation on both the merchandise and the fish, always to their own advantage. Money never changed hands and the fishermen were perpetually in debt to the merchants. To enforce this scheme upon the sealers, the merchants brought a lawyer from Nova Scotia to draw up a legal agreement for the sealers to sign. The sealers, notoriously an independent group, rebelled against this imposition, and on January 9 and again a month later, some 3000 of them met at Saddle Hill, half-way between Carbonear and Harbour Grace, to pledge themselves to refuse to accept the truck system. Excitement ran high. One merchant, Thomas Ridley of Harbour Grace, refused to attend the meetings, and, in retaliation, the mob marched on his schooner *Perseverance* and cut down its masts. Other people, who were also suspected of non-cooperation, were beaten. Thoroughly alarmed, the magistrates swore in about 100 special constables for Harbour Grace and 130 for Carbonear, but this move proved useless. The frightened merchants now demanded the intervention of the military. Unfortunately, Governor Cochrane was then in England seeking to dissuade the British Government from granting representative government to Newfoundland and Judge Tucker was acting Governor. He was led to believe that the sealers were trying to impose a new type of agreement on the merchants, and issued a Proclamation declaring the meetings illegal and offering a reward of £100 for information leading to the arrest of those responsible for damaging

Ridley's schooner. Placards to this effect were posted in both Carbonear and Harbour Grace but were immediately torn down. Demonstrations continued in both towns to reinforce the sealers' demands. Faced with this determined opposition, the merchants surrendered and reinstated the former method of payment.

However, **Henry Winton,*** the editor of the *Public Ledger*, became involved. Winton published an article about the meeting at Saddle Hill in which he berated the Irish who formed the major group among the sealers. Those attacked became enraged, and a riot was threatened. Placards again appeared this time threatening Winton with death and containing equally dire threats against anyone who would dare to remove those notices.

Winton became alarmed at the threats on his life and came to the Bishop to protest. Whatever his own sentiments, the Bishop did not hesitate to respond. He took Winton by the arm and publicly strode through the town with him. Before the glowering eyes of the inhabitants, he tore down each threatening placard as he came upon it while persuading the angry sealers to return to their homes. He instructed his priests to do the same in Harbour Grace and elsewhere. The Bishop's actions required considerable moral and physical courage. He could not be sure that the physical threats against anyone who would interfere with the placards would not be carried out upon him though he might depend on his episcopal state for protection. Nor could he tell what impact his bold actions would have on his still untested influence over his people. When he had confronted them previously in such matters as drunkenness and immorality, he had been acting well within his spiritual authority. Here, however, he was intruding in political and social affairs, and, with emotions running high, his people might well turn against him. Fortunately he was successful and the agitation died down. In spite of this act of kindness,

Winton and the *Public Ledger* were to prove a major thorn in the Bishop's side for many years to come.

It was in this turbulent atmosphere that Governor Cochrane, his opposition to representative government having proved futile, returned from England, reluctantly carrying with him the bill to introduce this new type of government to the Island. There were to be two chambers: one, a Legislative Council, consisting of the top Government officials and other members appointed by the Governor; the other, an elected House of Assembly.

The elections for the new House of Assembly were announced in September 1832. In both England and Ireland, the right to vote had been restricted to the middle classes by the use of appropriate property qualifications. But in Newfoundland there was no such middle class. Consequently, to obtain any kind of a representative Assembly, the vote had to be extended to almost all adult men - women having not as yet achieved the right to vote. The only restrictions were that one must be a British subject, twenty-one years of age, and occupying a dwelling house as owner or tenant for at least one year prior to the election. To be eligible as a candidate for election, one had also to have lived in the colony for at least two years previously. The result, as Governor Cochrane complained bitterly to the Colonial Office, had practically the effect of establishing nearly universal suffrage.

In St. John's, three seats were at stake and eleven candidates entered the contest. The establishment put forward the names of William Thomas, a highly respected businessman, and William B. Rowe, an English lawyer. Doctor William Carson, the main inspiration in the drive for representative government, also put his name forward. But a shock ran through the establishment when **John Kent**,* a young Irish Catholic businessman, just twenty-seven years of age, announced his candidacy. Kent was a nephew of Patrick Morris, the leading Catholic merchant on the island.

Since eventually he was to become Prime Minister of
Newfoundland, he clearly possessed the necessary talent for
the position to which he now aspired. However, his candidacy placed Bishop Fleming in an embarrassing position. The
Bishop agreed with Governor Cochrane in his opposition to
the grant of a local Assembly. "My opinion remained
unchanged as to the evil effect likely to be produced on the
peace of the Colony and the harmony of private life, by the
establishment of the House of Assembly." He believed that,
given the way in which the rivalry between the different
Irish counties had spread to Newfoundland with its already
bitter divisions, entrusting the government into local hands
was a recipe for chaos. He had a more personal reason for
opposing Kent's candidacy. Kent was shortly to marry his
sister, Johanna, and the Bishop considered that, in view of
Kent's coming responsibilities, he could not afford to take so
much time away from his fledgling business as a commission
agent.

However, the one who reacted most stridently to this
"presumption" on the part of Kent was Henry Winton, and
a strident debate ensued in the public press between Winton
and Kent. Bishop Fleming determined to stay aloof from the
election, confining himself and his clergy to exhortations to
the people on their duty to vote responsibly. He resisted the
requests of several delegations to name those he thought
most suitable. But eventually the repeated statement by
Winton that he had no right to become involved stung him
into action. Unfortunately, while still angry, he published a
letter in the press in which he expressed his resentment in
extremely strong terms.

> Were I conscious of having incurred the enmity of
> any individual in the world—which, thank God! I
> am not—I would pitch on the Editor of the *Ledger*
> as the man, from the unwarrantable and unjusti-
> fiable manner in which he brought my name

before the public in his paper of Tuesday last. In
his stricture upon Mr. Kent's letters, he has conveyed to the public insinuations injurious to my
character, and tending to impress upon the minds
of his readers, an opinion of my clergy, and of me,
which I trust we do not merit.

He then announced his support for three candidates. At
first sight, his choice would appear to be very judicious, for
he named Doctor Carson, William Thomas, and John Kent.
He could hardly be accused of religious prejudice since
Carson was a free thinker, Thomas an Anglican, and only
Kent a Catholic. He gave as his reason for this selection that
those three were the candidates most interested in the
needs of the working-class poor. It was this latter group
whom the Bishop had repeatedly urged to vote for those candidates who had their interests at heart and not merely bow
to the choice of their employers. It must have been a revela-
tion to those poor people to realize that they now possessed
political "clout" in their own right no matter how difficult it
might be in practice to exercise it.

There was an outcry among the establishment against
this "interference" of the Bishop. Again Winton was in the
forefront. He attacked the Bishop even more irresponsibly.
He wrote:

...You have openly turned your back upon all the
respectable inhabitants of this community, both
Catholic and Protestant, and have thrown yourself upon the rabble... What shall be said of you
when you can so far prostitute your sacred calling
to secular purposes of so unworthy a character.

As might be expected, the Catholics indignantly rallied
around their Bishop and in public meetings denounced
Winton. He, however, was not daunted. When the Bishop

responded in the press, he described the response as "as foul a tissue of falsehood and misrepresentation as ever flowed from the pen of a gentleman."

The whole tempest in a teapot took on the shape of a comic opera when John Kent's brother James challenged Winton to a duel. Winton refused though he stated that he could always be found in the streets, where, if molested, he had both the ability and the courage to defend himself. One critic took advantage of the heated atmosphere to point out that the Catholic Bishops had traditionally been supported financially by deductions from the workers' wages by the Protestant merchants, and he complained that the Bishop showed little gratitude for such service of their part. The Bishop's answer was what might be expected. He stated that although he was extremely grateful to some merchants for their assistance, he felt that the system was unhealthy. He asked that it be abolished and that in future the fishermen and longshoremen would pay him what they could afford. He added that he had no hesitation in saying that he believed they would do so more generously than ever.

In the midst of all this useless trading of insults, the Governor issued a proclamation calling upon all the inhabitants of the island for a day of "fast and humiliation" and of prayer to God to avert the threatened onslaught of a cholera epidemic which had already invaded Canada. Perhaps as a result, the threat did not materialize, but it may well have helped bring everyone to their senses.

The English "rotten boroughs," whereby one landlord controlled the appointment of as many as nine members of Parliament, had been all but abolished in England by the Reform bill of 1831. But the 1832 elections transported these rotten boroughs, albeit in another form, into Newfoundland. Whereas in England these boroughs had been controlled by immensely wealthy landlords, in Newfoundland they became the fiefs of the few wealthy merchants. Most of the newly enfranchised voters were completely dependent on the merchants for their livelihood, and the latter were determined to maintain the power this gave them. Two circumstances made this possible. First, there was no such thing as a secret ballot. Voters were brought (perhaps "herded" would be a better word) to the polling booths in groups of ten and there announced their vote publicly. Second, each candidate published a list of those merchants and other employers who supported him. To vote contrary to the wishes of one's employer was to court almost certain dismissal and hence starvation.

It did not take the Catholic clergy long to realize that, if the elections were not to be a mere farce, some method must be found to give the voters the courage to vote against the wishes of their employers. Consequently, they now began to take a very active part in the election campaign— encouraging the voters from the altar and even taking part in parades. This development aroused great indignation among the "respectable" people for whom such clerical conduct was unheard of. The establishment became concerned. In a shrewd ploy, they spread word that the Bishop was betraying the interests of his fellow Catholics. Because of the number of Catholic voters, they claimed, at least two of the members from St. John's should be Catholics, while the Bishop had nominated two non-Catholics. They claimed, moreover, that he had nominated Doctor Carson just because he was a particular friend of his. They then put forward the name of **Patrick Kough**,* a prominent liberal Catholic and the main Government building contractor.

The elections began on Monday, November 5, and voting lasted the entire week; the Catholic clergy lending the support of their presence at the polls. In St. John's, Kent won easily with 893 votes, Thomas was second with 762, but Carson was beaten by Patrick Kough who obtained 647 votes to Carson's 622. Since of the fifteen members of the new Assembly, only five were Catholics and, of these, one, Patrick Kough, was aligned with the establishment, the

Catholics could hardly exert much power. Nevertheless, they
had a foot in the door and could make their presence felt.

The Assembly opened on January 1, 1833, amid much
fanfare. Paul O'Neill, in his work, *The Oldest City*, vividly
describes the squabbles which ensued, much as both
Governor Cochrane and Bishop Fleming had foretold.

> The new Legislative Assembly... proved a hen-
> house to the British Colonial administration, and
> the chickens of centuries came home to roost
> within hours of its opening. The bitter years of
> English oppression, the denial of human rights to
> settlers, the inequalities faced by servile
> Irishmen, the harsh penal laws against Roman
> Catholics, the restrictive interdicts against reli-
> gious dissenters, the gross illiteracy of the elec-
> torate, and the political inexperience of the elect-
> ed manifested themselves in a pettiness and fick-
> leness that was to be a cause of violent party strife
> for three decades.

Yet Bishop Fleming availed of the opportunity to show
his concern for those of other faiths. At the first sitting of
the new House he presented a petition that the law forcing
Dissenters, i.e., the Presbyterians and Methodists, to have
their marriages celebrated by Anglican clergymen be
repealed. This appeal was successful and perhaps helps us to
understand why Bishop Fleming was able to elicit the affection and support of all classes of ordinary citizens.

One result of this legislative bickering, a most unfortunate one for the Colony, was that in March 1833, Chief
Justice Tucker resigned and his place was taken by **Judge
Henry J. Boulton*** who, like Henry Winton, was to become
a major antagonist to Bishop Fleming. Boulton had just
been dismissed as Attorney-General of Canada and was a
most unsuitable choice. According to Prowse, "His views,
both of law and legislation, were most illiberal . . . his harsh

sentences, his indecent party spirit, and his personal mean-ness caused him to be hated as no one else was ever hated in this Colony." Soon, in his position as President of the Legislative Council, he and the Assembly were at logger-heads, bickering over the most trivial matters. At the same time, the two parties within the Assembly—one supporting the Establishment and the other sponsoring reform—were also daggers drawn; consequently a roadblock to any pro-gressive legislative action ensued.

The election campaign of 1832 marked the point of no return in the life of Bishop Fleming. Until this campaign, the establishment, though irritated by some of the chal-lenges he had made to their authority, could not but respect him for the strenuous efforts he was making for the moral and spiritual improvement of his Catholic people. But this regard lasted only as long as he remained within the sphere of his spiritual authority. With the 1832 campaign, he emerged as an important player in the political world, so much so that Governor Cochrane was later to say of him that "his power was greater than mine." The exercise of this power not only earned Bishop Fleming the hostility of the civil authorities in both Newfoundland and England but also severe rebukes from the highest Church authorities. Be that as it may, the establishment was not prepared to accept his growing influence and from that time onward joined with the dissident Catholics in a determined effort to destroy him.

CHAPTER FIVE
VALIANT WOMEN

There is a grey eye that will look back upon Erin,
Never again will it see the men of Erin or women.

- Columcille

ishop Fleming was intensely interested in education, particularly religious education, as the best
means of raising the poor from the squalor and
misery to which they were usually subjected.
While still a curate in Ireland, he had seen the success of the
various Religious Orders which had been recently founded
there for the education of the poor. In Carrick-on-Suir itself,
he had witnessed the dramatic effect on the boys of a school
established there by the Christian Brothers. Moreover, his
understanding of the power of education went still deeper.
He realized that the foundation on which he must build an
enduring, vibrant Catholic community was the education of
its future mothers. He had a sensitive understanding of the
differing needs of boys and girls, and of the special reasons
for educating them separately which existed in
Newfoundland where the boys were accustomed from an
early age to inhabit the wharfs where they imbibed, together with their thrice daily "noggin of rum," the coarse customs and language of their elders.

> I judged it of essential importance to fix the char-
> acter of the female portion of our community in
> virtue and innocence, by training *them* in partic-

ular in the ways of integrity and morality, by
affording them the very best opportunities of having their religious principles well fixed, by impart-
ing to them, while their young minds were daily
receiving the elements of a general and useful
education, a course of religious instruction, that
should teach them the true value and the proper
use of those mental treasures by which they were
being enriched.

But how to obtain suitable teachers for these children?
Bishop Fleming was convinced that, to get the results he
desired, he must persuade the Superiors of one of those Irish
Congregations to send a community to Newfoundland.
Accordingly, early in 1833, glad no doubt to escape the political bickering that consumed the Assembly, he set sail once
more for Ireland. His destination was Galway City where
there was a convent of **Presentation Sisters**.* Arrived
there, he approached his objective obliquely. Carrying a car-
pet bag, he appeared at the convent gate and, saying that he
was an American bishop, sought permission to celebrate
Mass. Afterwards he asked to see the schools and declared
himself delighted with everything there. When the Sisters
then assembled in the community room to learn of his mission, the Bishop made an impassioned plea on behalf of the
neglected children of his vicariate. Inspired by the picture he
painted, four Sisters immediately volunteered to accompany
him. They were Sisters Magdalene O'Shaughnessy, Bernard
Kirwan, Xavier Molony, and Xavier Lynch. It is difficult for
us now in the twenty-first century to appreciate the heroic
generosity of these Sisters. Not only had they no preparation for the difficulties of climate and culture that would
face them, but going to Newfoundland meant leaving forev-
er their homeland, their community, their families and their
friends, everyone and everything that they held dear.

The Bishop of Galway, Doctor Browne, when approached by Bishop Fleming, gave his consent for the venture and appointed Sister Bernard Kirwin as Superior. Bishop Fleming, on his part, agreed to provide the Sisters with a convent and school in St. John's and £100 a year until they could support themselves. He set off immediately for Dublin to make arrangements for the voyage. While in Dublin, too, he ordained five clerics who had volunteered for the Newfoundland mission: Fathers Bernard and James Duffy [not related], McKenna, Ward and Waldron.

Anxious as he was to return immediately to Newfoundland, he yet found it unusually difficult to obtain suitable passage. This was no easy matter in any case, for the Sisters belonged to a cloistered Congregation and, as such, were expected to have no contact with the outside world even when travelling. In Dublin, he discovered that the boat he had intended to use was too small. He crossed to Liverpool but several arrangements that he made there broke down. Then Mother Power, the Superior of the Galway convent, suggested a vessel leaving from Galway. He returned to inspect it but decided that it was unseaworthy. Returning once more to Liverpool, he finally convinced the Brocklebank Shipping Company to have one of their ships call at Waterford on its way to St. John's. However, the company struck a hard bargain. The Bishop had to accept liability for any accident the vessel might suffer on the way to Waterford. He had also to pay for the Sisters' passage across the Atlantic even should they miss the boat. Nevertheless, he was determined that the Sisters should, as far as possible, be able to live their normal conventual life on shipboard with dignity, comfort and privacy. He therefore stipulated, at what must have been considerable further expense, that they and he be the only passengers. He even sent the newly ordained priests to Newfoundland by another vessel.

The immediate problem was how to get the Sisters to Waterford on time. Galway was almost 150 miles from

Dublin with another 100 miles to Waterford along winding pitted gravel roads, with the mail coach the only suitable means of transportation. From Dublin, on Monday, August 5, he wrote to Mother Power, alerting her to his pending arrival in Galway and asking her to have the Sisters ready to leave as soon as possible. He arrived on the following Sunday, August 11. At 4 a.m. on Monday, after having celebrated Mass to beseech God's blessing on their journey, they set out for Dublin, the four Sisters having bade a tearful farewell to those staying behind. In Dublin, they remained for a few days to rest and obtain needed supplies. Continuing to Waterford, they were welcomed there by a sister of one of the Galway communities. While they waited for their chartered vessel to arrive, they were besieged by visitors with presents and articles for relatives in Newfoundland. As has been noted, there was a great deal of passage between Waterford and St. John's.

Eventually, their ship, the *Ariel,* appeared, and on Wednesday, August 28, they set out on their voyage with the Sisters in possession of the lone cabin. The passage proved to be a most perilous one. For the first three days, they were all violently seasick. Just as they were recovering and getting their sea legs, they were overtaken by a storm so fierce that the monstrous waves smashed one of the ship's masts and damaged the others. Throughout this tempest, which lasted for three days, the Bishop cared for them, as they reported later, "like a tender parent," while the Sisters were too seasick to be frightened. But this gale was only a harbinger of a hurricane which followed shortly after. Though it lasted only a day and a half, it did enormous damage to the vessel. The sails were torn to pieces. The waves which swept over the deck were so high that the passengers feared every moment would be their last. The tossing of the vessel made it impossible for them to stand. Forced to remain in their bunks, they spent the time praying fervently for the ship's safety. The sailors watched in helpless dismay as the

remaining masts were swept away and the ship became an
unmanageable hulk. They could only trust the vessel to the
mercy of the waves and the Providence of God. Eventually,
the storm wore itself out, the sturdy ship righted itself and
makeshift sails were rigged. Fortunately the winds became
favourable and the remainder of the twenty-five day voyage
passed quietly, enabling them to recover from their harrowing experience.

When they reached St. John's, they were again frustrated for a dense fog and contrary winds prevented the vessel
from entering the harbour. For three days, they sailed continuously back and forth, impatiently waiting for the wind
to change. Finally, at 6 a.m. on September 21, they were able
to enter the harbour. The sight that met their astonished
eyes, as they watched from the deck, more than made up for
the delay. Even at that early hour, the harbour was crowded
with boats filled with welcomers. The shore and hills were
equally thronged. While they cleared quarantine, many people came out in small boats to greet the Bishop, among them
the members of the Assembly. Others brought breakfast for
him and the Sisters. Even the quarantine was a formality;
the inspectors merely looked up at the Sisters lining the
rails and passed them through. By a coincidence, the vessel
carrying the five new priests for the mission had arrived the
day before, although it had not been sighted during the
entire voyage. The priests had been delayed in the customary quarantine but they were now released so that all joined
in the celebrations.

The Bishop had to endure an Address presented by the
members of the Assembly, and it was noon before all was
packed and ready and the Sisters, encouraged by the Bishop,
descended timorously into small boats to reach the shore.
Arrived at the wharf, the Bishop and the Sisters received a
tumultuous welcome, people of every denomination waving
their hats and shouting, "You're welcome, my Lord, and
may you live long." The welcome and the obvious love of the

people for their Bishop more than made up for all the hardships the Sisters had endured on the voyage and filled them with hope for the success of their new mission.

A carriage, with the Bishop's coat of arms emblazoned on its doors, awaited them on the wharf. But it no longer belonged to the Bishop. Some time before, he had been forced to sell it to Doctor Carson to help pay his debts, and the latter had graciously offered it for the occasion. Ensconced in this carriage, the newly arrived were led in triumphal procession through the streets adorned with the flags of the various mercantile premises. Glad as the people were to see their Bishop back safely after his lengthy absence, the arrival of the Sisters in their habits—the first Religious Sisters ever to set foot on the island—had a most dramatic effect on them. Many of them broke into tears, among them hardened sinners whom the Bishop had previously tried in vain to convert. Arrived at the Bishop's residence which was to be their temporary home until a permanent residence could be found for them, they unpacked and tried to relax. But some pious women burst into the room and, to the embarrassment of the Sisters, threw themselves on their knees before them, asking their blessing, kissing their hands and welcoming them with the greatest fervour. Finally, the devotees retired and the Sisters were left in peace to recover from their long ordeal.

In the following days, when the fog cleared away, the Sisters were enchanted by what they could see from the Palace window:

> The view of the harbour and surrounding country
> is most picturesque and beautiful on whatever
> side you turn and appears to be in a perfect state
> of cultivation. The harbour is covered with vessels
> and small boats. All around there is to be seen
> hills and mountains, perfectly green, interspersed
> with houses, green fields and small gardens. At

the foot of these hills at the very edge of the
water, there are houses and gardens, and as far as
the eye can carry you on the tops of these hills
and mountains there are houses to be seen and
cows and trees, and the water underneath gives
the whole a most romantic and beautiful appearance.

However, reality soon set in. A suitable residence was
not easy to find. Eventually the Bishop settled on an unused
tavern, the Rising Sun, and rented it for a year. The building, a one-time slaughter house, was old and decrepit and
needed extensive repairs. The Bishop did not realize the
hardships to which this arrangement was to subject the
Sisters. The Sisters had to find space for the large number
of young girls who were demanding entrance to this
makeshift school. To do so, they could reserve for their own
use as a convent only two bedrooms and a very small parlor
which had to serve them as kitchen, dining room, chapel,
and community room. There was a stable at the rear, the
only entrance to which was through the hall of the house,
and through this hall horses regularly came and went. They
had only a very small garden and that so hilly that their
walking area was only about the length of a room [As an
enclosed Order, they could not leave the property.] With
admirable self-sacrifice, the Sisters endured these hardships
until one day, about six weeks later, the Bishop, during one
of his visits, had to make way for a horse in transit through
the hall. Realizing finally the discomfort and indignities to
which the Sisters were being subjected, he determined to
move them immediately. By a stroke of luck, a large dwelling
house near King's Road belonging to the Anglican
Archdeacon Wix* became available. The Bishop rented
this house and the Sisters transferred there while the
Bishop set about building a commodious school next to it.
The Sisters were very happy with their new abode. It was

set apart from the other houses in the area and had a garden in front and a large meadow in the rear. On the front of the house, there was a large balcony with a magnificent view of the harbour. Here they could walk and watch the boats leaving and entering the Narrows when the weather prevented them from walking in the grounds.

The numbers in the school grew dramatically. To their surprise, they found the young girls to be well-off in comparison with their Irish cousins. They were well-dressed, fond of jewelry, necklaces, ear-rings, and so forth, not a bare foot among them. To the relief of the Sisters, they found them docile and eager to learn. Before the end of November, 50 of the children received Communion at Sunday Mass.

Bishop Fleming was supremely happy at what he had achieved, but wondered where he was to find the money for his mounting expenses? Fortunately, he had tremendous trust in Divine Providence. As he wrote to the Cardinal Prefect of Propaganda Fide in Rome:

> I really don't know how I procured the means to do all of this. I never received from any person a single penny to bring about my plans. All that I am able to say, and I say it with gratitude, is that God has assisted me to bring into effect these great designs which were conceived for His glory... without my being a penny in debt to a living soul with the exception of a little sum loaned me for my travelling expenses to Ireland.

It was to meet these expenses that he had to deprive himself of most of the 'trappings' of his position, but, as he said: "For the present it is enough if God will accord me the means to be able to subsist. I will count myself fortunate to be able to divide with these edifying Religious my last farthing."

This joy, however, contrasted with heartbreak in Galway. Immediately after reaching St. John's, the travellers had sent back word of their safe arrival. By some misadventure, however, their letter was mislaid in Liverpool and no comforting word reached the Galway community. As weeks and then months went by with no news of the travelers in spite of all inquiries, the Sisters grew more and more worried and finally, fearing the worst, became disconsolate. After four months with no word, the community gave the travellers up for lost, assuming that they had perished on the voyage. The services for the dead were celebrated for them, copies of their vows burned as was the custom, and a general mourning prevailed. We can imagine how the Reverend Mother must have reproached herself for approving such a hazardous venture, blaming herself for the loss of her Sisters, while every room of the convent must have reminded the Sisters of their missing companions. Eventually, when the good news of the safety of the travelers arrived, the joy and relief of all and their prayers of gratitude to God must have been unbounded.

CHAPTER SIX
THROUGH OTHER EYES

He takes no care of himself, his whole heart being on the good of religion.

- Sister M. Xavier Lynch

he arrival of the Presentation Sisters in Newfoundland had an unexpected but fortunate result for a historian. Their letters home to the community in Galway provide a treasure trove of information about life in Newfoundland. They also give an intimate view of the spiritual ideals of Bishop Fleming and of his relations with his people, a portrait not available from other sources. In their correspondence, the Sisters described the deplorable spiritual condition of the Catholics of St. John's and the Bishop's fatherly care for them. One of the Sisters, Sister Mary Magdalene, wrote that the Catholics, while well disposed, were very ignorant about religious matters. Since they were surrounded by people of other faiths, she considered that, were it not for the great exertions of the Bishop and his watchfulness over their spiritual concerns, there would scarcely be a vestige of Catholicity left among them. His labours for the promotion of the faith, she wrote, were almost incredible.

> He seems to be the "Man of the People" here, enters into all their grievances and at the same time has a resolute, unbending firmness of manner by which he has acquired a great ascendancy

over them.... He appears not to care for anything
in this world. His only breathing seems to be for
the good of Religion and salvation of souls.

Remember that this judgement was made even before his
herculean labours in the building of his Cathedral or his
death-defying visitations to the farthest reaches of his vicariate.

As an example of his self-forgetfulness, Sister M. Xavier
Lynch described his supervision of the building of their new
school:

> Night and day he is continually over the workmen
> who are giving their work for nothing and by his
> own exertion he is getting all this done. We some-
> times think he will be famished with cold for in
> the most severe weather and the snow coming
> down in flakes he will be with the workmen in the
> open air and perhaps will not eat a bit until five
> or six o'clock and sometimes not then. We wonder
> how he lives for he takes no care of himself, his
> whole heart being on the good of religion.

The correspondence of all the Sisters emphasized how
attentive he was to their needs both on the voyage across
the Atlantic and after their arrival in St. John's. This kindness, however, did not extend to indulgence. The Sisters
observed that, just as the Bishop was uncompromising in his
demands upon himself, he was equally exacting in his expectation that the Sisters live the requirements of their religious life to the full. He ensured also that they had daily
Mass and weekly Confession, no matter how pressing other
priestly commitments might be. He often shared with them
his understanding of the perfection to which a Religious
should aspire. For instance, in one of his frequent conferences to the community, he reminded the Sisters that, by the
vow of poverty, they had given up all for Jesus Christ and

disengaged their hearts from this world and all that was in it, so that even to look back with regret on the home they had left would be contrary to their vow. The Sisters were deeply impressed by the Bishop's conferences not only because of their content but also because of the beauty of his language and the great feeling with which he spoke.

Bishop Fleming was sufficiently psychologically aware to take advantage of suitable occasions to deepen the spiritual impact on the people of the Sisters' presence. For instance, on the first New Year's Day after their arrival, he arranged for the Sisters to renew their vows publicly though it meant an additional commitment for him during a very demanding season. After celebrating his accustomed High Mass in the Church, he came to the community for the vow ceremony which the people had been invited to attend. The Sisters did not yet have a chapel, so the eager throng crowded the room where the ceremony was to be held and filled the adjacent hall as well. The Bishop began the ceremony by celebrating another High Mass during which the Sisters, for the first time, provided the liturgical singing. Then he presided while the Sisters processed to the foot of the altar, knelt and solemnly renewed their vows. The Bishop concluded the ceremony by preaching a sermon which lasted almost an hour. He spoke of the great happiness of the Religious life and the great perfection to which the Sisters were called. He reminded them that the part of a Religious is self-denial, continual renunciation and the thorns of the Cross. He spoke of the vows and of the danger of relaxation and the necessity of observing their Rule with the utmost fervour and exactness. The impact of this unique ceremony on those who witnessed it must have been awe-inspiring.

The Bishop's demand for exact observance is illustrated by the following incident. At that time, it was the rule in Religious Congregations that all letters, whether outgoing or incoming, must undergo the scrutiny of the Superior before being passed to their destination. On one visit to the

community, the Bishop brought a letter from Ireland to
Sister M. Xavier Lynch. In her happy excitement, as she
turned it over and over in her hands, she fumbled with its
seal, hardly aware of what she was doing. She was quietly
brought to task when the Bishop pointedly but gently asked
if she was going to open it herself even though the Mother
Superior was present. Needless to say, the prescribed proce-
dures that day were duly observed. Incidentally, this incident helps to explain why, as we shall see, the Bishop was to
take drastic action some years later when faced with a somewhat similar situation.

The Sisters were very happy to be under the jurisdiction
of Bishop Fleming, and the great respect they had for him
they soon learned to extend to the priests who assisted him.
In a letter home, Sister M. Xavier described the Sunday routine of these clerics. After saying Mass at an early hour, they
would walk to a "station" several miles away. [Stations were
places in isolated districts where Mass was celebrated when
a chapel was not available.] In winter, unless travelling by
dog-sled across the lakes, they had to trudge through snow
as high as themselves. Answering sick calls in the remote,
isolated communities demanded a similar endurance. Sister
M. Xavier related how, on Christmas Eve and again at New
Year's Eve, one of the priests had to walk several miles to his
"station" to celebrate Mass for the people of that locality,
then plod back to St. John's for the High Mass at noon. But
his duties were not yet completed for, at five p.m., he had to
visit the convent to say still another Mass for the Sisters
since they could not attend the midnight Mass in the
church. Jokingly, Sister M. Xavier remarked how different
this was from the situation in Ireland where a priest might
complain about having to go from one street to another to
answer a sick call.

The ignorance of the people regarding the nature of the
religious life continued to amuse the Sisters. When they first
arrived, they were asked whether they would be going to the

"out-harbours" to say Mass and hear Confessions. Some thought the Sisters would live underground. Even some of the better educated asked whether they would ever speak or laugh, while the poorer people regularly knelt to them in reverence. Because Sister M. Xavier Lynch wore glasses, giving her an air of authority, she was thought to be the Superior. Still, in spite of their ignorance of spiritual matters and their moral weaknesses, the Catholic people of St. John's were seen by the Sisters as fundamentally pious. Their regular use of the Sacrament of Confession, acknowledging their weaknesses and requesting forgiveness, made constant demands on the priests' time.

When winter came, the Sisters soon learned also to respect the power of its bitter cold and its raging storms far beyond anything they had experienced in their mild-weathered homeland. Everything froze. The water in their dining room froze even though they kept a good fire going. If they set down a mug of tea, it froze solid in a few minutes; jugs and mugs froze to the table. Dishes piled on top of each other froze together. The milk they used for tea froze like lumps of sugar and had to be cut with a knife. The meat froze and had to be sawn so that it could be cooked. The water used by the priest at Mass froze before he could use it even though set out just a few moments before. When they tried to write a letter, they had to keep blowing on the pen and the ink bottle to keep them from freezing. They suffered severely from chilblains and used the traditional remedies of oil and goose grease to relieve the pain. When Sister M. Xavier Lynch came downstairs one morning carrying a brass candlestick, it stuck to her hand and caused her as much pain as if hot sealing wax had fallen on her. Biddy, the cleaning woman, when mopping the stairs, found that they became like sheets of ice although she was using boiling water. When they walked outside, their breath froze on their cloaks, at night it froze to their sheets. 'Twas a wonder, as one of the Sisters wrote back to Ireland, that they did not

freeze themselves! They must have been very thankful for
the gift of several yards of the finest flannel which a friend,
Mrs. Hughes, had given them as they were leaving Ireland.
The adaptations of the townspeople to the winters
intrigued the Sisters. Never before had the Sisters witnessed the colourful sight of sleighs drawn by horses or dogs
festooned with bells and moving merrily and rapidly over
the snow. They were fascinated by the footwear of the people which the Sisters called "moggissons"(mocassins) or
overshoes made of wood and "creepers" —a piece of wood
tied to the shoe with an iron spike protruding from it to prevent slipping. The Sisters observed that, as a further pre-
caution against falling, the men carried long poles with a
spike at the end. But here they may well have been misled
by sealers carrying their poles. Nevertheless broken bones
were a frequent occurrence and bone-setters were in great
demand.

The Sisters were also surprised to find that there was no
town clock in St. John's as there was in Irish towns. The
reason, they were told, was that the extreme cold interfered
with the clock mechanism. Instead, time was indicated by
the firing of guns at stated times during the day. This practice, in modified form, lasted until fairly recent times.

In their letters home, too, the Sisters recounted their
amusement at the curious sayings they overheard. The head
of every household was the "skipper"; when anything was to
be thrown out, the townspeople said "Leave it out." When
something was to be lifted, the request was "Haul it up"; if
a lad had a stone thrown at him, he complained "Don't be
throwing rocks at me"—all expressions familiar to the mod-
ern-day Newfoundlander.

Coming, as the Sisters did, from a farming country with
its abundant, inexpensive food, they were amazed at the cost
of food in St. John's. Eggs were six shillings a dozen; a
turkey cost ten shillings, chicken a great treat, cream and
butter were a luxury. Fortunately the Bishop kept them well

supplied with meat, no doubt from that contributed by the people for his own table.

Yet there were compensations. The Sisters were entranced by the beauty of the clear sky and the brilliancy of the sun and were pleased to find that the winter days were longer than those in Ireland. They were surprised to find that, in spite of the discomforts which they had to endure and the rigors of the harsh climate, they enjoyed excellent health. And soon, good news lifted their spirits. By January, the new school was ready. It contained two class-rooms with high ceilings and each with five Gothic-styled windows on either side. The Sisters must have been delight-ed with the advantages this new school gave them. Already in their letters home, they were asking for materials to begin the teaching of music by which they were afterwards to make such an incomparable contribution to the cultural life of Newfoundland.

The Sisters stayed in their "temporary convent" for eight years giving to the location the name Nunnery Hill which it still bears. Even then, as we shall see, their travels would by no means be over. Bishop Fleming had hoped to press ahead with the building of a permanent convent for them soon after their arrival, but many matters frustrated his intention and to these we must now turn our attention.

CHAPTER SEVEN
RIOTS AND BAYONETS

Not only has he (the Bishop) *abused us,*
but he has abused the respectable portion of his flock—
nay, he has abused the whole community.

- Henry Winton

I t was not long before political turmoil again engulfed Bishop Fleming. In the fall of 1833, Mr. Thomas was appointed to the Legislative Council, and a by-election became necessary to find his successor in the Assembly. There were two candidates: one, **Doctor Carson**,* undeterred by his previous failure; the other, **Timothy Hogan**,* a dissident Catholic, merchant and President of the Benevolent Irish Society. It was Hogan who had chaired the meeting which nominated Patrick Kough during the previous election in 1832—so the motives of those behind his nomination were clear. As before, the Bishop supported Doctor Carson. The people, realizing how, in the previous election, they had been manipulated on behalf of Kough, turned against Hogan. He eventually withdrew from the contest alleging, in a public statement, that the Bishop had announced from the altar that it would promote the interests of religion to elect Doctor Carson. Moreover, he claimed that the Bishop had declared that he would make grass grow before the doors[1] of anyone who voted against him. As a consequence, Doctor Carson was elected unopposed.

Henry Winton was again outraged at this continued interference by the clergy in the political process. He began another series of bitter attacks against them in *The Ledger*. On December 10, for instance, he wrote that Father Troy, who was the Bishop's right-hand man, had brought disgrace upon the Catholic Church and scandal upon the community. He claimed that the Roman Catholics were so thoroughly under the control of the priesthood as to be deprived of the free use of their civil rights. He regretted that the town did not have an enlightened Roman Catholic Bishop and a well-educated man. Instead, he wrote, the priest is found "in the streets at the head of a mob, busily engaged in the scenes of contention . . . and, in church, in uttering horrible denunciations against those who oppose his political favorites, and is filling their ears with the language of abuse and obscenity!"

A week later, Winton returned to the attack: "Not only has he (the Bishop) abused us, but he has abused the respectable portion of his flock—nay, he has abused the whole community... He will be regarded in every instance as the *ruffianly* offender." Winton then went on to accuse the clergy of instigating attacks upon his and others' properties, especially Mr. Hogan's: "The altar which was once dedicated to the service of the living God has been of late desecrated to the service of Mammon". While *The Patriot*, a newspaper begun by Doctor Carson, was every bit as vituperative in its reply to Winton's charges, the Bishop remained aloof. If the Government had wanted Winton to moderate his attacks and thus avoid civil discord, it could easily have done so since he was dependent on Government advertising to finance his paper.

Towards midnight on December 22, inflamed by these continued tirades against their clergy, a group gathered outside Winton's home, threw stones and broke some of his windows. Winton was not deterred. In his Christmas Eve edition, he defied his attackers and once more attacked the

Bishop and clergy stating that "the laboring population of
this country are under even greater subjection to the domin-
ion of ignorance and priestcraft than are the corresponding
inhabitants of the most unenlightened parts of Ireland; a
fact which can only be accounted for by the unhappy circumstance that for years past the Roman Catholic priesthood in this country have themselves been anything but an
ornament to the church to which they belong."

That night his house was again attacked and some damage was done. On the following day, Christmas Day, a threatening crowd once more gathered before it. The magistrates
and constables tried to control the situation but were inef-
fective. Within, the house was defended by about twenty
men with guns. When night drew near, a detachment of
some eighty soldiers under Lieutenant Rice was sent to the
scene to protect Winton and his family. The soldiers formed
three sides of a square in front of the house and the area
began to resemble a war zone. A rumor spread through the
town that the military had attacked some youths playing in
the street, and the crowd grew constantly. Fear was
expressed for the safety of the military and even for the
town, since every house was built of wood and a single mus-
ket shot could start a conflagration. The Riot Act was read
repeatedly, but the crowd refused to disperse. Some influential citizens, highly alarmed by what was happening,
appealed to Bishop Fleming to intervene, but he hesitated to
do so. He feared that, in the excited state in which the people were described to be, his authority and presence would
be unheeded, while, if he failed to calm them, his well meant
efforts would expose him to calumny and misrepresentation
as it had on other occasions. Clearly, he was still unsure how
far his authority extended over the people.

Eventually the military succeeded in partially clearing
the street and then retired to the court house, leaving sen-
tries around Winton's dwelling. Apparently James Kent had
guaranteed that, if the soldiers withdrew, the crowd would

disperse. But, if so, he had overestimated his influence, for soon afterwards the crowd began to reassemble, and the military were forced to return. Eventually, in a desperate attempt to clear the street, the soldiers fixed bayonets and charged. Some of the crowd were bayoneted, others arrested. The danger reached such a pitch that many people came to the Bishop's residence to plead for his presence. Given the situation, he considered himself bound to make the effort regardless of consequences to himself. He proceeded to the scene accompanied by his priests and, with considerable difficulty, succeeded in quieting the people and persuading them to retire to their homes.

Alarmed at the swelling unrest, Governor Cochrane, the following day, summoned Bishop Fleming to Government House to discuss how to defuse the situation. Following their meeting, the Bishop issued a circular letter to the "Catholics of St. John's", appealing to them "with all my might...to maintain that respect and obedience to the Laws which the principles of our Holy Religion inspire and command." He attempted to soothe them by stating that he had had an interview with Governor Cochrane in which, he claimed, the Governor had strongly disapproved of those "who wantonly prostitute the press to base and abusive purposes." The Governor had apologized for the actions of the military, he said, and had promised an inquiry. On the same day, December 27, a group of leading Catholics gathered in the Orphan Asylum School to protest this "despotic attempt to infringe upon our liberties." The meeting, with Doctor Carson in the chair and with his son, Doctor Samuel Carson, in the group, passed resolutions to be laid before the Governor, expressing their indignation at the introduction of a large military force into the town, calling for "signal punishment of the delinquents," and expressing grateful thanks to Bishop Fleming "for his prompt, judicious, and efficient service in calming an incensed multitude, maddened by insult and outrage."

Incredibly, the *Ledger* still breathed defiance, and, on the following Tuesday, December 31, Winton mocked the Bishop's interpretation of his meeting with the Governor, claiming that he "is charged with having been guilty, if not of a wilful, at least of a gross misrepresentation of the conversation which really did transpire." The Governor's subsequent actions supported Winton's contention for, in answering the Carson petition, the Governor repudiated the Bishop's version of their conversation, stating that the Magistrates were right in calling for the Military. The Bishop was both indignant at the Governor's insulting contradiction of his report and dismayed that now the people might well be stirred up again.

In spite of his ambiguous actions in this difficult situation, it is generally accepted that Sir Thomas Cochrane was one of the best governors ever to come to Newfoundland. He possessed a progressive spirit, as witnessed by the program of road-building that he inaugurated as well as by the magnificent (and costly) Government House he built for himself on Military Road. He was sincerely interested in Newfoundland and the betterment of its people, though this did not prevent him, in a later interview, from claiming that "a more desolate, unproductive, unmanageable country except Labrador, does not, in my opinion, exist on the face of the earth." Nevertheless, like the vast majority of the ruling class, he was entrenched in the traditional order of society where it was the responsibility of the upper classes to govern and that of the "lower orders" to obey. He would have agreed with the person who complained that he could not agree with the "French philosophy" that all men are born equal, because "he had been born a gentleman."

He had, moreover, a very poor idea of Roman Catholics in general. "There are very few respectable Roman Catholics in the colony," he declared in his evidence before the *Select Committee* of the British Parliament, "not one Roman-Catholic in the colony fit to put in it [*the advisory*

Council], either of intelligence, or property, or station. This view was in stark contrast to the flattering tone of his letter to Bishop Fleming in which he spoke of "the numerous and highly respectable body of the Roman Catholics in the island." Obviously the Governor was quite capable of making very different statements in public from those he made in private—a deviousness that was unhesitatingly challenged by Bishop Fleming. In spite of his antipathy to Roman Catholics generally, the Governor had been on good terms with Bishop Fleming's predecessor, Bishop Scallan, whom he described as "very conciliatory and very quiet." Hence he must have been disconcerted by the new breed of clerics represented by Bishop Fleming.

In spite of his many excellent qualities, Governor Cochrane, as the first career governor of the island, was often influenced by self-interest. Some time previously, he had applied for the governorship of Nova Scotia when it should become vacant. He was therefore anxious to avoid anything which might reflect on the conduct of his administration. At the beginning of December, alarmed by the possibility of violence, he had written Major General Campbell in Fredericton, the commander of the armed forces in Nova Scotia, asking for reinforcements. Campbell had refused this request, citing disturbances in Sydney "headed by a Priest." On the day after the riots, Cochrane wrote Campbell again, protesting against this refusal and placing the blame for the disturbances squarely on the Catholic clergy. The riots, he wrote, proceed "from the growing evil of political differences mixed up with the religious antipathies in which the Roman Catholic Priesthood are the chief instigators to violence with a bigoted flock. "Significantly," he continued, "It is, however, satisfactory to me to feel that whatever may result from the present position of the Colony, the strong and repeated representations I have made . . . will fully exonerate me with His Majesty from all blame and responsibility."

On the same day, in a dispatch to the Colonial Office, he repeated this theme: "whatever may result from the inadequacy of the force at my disposal to meet the present disposition to outrage, that His Majesty's government will consider it has not arisen from any supineness on my part duly and constantly to urge its augmentation." He seems more concerned about his reputation than about the safety of the people. The most significant part of these dispatches is what he does not mention. There is no reference to the bayoneting incident which could easily have caused full-scale riots.[2] He merely wrote that: "Last night a most serious disturbance took place in the Town which although suppressed for the instant, I have every reason to fear is succeeded by only a momentary tranquillity." In view of all this, we may be justified in speculating that the Governor did, indeed, say one thing to the Bishop and another to the military, and that when his failure to report truthfully the bayoneting incident came to the attention of the Colonial Office, it may have been a major reason for his recall the following year. In any event, the result of the Bishop's intervention was a temporary cooling of the political temperature. However, it rapidly boiled up again though in a different direction.

CHAPTER EIGHT
His Enemies Unite

"Who does not affirm that so long as Bishop Fleming and Mr. Troy are allowed to remain in Newfoundland there can be no peace for them (i.e., the people of Newfoundland.)"

- Governor Cochrane

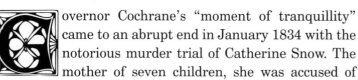overnor Cochrane's "moment of tranquillity" came to an abrupt end in January 1834 with the notorious murder trial of Catherine Snow. The mother of seven children, she was accused of conspiring with her lover, Tobias Mandeville, and a servant, Arthur Spring, to murder her husband. The trial took place on Friday, January 10, and after "a long(!) and patient investigation," which ended during the late evening of that same day, all three were found guilty and death sentence passed upon them. Both Mandeville and Spring admitted their guilt and were hanged from the Court House on the following Monday. Judge Boulton, in his address to the jury, stated that although neither Spring nor Mandeville had implicated Catherine in the murder, still "if upon other evidence you will find that she instigated one or both of them to murder her husband, you will indict her as accessory before the fact." When Catherine was found guilty, she revealed that she was pregnant, and her execution was postponed until her child was delivered.

All three accused were Catholics, and Bishop Fleming had the sad duty of preparing them for their execution. He remained in the cell with Mandeville and Spring for the two nights preceding their execution, and celebrated Mass there each morning. On Monday morning, Fathers Troy and Ward accompanied them to the scaffold. Part of the usual punishment for such offences was the performance of an autopsy by the Surgeon General after which the bodies were exhibited on a gibbet. Governor Cochrane, reporting shortly afterwards to the Secretary of State for Colonial Affairs, was indignant that "on the interference of the Roman Catholic Priests...the hanging in chains was remitted, that an anatomical form was gone through of making a scratch with penknife on their necks, and that the parties had a public and rather imposing funeral." It would appear that the surgeon, who was also a Catholic, feared for his life if he attempted to carry out the prescribed operation.

Catherine was ill for some time after the delivery and, ironically, her execution was further postponed until she should regain her health. There was strong circumstantial evidence linking her to the crime, but the priests were convinced of her innocence and, after the trial, made great efforts to have the Governor remit her sentence but without success.

In July, her child having been delivered and her health restored, Catherine Snow suffered the same fate as the others. Father Waldron, in the absence of the Bishop who was visiting the northern extremities of his Vicariate, assisted her for the last few days, and at 3 a.m. in the morning of Monday, July 21, offered Mass in her cell. At 5 a.m. came the gruesome ceremony of putting on her "grave garb." At the sight of her shroud, she became hysterical but later recovered her calm. At a quarter to nine, Fathers Troy, Ward, and Waldron accompanied her to the scaffold "to which she advanced with firm step." She died, declaring "that she was a wretched sinful woman, but as innocent of any participation in the crime for which she was about to suffer as her child unborn." Convinced of her innocence, the priests had her buried in consecrated ground, though this was against

Canon Law in the case of convicted murderers. So died the last woman to be hanged in Newfoundland.

In between these painful events, the Bishop performed more pleasing functions. In April he acquired five adjoining pieces of land to form a farm. This farm located at the back of the town, he called 'Carpasia' after his titular Bishopric, the approach to it is now called *Carpasian Road*. On the 6th of the same month, he presided at the marriage of his sister Johanna to the rising merchant and politician, **John Kent**.* For the Bishop, this ceremony provided a peaceful moment amidst the social turmoil and his constant confrontations with Governor Cochrane.

To Governor Cochrane, these confrontations were a source of growing irritation. He blamed the Bishop for being the major cause of the unrest prevalent in the Colony. Originally his objective had been simply to force the Bishop to restrict his activities to purely spiritual matters. His reports on the political activities of the Catholic clergy during the elections of 1832 had greatly disturbed the officials at the Colonial Office. Reacting to one such report, **Lord Stanley**,* the head of the Office, wrote **Lord Palmerston,*** the Secretary of State for Foreign Affairs, to ask him to request the Vatican "to put a stop to the objectionable course adopted by the clergy of Newfoundland." He urged that this be done through a suitable British agent on the continent but warned that it must be done "in a manner perfectly free from all legal perils." This last request was important since legally there could be no direct diplomatic contact between England and Rome, such contact having been broken off from the time of Henry VIII.

Urged by his advisors, the Governor eventually decided to try to oust the Bishop from the Island. His reports on the priests' activities in the by-election of December 1833 and consequent events were increasingly critical. By August 1834, the Foreign Office was persuaded that definite action must be taken. Because of the legal complications, the chain

of communication was a tortuous one, from **Spring Rice***
(now Secretary of State for the Colonies) to Lord Palmerston
(still at the Foreign Office) to Seymour (British representative in Florence) to Aubin (British agent in Rome) to
Monsignor Capaccini* in the Secretariat of State, to
Cardinal Fransoni,* the Prefect of Propaganda Fide.
Monsignor Capaccini, taken aback by the lurid presentation
made to him by Aubin of Bishop Fleming's misbehavior,
promised that Propaganda Fide would put a stop to such
practices. Nevertheless, he decided on a more gentle intervention. Instead of conveying his misgivings to the Prefect
of Propaganda Fide, he wrote a personal letter to Bishop
Fleming on November 9, 1834, reminding him of their meeting in the Netherlands when he had been Internuncio there.
He noted the part which the clergy were reported to have
taken in the recent election and strongly urged that upon
any such future occasion, the Bishop would take firm steps
to prevent similar occurrences.

The dissident Catholics in St. John's now joined in the
attack. It seems probable that they were in the confidence of
the Governor and knew what measures were being taken by
the British authorities in the matter. Mrs. Eliza Boulton,
wife of the notorious Judge Boulton, herself a Catholic but
hardly sympathetic towards the Bishop, wrote to
Propaganda Fide in September 1834, complaining of the
conduct of Father Troy and belittling the Bishop who, she
said: ". . . set out with good intentions, but being a weak
man, and having no reason formally to expect his present
elevation, he has become dizzy." She revealed her bias when
she claimed: "Since the election of the present bishop, every
educated priest has left this town. But one, I hear, remains
in the Island. He is the Reverend Mr. Browne of Ferryland."
Father Browne*, as we shall see shortly, was sadly another and a pivotal member of the clique opposed to the Bishop.

Later, Bishop Fleming was to describe the hatred of
those dissident Catholics towards him. They went from

house to house contradicting the Bishop's condemnation of rash oaths (the practice of "taking the pledge") citing the silence of his predecessors on this matter. They distorted his teaching as favoring drunkenness. His constant reproof of their laxity in religious matters brought on him their "venomous rancor," a bitterness which increased when he defied their authority and began giving religious instruction to the children in the Orphan Asylum School. When he set out to combat the spread of sexual immorality in all its varied forms, they became still more hostile, for their own relatives and friends were among those whom he was condemning. As he said in a picturesque, if mixed metaphor, "to disturb their dens of lewdness was to thrust my hand into a nest of hornets."

Soon the campaign against him progressed to the point that his dismissal from his post was being demanded. When Governor Cochrane was recalled to England in October 1834, even while still at sea, he complained to the Colonial Office: "Who does not affirm that so long as Bishop Fleming and Mr. Troy are allowed to remain in Newfoundland there can be no peace for them (*i.e., the people of Newfoundland*)." However, the severity of his denunciation may be explained by the fact that, while the governor and his family were on their way to embark for England, he was jeered by the mob and his carriage pelted with mud.

Governor Prescott,* Cochrane's successor, started off well by dropping charges which Cochrane had instituted against Father Troy, but soon revealed his real sentiments— or perhaps the way he had been influenced by those around him. Less than two months after his appointment, he wrote to the Earl of Aberdeen who had replaced Spring Rice as Secretary for the Colonies, "We have unfortunately an illiterate and vulgar RC bishop whose dependent clergy being principally of his own choice would lead one to believe that there was a common influence behind them." When some years later, the Bishop was given the opportunity to read

Prescott's dispatches concerning him, he was infuriated at the duplicity of the Governor, for that damning judgement was written on the same day that the Governor, in receiving him at Government House had exclaimed: "My dear Doctor Fleming, I [have] just been writing my dispatches and telling His Majesty how easy I find the government in consequence of the kind assistance you afford me." If this incident is true—and we have no reason to believe otherwise—it is indicative of the atmosphere of deceit with which the Bishop was surrounded in his dealings with the civil authorities. At times, he seems to have felt like a bewildered fly caught in an invisible web.

Another participant in the campaign against Bishop Fleming now arrived on the scene. He was **Michael McLean Little**,* a minor Catholic shop-keeper who had opposed the Bishop's nominations for the Assembly. The Bishop later described him as "a reputed Catholic, but one who was a notorious infidel." He complained to the Governor that, as a result of his opposition to the Bishop, his business was being boycotted by the Catholics of the town and he was being forced into penury. The truth of this complaint, however, is dubious since Prescott's successor, Governor Harvey, later suggested that, in fact, the additional business McLean received from the Establishment more than made up for his losses. Governor Prescott* took the unprecedented action of forwarding McLean's petition to the Colonial Office calling him "one of the most valuable individuals of our Society, an industrious tradesman and member of the house of Assembly, the father of ten children, the sole prop and stay of two ancient relatives, (he) is meditating a removal from this his native land in consequence of the persecutions he has suffered." Prescott added that he had been told, before leaving for Newfoundland, that measures had been taken to prevent Roman Catholic clerical interference, and suggested that the best remedy for Newfoundland would be the removal of Bishop Fleming.

This letter of Governor Prescott's is another indication of the lengths to which the Bishop's enemies were prepared to go to obtain his removal. McLean was never a member of the Assembly and it was not possible for Governor Prescott to be ignorant of this fact. Yet the Governor was prepared to deceive his own government in order to influence its decision. Of all these plots, Bishop Fleming had as yet no knowledge. This innocence, however, was not to last much longer.

CHAPTER NINE
NORTHERN ADVENTURE

Five days and nights passed in an open boat with no protection from the weather, unable to stand or even change positions without putting the boat in danger of overturning, enduring the constant smell of putrid fish, and with a bare minimum of food.

- Bishop Fleming's description
of his northern voyage

ompletely unaware of these secret plots against him, Bishop Fleming decided early in 1834 to begin the visitation of his far-flung Vicariate, many isolated parts of which had never seen a priest, let alone a Bishop. Immediately after presiding at the wedding of his sister in April, he set out on a three-week visitation of the settlements in Conception Bay. It is probably on this trip that he had his first real experience of the difficulties of travel in Newfoundland and that he displayed his extraordinary stamina and endurance of severe hardships. He made this journey on foot through thick forests where there was no hint of a road. For most of the trip, he walked barefoot—his one pair of shoes having given out before he had finished a third of the way. He waded through fast-rushing rivers, ice-covered lakes and clinging bogs, his clothes torn by the trees and thorns through which he had to force his way. With no means of changing, he had to let his garments dry on his back. For ten nights in a row he slept in the woods, his only bed was a few branches thrown on the ground, with no other covering than the sky. His only food was hard biscuit washed down by black tea.

As might well be expected even for a man of his stamina, when he returned to St. John's from this trip, he was exhausted. Writing **James Crowdy***, the Colonial Secretary, on April 29, he apologized for the delay in answering his communication of the nineteenth. He explained that he had been away for the past three weeks, and had only returned on the previous Saturday night, having walked along the shore of Conception Bay from Harbour Main to Portugal Cove—a distance of about fifty miles which he covered in a single day! "The great fatigue which I felt," he wrote, "with pains in every joint of my body after the last day's journey . . . that I was unable to hold a pen in my hand yesterday." This harrowing experience, however, did not deter him from his long intended project of visiting the northern parts of his far-flung Vicariate.

In June 1834, he set out for the north without any idea how he was to get there. The government provided a naval vessel for the Anglican Bishop when needed, but had refused a similar request from Bishop Fleming. He was grateful, therefore, to accept the offer of free transport from the owner of a fishing schooner that was returning from St. John's to Tilting Harbour on Fogo Island. He took with him his young fellow Franciscan, Father Charles Dalton, whom he had recently appointed Parish Priest of Harbour Grace. When he boarded the vessel on June 20, it was crowded with men and women hired for the fishing season and, as well, was loaded to the gunwales with the needed equipment. Although the winds were favourable, the trip from St. John's to Tilting lasted two full days. It was very uncomfortable sailing in those crowded conditions utterly lacking in privacy.

They arrived in Tilting to find a small, well-sheltered harbour, skirted by numerous small homes, each with its fish flakes and small vegetable plot, the area being suited for farming. Tilting had been settled by Thomas Burke, a native of Dungarvan, an Irish port some miles from the Bishop's home town of Carrick. Consequently, Tilting was a Catholic enclave in the midst of a generally Protestant area, and the Bishop remained there for four days confirming 300 candidates from the community and nearby settlements.

His goal was Fortune Harbour on the west side of Notre Dame Bay, or Green Bay as it was popularly known at the time. This port marked the northern boundary of British territory on the Island. All beyond this point being under the control of the French. A small fishing boat was about to set out from Tilting for this harbour and offered passage to the Bishop and his companion. Notre Dame Bay is very exposed to the winds and notoriously stormy. Having been battered by adverse winds for an entire day and not having even cleared Fogo Island, the weary travellers were forced to seek refuge in Joe Batt's Arm on the north side of the same Island. They were not the first to find shelter here for the port derived its picturesque name from its first settler, supposedly a deserter from Captain Cook on one of his northern trips. The Bishop, taking advantage of the opportunity his forced refuge provided, celebrated Mass for the people and confirmed another 100 candidates.

The delay, however, forced the boat on which he had been travelling to return to Tilting for the fishery. Seeing the Bishop's predicament, Henry Stark and his crew of two offered to bring him on his way in their little vessel. So, the next morning, they set out once more through rough seas with contrary winds still beating upon them. All through that day and the following night they struggled on. Finally, with the crew exhausted, a storm threatening, and very little progress made, the Bishop decided to put into some port so as to obtain another vessel with a fresh crew and release Stark and his crew to return to their home. He was full of remorse due to the length of time he was keeping them from their fishery—their only means of livelihood. This remorse which was later increased when he learned that the week's fishing they had lost had been the only really successful week of the season. Consequently, when daylight came, they put into Fogo Harbour, still on the northern part of Fogo Island. Stark and his crew had been hurt at the Bishop's intention, however well meant, to release them. They were delighted to learn that no other boat was available and that the Bishop was forced to continue to use their services.

That day, fortune smiled on them and they made considerable progress reaching New World Island. Another storm, however, which sprang up just as evening came on, forced them to seek shelter once again, this time in Herring Neck, a bleak area on the north extremity of this Island. Though Herring Neck is a sheltered harbour, its approach is through a treacherous inlet and it was from this peculiarity that the area got its name. The ocean nearby abounded in herring and the fishermen were accustomed to carry their catch over a narrow neck of land to the village, rather than tempt the treacherous waters of the inlet. However, our travellers were fortunate enough to navigate it safely and were welcomed by the Kent family. The Bishop was happy to enjoy the luxury of a bed and proper food which they provided.

The next morning, conditions having improved, they set out again and, at long last, succeeded in reaching their destination, Fortune Harbour. The journey from Tilting had taken them five days, four of which they had spent beating around all sides of Fogo Island. It had been an unpleasant and dangerous voyage. Five days and nights passed in an open boat with no protection from the weather, unable to stand or even change positions without putting the boat in danger of overturning. In addition to this they had to endure the repulsive smell arising from the fish putrefying in the heat of the sun, with a bare minimum of food and racked with thirst. This was an ordeal calculated to tax the endurance of any traveller let alone a sailor as subject to sickness as was Bishop Fleming.

When they eventually arrived at Fortune Harbour, the scene had an overpowering effect upon the Bishop. Later he described its impact upon him:

> It was evening on the first of July when we slowly approached the high and commanding shores on the north west side of Green Bay, and weary as we were, our limbs crippled from constant sitting, our eyelids closing from want of sleep, our spirits depressed, and our crew at length exhausted with exertion, yet subdued as we were, we could not refrain from admiring the sublimity of the prospect before us: the majesty of the mountains crowned by eternal forests as the setting sun poured its "liquid light" through the foliage.

Frustratingly, the inlet was very narrow, the wind had died down, and they were unable to make their way in. Fortunately, they were seen from the shore and curiosity brought out a boat to see them. When it was learned who the distinguished visitor was, the investigating boat returned rapidly to shore and soon several skiffs came out to tow them in. Amid great rejoicing, every man, woman and child left their employments to welcome them. The evening was given over to festivities and ended with a prayer of thanksgiving for this great blessing since, in living memory, they had only twice before been visited by a clergyman.

The Bishop found some forty families there, principally Irish or of Irish descent. Now at last, he was able to send Henry Stark and his crew back to their home in Joe Batt's Arm. For the next three days, all work in Fortune Harbour ceased as the people prepared for Confirmation. The Bishop was both pleased and amazed to discover how well versed the people of the settlement were in their religion and how fervently they practiced it. The fathers of three families were accustomed to assemble the people alternatively at their homes for prayer and spiritual reading on Sundays and holidays, while during Lent and Advent, each evening was devoted to a spiritual lecture and to the saying of the Rosary. On Sunday mornings, one of the ladies of the place, a Mrs. Power, who had received her education from a community of Nuns in her native Germany, would take the children for religious instruction and prayer. No wonder that the Bishop could speak of them as "a people . . . among whom reigns so much virtue . . . where vice is so little known." He gave thanks to God that he had been given the courage and strength to survive such a hazardous enterprise, and he looked forward to the day when, having received instruction from the Presentation Sisters, each settlement in Newfoundland would have women similarly prepared to undertake this work.

But three days was all the Bishop could spare, and soon, too soon, he had to leave. He wrote: "I met these good people in joy, and parted them in pain," while the people were in tears at his departure after such a short visit, even the weather-beaten fishermen had tears rolling down their cheeks. As the Bishop prepared to make his meandering journey homewards, he discovered one immense difficulty— there was no sail boat in the harbour. So, having no other choice, he boarded a small skiff or punt, as the local people called it, and set out. Not much bigger than a dory, it was crammed with himself and Father Dalton, and a crew of four oarsmen. Loaded with their provisions and other supplies, the boat was dangerously low in the water. Rather than try to cross the stormy Notre Dame Bay directly, and since he intended to visit as many settlements as he could on the way home, they skirted the shore. On the first evening, they put in at a place called Ship-run. Here, there were only two families but he must have found a sail boat for he says that "I exchanged a couple of hands for a younger and fresher pair, and having passed the night there, sailed in the morning for Moreton's Harbour." Morteon's Harbour was located on the west side of New World Island.

By this time, his muscles had begun to rebel from having spent so much time sitting in a cramped position. When they landed at Moreton's Harbour, his legs refused to hold him up. A local Protestant settler, a Mr. Taylor, hearing of his arrival, pressed him to remain to recover his strength, but, not being able to procure a fresh crew, and knowing that there was no place between Moreton's Harbour and Fogo where he could hope to find a boat or a crew, he was forced reluctantly to refuse his kind invitation and to press on to Fogo. During his short stay, however, he met a Mi'Kmaq Indian and promised to meet his people at their headquarters at Conne River on the south coast of Newfoundland during the following summer.

On the way to Fogo, they encountered constant headwind so that, with night coming on, the crew getting exhausted and his own physical condition deteriorating, the Bishop asked the men to put in to land. They lit a fire, ate what they could, and slept on the rocks until the following morning. The Bishop was so exhausted that he could later describe this sleep as "the soundest and most refreshing sleep we ever in our lives enjoyed." Next morning they set out again and reached Fogo without incident. The trip from Moreton's Harbour had taken them twenty-four hours.

By now, the Bishop must have learned his lesson that it was foolhardy to venture into these treacherous waters in such small boats. Consequently, at Tilting Harbour, he ordered a schooner to be built—probably by the Burke family which had taken up ship building. The vessel was to be delivered to him in the following spring when he intended to visit these northern regions again, since he was not satisfied with the haphazard way in which he had been forced to cover this territory on this first attempt.

The Bishop gave only a summary account of the rest of his trip homeward. From Fogo, he visited briefly Greenspond in Bonavista Bay where he was hospitably received. King's Cove, located on the rocky slopes of a sheltered cove on the opposite side of the same bay, was the largest settlement he encountered in his travels. It was the headquarters of the MacBraire Company whose owner, James MacBraire, had also been one of the founding members of the Benevolent Irish Society. The company had experienced a swell of prosperity during the Napoleonic wars when salt fish was in great demand everywhere, and James MacBraire, although a Protestant, had encouraged Catholic immigrants from Ireland to settle in King's Cove. By the time of the Bishop's visit, the Catholic community had grown to almost 300 members out of a population of about 420. Moreover, the agent of the MacBraire Company, a Mr. Mullowney, was a native of Cork. Consequently, the Bishop received a very warm welcome and was provided with every comfort. Mr. Mullowney even provided them with a boat and a crew for the rest of their journey. So, in relative comfort, they visited various harbours in Trinity Bay and finally reached Bay de Verde at the northern extremity of Conception Bay. Here the Bishop sent the boat back to King's Cove while he concluded his visitation by visiting the various harbours in Conception Bay before returning to St. John's. He gave some idea of the hardships he had endured when he summarized his travels thus:

> I accomplished a journey of at least more than twelve hundred miles, visiting forty-six harbours in my circuit through Green Bay [*Notre Dame Bay*] Bonavista Bay, Trinity Bay, and Conception Bay, I administered the sacrament of Confirmation to upwards to 3000 persons, of Penance and Eucharist to more than that number. For the great part of the time I knew not the

luxury of a bed, while for days and nights together, I had not an opportunity of reclining even on
the thwart of the boat. I have not been able for
days to take off my clothes, I seldom met with better fare than a hard sea biscuit and a little fish,
sometimes a bit of fat pork out of the pickle, while
I had not an opportunity of indulging myself in
my exhaustion with a single glass of wine—no
variety of food whatever, except when the men
would land on some desolate rocky island, and
robbing the sea-fowl of their eggs, strike a fire
and roast them on the rocks, while at the same
time the stench of the boat from bilge water,
mixed with putrid fish, so affected my stomach as
to induce a severe bilious attack, which developed
itself upon my return.

By early September he was back in St. John's hard at
work, apparently recovered from the hardships of his journey. But it may well have been that it was on this journey,
living in wet clothes for days at a time with inadequate food,
that he first contracted the dreaded disease of tuberculosis
which was eventually to cause his death.

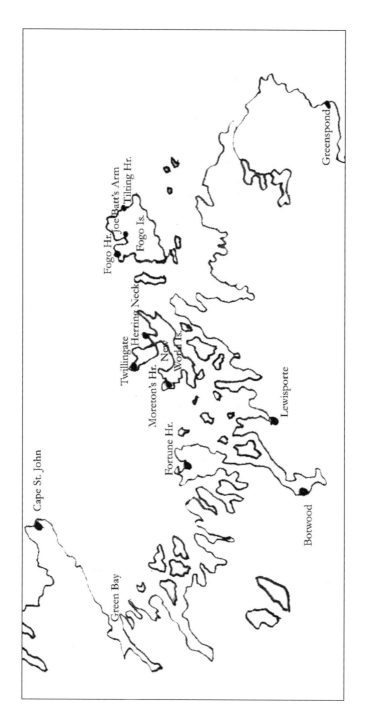

Map of Bishop Fleming's Northern Adventure

CHAPTER TEN
THE CROPPY BOY

Now Orangeman gentry wherever you be,
Whether in Newfoundland or home over the sea,
Don't treat the poor Papist with scorn and with jeers
Just remember what happened to Winton's two ears.

- "Sectarian Ballads"
collected by Doctor James M. F. McGrath

he same pattern of involvement in political turmoil followed by a lengthy ocean voyage prevailed for Bishop Fleming during the following year, 1835. When he returned from his northern voyage in September 1834, he found that the Assembly and Legislative Council had descended into such bickering as to be mocked in the English press. A cartoon in one of the English papers depicted the members of the Assembly as Newfoundland dogs in legal dress and described the Assembly as the "Bow Wow Parliament." The reformers, claiming that several of the members had been elected illegally, were clamoring for the Assembly to be dissolved and new elections called. On the other hand, the Conservatives had introduced a bill to increase the membership of the Assembly to twenty five hoping, thereby, to ensure their control of the Assembly for the foreseeable future since the additional members would be elected from areas under their control. The Assembly itself was at loggerheads with the Legislative Council particularly over the exorbitant salaries allotted to the Government officials, £10,000 out of a total budget of £27,000.

Judge Boulton's decisions and the new laws he introduced as President of the Legislative Council were causing ever greater outrage. It became practically impossible for Catholics to plead cases before the Court or to act as jurors. Boulton introduced a bill that would give the judges the power of banishment, whipping, hard labour in leg-irons. His execution of Catherine Snow could only be called barbarous. His worst offence was to reverse the age-old custom of the fishermen having first claim on the proceeds of their fishery. This threatened the livelihood of every fisherman in the Island since the merchants could claim these proceeds for their own profit. In view of all this, it is no wonder that Bishop Fleming felt himself forced to intervene, as he did on several occasions. For instance, he signed the resolution protesting against the bayoneting of the gathering at Winton's house, the petition to have the Assembly dissolved, the petition to have Judge Boulton removed and took an active part in the attempt to implement that petition. As he complained on one occasion, he was "in the unenviable position of being obliged constantly to stand between my flock and their oppressors." He alleged that, but for his intervention, political agitation would have been far worse: "...the only reason why intense agitation does not prevail here is because I have constantly discountenanced agitation, constantly discountenanced meetings except when irritation produced by gross ill-treatment from the Executive rendered them expedient as political safety valves."

The relations between Bishop Fleming and the authorities were further damaged when word of Monsignor Capaccini's letter of November 9, 1834, was "leaked" to the press. In the *Ledger* of December 16, Winton wrote: "It has, within the last week, been rumored that our most particular friend, 'His LORDSHIP of CARPASIEN' has . . . been cited to appear before His HOLINESS, to account for certain mis-

doings since the unlucky day that he was placed at the head
of the Catholic church in the Colony." After much more in
the same vein, he concluded: "WE SHALL NEVER MISS
HIM."

The following week, the *Patriot* retorted to Winton's
abuse of the Bishop. Its editorial ended ominously: "The
Editor of *The Ledger* . . . has committed an enduring, a
burning insult upon every Catholic in the Island—an insult
that must fester and rankle in every bosom, until erased by
ample expiation—when and how this will be accomplished
remains to be seen."

Bishop Fleming himself refused to be drawn into the
affair. Indeed, *The Patriot* on one occasion commented: "we
cannot withhold our just approbation of the Catholic Bishop
for the spirit of forbearance which he has manifested
towards his base and unprincipled maligner."

On February 3, 1835, Winton went far beyond the limits
of acceptable comment even for those outspoken times. He
wrote: "A correspondent obscurely hints that the ecclesiastical appointment of a RANGER[1] OF THE NUNNERY is
about to be established, and modestly inquires if the House
of Assembly will not provide for ———— young Nuns."
[*dash in the original.*]

This atrocious insult to Religious so highly respected by
all classes brought forth an immediate outcry. In the next
issue, Winton apologized, but the damage was done and only
the opportunity was awaited for "ample compensation" to
be made.

Winton's column in December 1834 in which he claimed
that Bishop Fleming was being summoned to Rome must
have alerted the Bishop that "something was in the wind."
He could not but realize that he was the subject of discus-
sions between Rome and the British Government. He was
indignant that this was happening without his knowledge
and dashed off a letter to Lord Aberdeen, the Secretary of
State for the Colonies, demanding to know what the charges

against him were. When he received no reply, he wrote again to know the cause of the delay: "Six weeks have elapsed since I have addressed Your Lordship on the imputations to my character." But again he received no answer. In the meantime, the British government had fallen and Lord Aberdeen had been replaced by **Lord Glenelg*** who was to prove much more sympathetic to the Bishop's position. In an internal memo of the Colonial Office, attached to the Bishop's letter, **Sir James Stephen*** wrote that he thought an answer had already been sent, and "if not, it is of great moment that no further delay should take place."

In the middle of May, the "ample expiation" promised to Winton finally took place. Winton rode to Carbonear with pistols in his pockets and defiantly made himself conspicuous there. On the afternoon of May 19, he left Carbonear for Harbour Grace with a friend, Captain Churchward. As they reached Saddle Hill, midway between the two towns, they were ambushed by a group of men, their faces disguised with yellow ochre. Captain Churchward was pinned down; Winton knocked unconscious with rocks. Then his left ear and most of his right were cut off. When he regained consciousness, Churchward brought him to Harbour Grace where his wounds were attended to by the local doctor. A reward of £200, later increased to £500, was posted for the arrest of the culprits, but they were never found. Governor Prescott reported to the Colonial Office that "the bad feeling of the lower class of Catholics, here as well as at Harbour Grace, has been manifested by the speedy removal of the proclamation from the walls, and by savage expressions of satisfaction at Mr. Winton's mutilation."

Although to our sensibilities, this act seems an outrage, it may have not appeared so to the perpetrators nor to the public generally. It was a time when, as we have seen, officialdom could order the execution of a pregnant mother of seven children. It was also common practice in the case of hanging, for the corpse to be subjected to an autopsy, have

its ears "cropped" and then hung on a gibbet for the edifi-
cation of the people. It was a time, too, when such an execution was the occasion of a public holiday and entertainment;
when a law could be passed providing for banishment, whipping, hard labour in shackles. In view of the above, the cutting off of part of a person's ears, particularly when done
with the care of a surgeon's knife, might not have seemed an
undue punishment for the outrage which Winton had committed. In fact, the punishment had a historic precedent.
When Sir Humphrey Gilbert took possession of
Newfoundland in the name of Queen Elizabeth, he proclaimed: "Anyone uttering words of dishonor to Her Majesty
should lose his ears and have his goods and ship confiscat-
ed." Governor Prescott complained to the Colonial Office
that "as he (Winton) has been repeatedly denounced from
the altar of the Roman Catholic chapel as an enemy to the
Bishop and Priests, it is much to be feared that the wretch-
es by whom the diabolical act was perpetrated may have
believed themselves to be performing a meritorious act."

Hardly was this incident over when passions were
aroused even higher by another such incident. An issue of
The Patriot contained an article severely critical of Judge
Boulton's conduct. The Judge had the editor, Robert
Parsons, arrested and brought to trial *before himself!* He
sentenced Parsons to three months imprisonment and a fine
of £50. In reaction to this patent injustice, tempers ran high.
A placard was placed on the Court House threatening dire
punishment to those involved in sentencing Parsons and, to
protect the Judge, Governor Prescott was forced to put a
military guard on the Court House while the Court was in
session.

Though Parsons was not a Catholic, his paper was very
friendly to the Catholic cause and this incident proved to be
the last straw for Bishop Fleming. He wrote a scorching letter to Daniel O'Connell, now a member of the British
Parliament, condemning the Judge's conduct and listing

many cases of his injustices. He called the Judge's appointment "a triple scourge—a violent Tory, he is in the Legislature a coercionist, on the Bench worse than a Jefferies[2] & everywhere a rank Bigot." In the same letter the Bishop asked O'Connell to present to the House of Commons petitions for financial assistance for the children of Catherine Snow "rendered orphaned from the unjust execution of their mother of a crime of any participation in which I must acquit her." He informed O'Connell that the people driven to desperation, had been on the verge of revolting and that to prevent this from happening, a society had been formed to direct their indignation into legal channels. This was the Constitutional Society which, according to Governor Prescott, was led by Patrick Morris, John Kent, Doctor Carson, John Doyle and Laurence O'Brien. An appeal was sent to the British Parliament where an emotional debate ensued. Eventually Parliament ordered that Parsons be released, his fine having been paid.

In the same month of June, the Bishop finally received Monsignor Capaccini's letter of admonition and realized, perhaps for the first time, the extent of the plot against him. Without delay, he dashed off a lengthy answer, defending his conduct and giving the history of the campaign against him—an answer which caused Capaccini to regret that the Bishop had thought it necessary to answer at such length. It was fortunate for Bishop Fleming's peace of mind that, at about the same time, he received a strong letter of support from Cardinal Fransoni which declared: "You indeed the Sacred Congregation will sincerely number among those Prelates of the Church of highest merit."

CHAPTER ELEVEN
THE MI'KMAQS

We felt as if we were touching an unexplored country, where all that can beautify or embellish, all that can cheer or animate the face of nature, is ever bright and ever verdant.

- Bishop Fleming

nce more Bishop Fleming was glad to get away from all this political turmoil, and when his long-awaited schooner finally arrived in the summer of 1835, he was eager to be off. He declared: "My heart was seized with the desire of visiting every creek and every cove of the entire Island." Unfortunately, it was now too late for him to venture the northern route again and so he determined to visit the south coast of the Island instead. Since he was particularly concerned about his promise to the Indians whom he described as "a people exceedingly jealous of the least attempt to deceive them," he took pains to get word to them that he would meet them at their headquarters on the Conne River on the south coast of the Island.

So, on Friday, July 17, 1835, as the Bishop embarked on the *Madonna* and saluted its captain and two-man crew, he must have been pleased with his new acquisition, a two-masted vessel of forty-four tons, forty-nine feet long and fifteen feet wide. He was again accompanied by Father Charles Dalton. Also on board was another of his clergy, Father Michael Berney, parish priest of Burin, who was on his way back to his parish. Besides its passengers and crew, the vessel was loaded with 6,000 feet of timber destined for the church in Petty Harbour.

It took them only an hour or so to reach Petty Harbour, to circumvent its treacherous entrance, and to anchor safely inside. The location of Petty Harbour so close to St. John's had, in earlier days, made it a favourite hiding place for pirates intent on attacking vessels bound for St. John's. For the same reason, in 1696, the French captured and sacked it as a preliminary for their successful assault on St. John's. The land is so rocky that it is almost impossible to grow any sort of crop there. Still, some 700 people, all dependent on the fishery and about half of whom were Roman Catholics, lived there in houses built wherever a sufficiently level spot could be found. The Bishop had begun a church there three years earlier and the lumber destined for it was now unloaded.

This should have necessitated only a brief stopover, but contrary winds caused a two day stay. Finally on Sunday morning after saying Mass for the people, he was able to set out once more. His first destination was Fermeuse about sixty miles farther south, but again the winds were contrary and, after battling gales all Sunday and Monday morning, the schooner was forced to put into Ferryland, a few miles short of his destination.

Ferryland presented a very different picture from Petty Harbour, the immediate neighbourhood being flat and fertile, though surrounded by rocky, barren hills. The harbour was large, the entrance well sheltered by islands. Both these factors had caused it to be chosen as the site of the historic settlement of Sir John Calvert (Lord Baltimore) in 1621, as a consequence of which, it can claim the longest continuous occupation in English-speaking Canada. Unfortunately, the Bishop could not enjoy these aspects of his visit. He had been having serious difficulties with the parish priest, Father Timothy Brownw, O.S.A., and he could not have been surprised to find him absent nor the people unprepared for

Confirmation. In order not to waste time, he decided to continue to Fermeuse, about four miles away. Since this settlement was located at the head of a long, narrow fiord, and he did not want to risk the *Madonna* in such confined waters, he engaged a skiff to take him there. Just as he was about to embark, he was joined by Father James Duffy, Father Browne's assistant priest. Father Duffy was responsible for the southern part of the parish and, suspecting that Father Brown might absent himself to avoid an embarrassing encounter with Bishop Fleming where his neglect of his spiritual duties would be exposed, he had hurried to Ferryland to receive the Bishop.

Arrived at Fermeuse, another of the historic fishing settlements in Newfoundland, the Bishop administered Confirmation to 120 people, whom he found well instructed by the same Father Duffy. Next morning, he ventured to Renews about six miles farther along the coast. This settlement, situated along the sides of a long fiord with steep rocky cliffs, was the nearest harbour to the fishing banks and hence also one of the oldest settlements in Newfoundland. The Bishop found it to be a poor fishing harbour but inhabited by very intelligent people. He confirmed about 140 candidates, all well instructed, most of whom were converts. In both these places, the people had built churches which, though large, were still only shells since the people did not have the financial means to furnish them. After the Confirmation ceremony, the Bishop returned to Fermeuse and rejoined the *Madonna*.

The next day, Thursday, the winds having changed, he set sail southward again. Violent gales, treacherous currents, fog, and drifting icebergs have caused this area to be known as the graveyard of ships, and the voyagers had good reason to fear the elements. They reached Cape Race, the southern tip of the Island safely, then, turning westward, the vessel crossed Trepassey Bay. As they reached Cape Pine on the western side of the bay, they were enveloped in a dense fog, became completely becalmed, and were forced to make a precarious anchorage. During the night, a breeze sprang up, and, because of the danger of their position, they decided to set sail again. Unfortunately, they were hardly under way when the breeze died down again and they were once more becalmed. To make matters worse, the tide, running at eight knots an hour, now bore them rapidly across the bay towards a ridge on its eastern side. The night was intensely dark and they could see nothing. They drifted farther and farther until eventually the roar of breakers warned them that they were in danger of crashing upon the rocks. In desperation, they let go their "kedge" anchor [*a small portable anchor used in warping and other light duties*]. Although this could not offset the force of the tide and the violence of the waves, still by hauling on the anchor rope, they were able to bring the bow of the boat around a little and to catch a slight breeze which had sprung up. Now they cut away the anchor and drifted along the ridge, the side of the boat all but touching the rocks, until they were able to make some headway and steer out of danger. Thus, according to the Bishop, by the intervention of Divine Providence, they were saved "from a fearful and instantaneous death."

As they resumed their voyage, these erratic winds veered again, and, for three difficult days, the *Madonna* battled its way westward against them. Eventually they reached Burin on the western side of Placentia Bay, near the southern tip of the peninsula which bears its name. There the weary travelers landed on the morning of Monday, July 27, thanking God for their safety and happy to enjoy the hospitality of Father Berney while they recovered from their fearful experience.

Burin is a large island about three miles in length surrounded by a number of smaller islands. As a consequence, the population was so scattered that one family could not visit another except by boat. The Bishop noted that, for the most part, the island was so barren that, to grow vegetables, the inhabitants had to bring soil from elsewhere. Of the population of about 1000 persons, one-half were Catholics. Father Berney had recently built a substantial church there, but one still bare of furnishings.

Since the dispersed people needed time to gather, the Bishop stayed in Burin for a week instructing the people and preparing them for the sacrament of Confirmation. Then he administered the Sacrament on Sunday, August 2, to ninety people "among whom there were not less that thirty-six heads of families converted to the Catholic faith." The following day, he confirmed another twenty people who lived so far away that they had not been able to get there in time for the previous day's ceremony.

On Tuesday morning, the *Madonna* set out once more towards the west, its departure accompanied by the salutes of the various batteries along the harbour. As before, the winds were unfavorable and, having battled another sixty-five miles along their way, they stopped at the island of St. Pierre. This island, though only some fifteen miles from the Newfoundland coast, is a colony of France and consequently was not within Bishop Fleming's jurisdiction. Therefore, he merely paid a courtesy call on the curate, Père Olivier, and the next morning, took advantage of a favorable wind to head almost due north for his ultimate destination, Conne River.

Conne River flows into Bay D'Espoir which, in turn, forms part of the much larger Hermitage Bay. The vessel reached Hermitage Bay in just one day's sailing, having covered approximately fifty miles. They landed at Gaultois, a small whaling station on its western side. To the delight of the people, word was spread that in two days' time the Bishop would celebrate Mass and administer Confirmation. To help spread the news, the local agent provided a whaleboat which sped along the various coves and harbours to notify the inhabitants of the coming event. Even at such short notice, the Bishop was able to administer Confirmation on Friday and to receive two converts. A poignant incident illustrated the extreme spiritual poverty of the inhabitants of the outlying districts. While preparing for Mass, he was approached by an old man and woman, leading their daughter, her husband and five children. He baptized the five children as requested and then was asked to marry the daughter and her husband. When that was done, the old couple begged him to marry them also. So in one day, the Bishop administered various sacraments to three generations of the same family.

The following day they set out for their long awaited encounter with the Mi'kmaq. Approaching Bay D'Espoir, they came to a narrow strait called Long Island Passage. The scene was breathtaking:

> We ran along before a light breeze, at the rate of five knots an hour... The sun had already ascended pretty high in his course, and as we brushed along rapidly, nearly touching both shores at the same time, I thought nature had exhausted all her powers to render the scene enchanting.
>
> The shore on the right and on the left rose precipitously, and the forests literally hung over the summit, while the sun poured through the foliage its liquid light, giving an ever-varying luster, shedding an eternally changing charm upon the landscape. We felt as if we were touching an unexplored country, where all that can beautify or embellish, all that can cheer or animate the face of nature is ever bright and ever verdant, and where darkness and sterility are unknown; such was the aspect of the country all along these uninhabited coasts.[1]

Reaching the head of the bay, they sailed across the mouth of the river Little, where they finally caught sight of the Indian habitat. At the entrance of the Conne River, a sand bar ran almost completely across, and it was on this sand bar that the Indians had erected their wigwams. At the approach of the ship, the inhabitants fled, having good reason to fear the advent of an unexpected vessel since the settlers were often accustomed to shoot them for sport. To reassure them, the Bishop had a banner bearing a cross displayed on the masthead. This restored their confidence and the Indians returned from the woods and, wrote the Bishop, "their joy at seeing us manifested itself in 1000 innocent extravagancies."

The Bishop was fascinated by the quality of life of these Mi'kmaqs. This tribe consisted of seventy-two members whose attachment to their religion and its ministers was truly edifying as was the simplicity, recollection and piety with which they prayed. In training their children, they were particularly careful to instill into their minds a love of purity and of all the virtues. When, in their wanderings, they settled in a particular spot, their first task was to erect a large wigwam which was to serve as a place of prayer. If any member of the tribe offended against public morals, he was excluded from this wigwam and not allowed to re-enter it until he had expiated his offence through confession. They possessed the principal hymns, psalms, and books of devotion in their own language, and in the mornings of Sundays and holidays, they assembled for about an hour, singing the opening parts of the Mass and then reciting the rosary and other prayers. In the evening they sang Vespers. The fidelity of the tribe to these religious practices was a remarkable tribute to the zeal of the missionaries who had first taught them in Nova Scotia.

Nevertheless, Bishop Fleming was extremely disappointed to learn that, although the Indians had been waiting there for two months, some mischief maker had informed them that no clergyman would be visiting them that year, and most of them had left. He had been expecting to meet 200-300 of them, but only twenty-eight remained. The Bishop stayed until the following Tuesday, instructing them through an interpreter, celebrating Mass every day for them, hearing their confessions, and finally administering Confirmation to those of them who had not been confirmed twenty years previously at their headquarters on Cape Breton Island before their migration to Newfoundland.

Hearing their confessions seemed to present an insolvable problem since they could not speak English and the Bishop did not know their language while it was necessary to maintain the seal of Confession. Bishop Fleming overcame this problem in an ingenious manner. He first prepared a list of the more common sins. Then, in the large wigwam which they used as a church, he had a partition of deer skins erected, on one side of which he and an interpreter sat. When the penitent entered and knelt on the other side of the partition, the Bishop reached around it and held the penitent's hand in his. As the interpreter called out the list of sins, the penitent would answer by squeezing the Bishop's hand if he or she had been guilty of this particular fault, or by relaxing it, if he or she had not. In this manner he heard the confessions of the entire tribe.

Finally came the time for departure. The Indians broke into laments and appeals for a longer stay. But on Wednesday morning, August 12, the *Madonna* raised her sails, and, realizing that their appeals were of no avail, the inhabitants proceeded to wish the travellers *bon voyage* by producing guns, about seven or eight feet long, and firing a continuous volley until the schooner was out of sight.

Their first stop on the Bishop's return journey was Great Jarvis Harbour on the east side of Fortune Bay where the Bishop administered Confirmation. However, realizing that neither the pilot nor the captain of the vessel was familiar with the coast, Bishop Fleming decided to turn back and visit more familiar harbours. So, on Friday, they set sail eastward, stopping briefly at St. Pierre. On the August 18, they reached the harbour of St. Lawrence. Here there was a church but, as elsewhere, its unfurnished condition testified to the poverty of the people.

From St. Lawrence, they set out for Placentia, stopping overnight at Burin to let Father Berney disembark. Although they reached Placentia, a distance of eighty miles, late on Friday, August 21, the winds forced them to stand off all during that night and next morning. Finally, they were towed in by boats sent out from the port.

From there they sailed to Little Placentia (now called Argentia), twelve miles away, where the Bishop was pleased to meet Father Nowlan whom he had recently appointed to that district and to hear the praises of the people for him.

From Little Placentia, they sailed north to Barren Island near the head of the bay. Then, turning back, they stopped at Merasheen where they remained from Wednesday, September 2 to Sunday, September 6. "In this island," wrote the Bishop, "there is no church, and although those pathetic people are well disposed to build one, the great majority of them being hired fishermen, they have no means, nor do they have the time, to transport building material from the mainland."

Hence the Bishop had to use a store as a church, and in these makeshift surroundings, he confirmed eighty-six people, of whom thirty-six were converts. As the Bishop left the store, he was met by two men who said that they were Protestants who had attended the ceremonies through curiosity, intending to ridicule them, but that the sermons given there had converted them. The Bishop deferred his departure to Monday in order to instruct them and another man who later joined them, and receive them into the Church. Next morning he confirmed them and nine other residents. Setting sail immediately after the ceremonies and, being favored with a following wind, he reached St. Mary's Bay on Tuesday, September 8, after twenty-four hours sailing. The Bishop found this settlement "like almost

every other harbour in Newfoundland, a collection of houses built at irregular distances, nor forming anywhere a
street or a lane, and commanding a good beach, backed by
rising ground, rather clear, which proved useful to the people for all public purposes."

On Thursday, he learned that a virulent epidemic had
broken out in St. John's. Embarking immediately, he
arrived at the capital on Saturday, September 12. His visitation to the south coast of the island had lasted over eight
weeks and during it he had confirmed approximately 1000
persons including almost 200 converts. "Thus," he wrote,
"we closed a visitation, in which we had undergone the
greatest labors, the greatest hardships, and had more than
once incurred the greatest dangers; but, nevertheless,
Heaven permitted us to land in safety, and with comparatively unimpaired health."

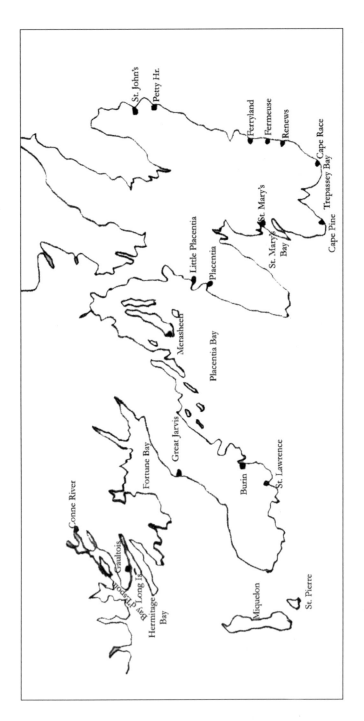

Map of Bishop Fleming's visit to the Mi'Kmaqs

CHAPTER TWELVE
AFFLICTED BY EPIDEMICS AND ECCLESIASTICS

*If the small-pox breaks out in any place, you find that the bishop
sets out directly, carrying off a cow or something of that kind for the
benefit of the people.*

- Captain Geary
"Evidence before Select Committee"

hen Bishop Fleming returned to St. John's from
his expedition to the Mi'Kmaqs, he found the
people ravaged by the inroads of a virulent
smallpox epidemic. Hundreds of the very poor
were swept away by its malignancy. Unfortunately, the
Bishop, in spite of his anxiety to help them, was severely
handicapped in his efforts to do so because his superhuman
exertions of the preceding months had brought on a severe
reaction which confined him to bed for several weeks.

Epidemics were perennial in St. John's due to the constant influx of sailors from overseas and were intensified by
its crowded tenements and lack of proper sanitation. These
epidemics quickly spread to outlying settlements. In the
case of smallpox, however, its impact on the Island was
somewhat assuaged by a fortunate circumstance. One of the
early medical missionaries in Newfoundland, the Reverend
Doctor John Clinch, had been a fellow university student in
England with Doctor Edward Jenner, the discoverer of the
vaccine for smallpox. Shortly after this discovery in 1796,
Jenner sent a supply of the vaccine to Doctor Clinch.
Consequently, for the first time in North America, the vac-

cine against smallpox was administered by Doctor Clinch in
Trinity in the year 1798, and later in St. John's and
Portugal Cove where the disease was rampant. However,
while the vaccine helped protect those who received it
against further infection, this immunity tended to lose its
effect over time, and by 1835, the pox was again raging violently throughout the island. That year, over 6,000 cases
were officially reported in St. John's out of a population of
19,000! Naturally, the people lost all faith in the vaccine's
efficiency and began their own amateur remedy, inoculating
themselves with the natural discharge from the sores. The
Bishop was bitter over the callousness of the upper classes
and the failure of the Government to act in this emergency.
He complained that the Executive had done nothing to
check the disease, particularly among the poor. Although
there was a surplus of £6,000 or £7,000 in the colony's treasury, not a penny was spent to open hospitals or dispensaries
or even soup-kitchens to help the afflicted thousands.
Instead a law was passed which, whatever its purpose, could
not but increase their suffering.

That law—passed by the notoriously inhumane Judge
Boulton—indicted anyone who left a house where the disease was present. Though his intention in thus trying to
limit the spread of the disease may have been good, to pass
such an Act, without making any provision for the needs of
those affected by it, was barbaric. Hundreds of persons were
going from door to door begging help to buy a coffin in which
to bury their loved ones. Others sought old linens or food or
clothing, or other comforts necessary to the sick or the con-
valescent. Furthermore, when some members of the Judge's
own family caught the disease, he himself did not abide by
the law he had promulgated. When, indeed, the disease
began to spread to the wealthier families, measures were
rapidly taken to deal with it. A house was commandeered
where the physicians were asked to inoculate the poor gratuitously although 2000-3000 people had already been inoc-

ulated with the natural matter and the disease was beginning to decline. At the opening of the House of Assembly, a
sum of £500 was granted to fight the disease when not one
case still existed in St. John's—a fact which the Bishop did
not fail to emphasize.

A second cause of distress was another law, passed by
the same Judge Boulton. Fishermen were usually hired by
"planters"—men who owned a fishing boat and had some
standing in the community. The planters themselves were
poor men, and, in practice, acted as agents for the merchants who were liable for the men's wages. According to
long established custom, the fishermen had first call on the
profit from the catch. However, the Judge now reversed this
law and ruled that the merchant was not responsible for the
fishermen's wages. If Boulton's ruling was followed, many
fishermen would be destitute. Fortunately, most of the merchants were more humane than the Judge and continued to
pay their employees as in the past.

In the first week of November, the epidemic, which had
begun to die out in St. John's, broke out with renewed violence in Petty Harbour, a few miles away. The Bishop knew
that the extreme poverty of the inhabitants of that settlement would prevent their getting medical aid or adequate
nourishment. He had by now acquired a basic understanding of the disease through the instruction of the doctors and
through his care for the sick in St. John's. So he immediately set out for Petty Harbour, taking with him his medi-
cine chest and a cow to provide the sufferers with fresh milk.
He declined to board with one of the families for fear of
spreading the disease as he ministered to the sick. Instead
he set up residence and a dispensary in an empty hut near
the church and arranged to have his meals prepared for him.
Here he remained throughout the winter, caring for the sick
and making no distinction between Catholic and Protestant.
As a result of his ministrations, when the disease eventually abated in February, only two deaths had occurred out of

400 severe cases. But, at what cost to himself from cold and improper nourishment this victory was won, we can only imagine.

The inhabitants greatly acclaimed his selfless devotion, and numerous conversions resulted. One such conversion is related by a modern descendant of the Osborne family:

> Although religious differences were of life and death importance in those days, he ignored them and looked after the Anglicans on the north side of the harbour as tenderly as the Catholics on the south. There was an Anglican minister there at the time, and tradition has it that he had fled with his family to escape the epidemic. ...Our family decided to join the Catholic Church out of gratitude to Bishop Fleming. Her (our grandmother's) earliest memory of the old bishop [sic!] was a child's-eye view of his waistcoat which was scorched from leaning over the cooking pots containing the food he prepared for the sick people.

Bishop Fleming was not content with his efforts to cure the disease; he wanted to prevent its return and to improve the condition of the people. The dead were being buried in a graveyard in the middle of the settlement, a most unhealthy practice. He found a suitable site about a half mile away, opened this as a cemetery, and had the bodies transferred there. The previous year he had begun to build a church in the settlement, and now he purchased a piece of ground in front of it, blasted away the rocks, and leveled the land for the convenience of the Congregation coming to Mass.

Even while thus deeply engrossed in caring for his people, Bishop Fleming could not escape the intrigues of his enemies. In the hope of applying more pressure to force him to withdraw from his supposed political activities, the Colonial Office approached Bishop James Yorke Brampton, the Catholic Vicar Apostolic of London, probably in the mistaken belief that Bishop Brampton possessed authority over Bishop Fleming. Complying with their request, and accepting, without checking, the truth of the government's complaints, Bishop Brampton wrote Bishop Fleming a severe reprimand. Having recalled that in their previous meetings, Bishop Fleming had expressed great satisfaction regarding the kindly relations between the Catholics and Protestants in Newfoundland, he then repeated the allegation made in Governor Prescott's dispatches that Bishop Fleming and his priests had caused a renewal of the dissension between Catholics and the Newfoundland Government. He reviewed the incident of the mutilation of Winton's ears, the threats to Judge Boulton, and McLean Little's alleged loss of his means of livelihood. While acknowledging that he possessed no authority over Bishop Fleming, he nevertheless stated that he felt it was his duty to pass on to Bishop Fleming the substance of the criticisms that he had received so that justice should be done to all parties concerned. He concluded by asking Bishop Fleming to write to both him and the Colonial Office to explain the situation in Newfoundland.

This letter was written on July 27, 1835. After waiting for some months and receiving no reply, Bishop Brampton must have concluded that Bishop Fleming was ignoring him. Consequently, on February 4, 1836, he sent a copy of his letter to the Colonial Office noting that he had received no answer from Bishop Fleming. Ignoring normal diplomatic confidentiality, the Government now forwarded an outline of Bishop Brampton's letter to Governor Prescott and it quickly became public knowledge, much to the delight of Bishop Fleming's foes.

The reason why Bishop Fleming had not answered was quite simple—he did not receive the letter until he returned from his southern visitation towards the middle of September, and by then he was both sick and engrossed in dealing with the epidemic in St. John's and Petty Harbour. Consequently, it was not until the end of January that he found the time and the opportunity to respond. His answer was civil enough as befitted one ecclesiastic writing to another, but it left no doubt as to his own views of the matter as he spoke of the "slanders" registered at the Colonial Office against him and his clergy. Brampton's letter alerted Bishop Fleming to the fact that Governor Prescott was behind these accusations. The realization of the "wily secrecy" with which the Governor had acted, expressing to him his warmest friendship while at the same time whispering away his reputation and the character of the mission, caused him deep anger. He explained to Bishop Brampton why these reports had been forwarded to England. Falsehoods issued in St. John's could be promptly answered. But, when they were sent to England, months must elapse before they could possibly be contradicted. Meanwhile they would take hold of the minds of their recipients. Indeed, because of the dignity of their accuser and the secrecy with which they were forwarded, they might remain entirely undetected. With a touch of sarcasm he concluded that if the Governor had acted with proper candour and fair play, the time and attention of His Majesty's Ministers would never had been wasted in dealing with a subject as humble as himself.

He was determined to confront the Governor about these allegations. In November, during one of his periodic visits to St. John's from Petty Harbour, he called on the Governor and asked for a copy of the dispatch containing the Governor's charges against him. He was flabbergasted when the Governor flatly denied the existence of such a document. Fortunately the Bishop had brought with him Bishop Brampton's letter. He produced it, and pointed out the reference to the dispatch in question. Trapped, the Governor had no recourse but to admit that he had indeed sent such a dispatch and promised to forward a copy to the Bishop.

Four days later when this promised copy had not arrived, the Bishop wrote the Governor a formal request for it. His answer was an invitation to call at Government House. There he was further amazed to hear the Governor deny that he had ever promised such a copy, claiming that he could not communicate the contents of his dispatches to His Majesty's Government without official sanction—a rather extraordinary position to take when one considers that this dispatch had already been shown to several other parties. On being pressed vehemently by the Bishop, he finally admitted that he had indeed forwarded McLean Little's petition and that he had condemned the denunciations made from the Roman Catholic altars against Winton. He attempted to conciliate the Bishop by declaring himself happy that these denunciations have been discontinued, and said that he could not imagine that the Roman Catholic clergy would use their influence to cause the attack on Winton. He then declared that he would ever conduct himself with strict impartiality and assured the Bishop that he felt as warm a regard for his fellow-countrymen of the Roman Catholic religion as of any other faith—sentiments very different from those expressed in his official dispatches to London.

In spite of the courteous manner in which he had written to Bishop Brampton, Bishop Fleming was outraged at his interference in the affair. Rarely has a public figure permitted his innermost feelings to be so openly revealed in official statements as did the Bishop in his *Relatio*[1] to the Holy See in 1837. In this report, he expressed his "lively indignation" at the interference of a "meddling ecclesiastic" who had unknowingly become the instrument of the "wicked machinations" of his political enemies in St. John's. The bitterness of his reaction is evident in the extravagance of his language:

> It happens that, at the same time as one of those worthies sat himself down to write this letter in which my conduct was condemned, I was a good

200 miles from St. John's after having finished
my visit to one part of the East coast of the island.
*(Here he describes in detail the great hardships he
had to endure on this trip and then continues:)* I
was condemned by those who had at their disposal, for the fulfillment of their ministry, gold coach-
es in which to travel in comfort on the level roads
of the metropolis of England and in the enjoy-
ment of all that can render life comfortable.

If, however, the Bishop was irritated by the charges of
his enemies in Newfoundland, and outraged by the interference of Bishop Brampton, he was devastated by the thought
that he might have lost the good opinion of His Holiness,
Pope Gregory XVI. If, he wrote, His Holiness should listen,
even for a moment to these calumnies, that would cause him
the most bitter distress.

In the midst of this controversy, he still had to attend to
his own religious duties. The people in his own district had
not had the opportunity to receive the Sacrament of
Confirmation for three years. So in April, he confirmed
almost 1,400 residents of St. John's, some adults, but mainly children. Already the impact of the Presentation Sisters
was becoming evident. The candidates for the sacraments
had been well instructed, and the behavior of the large congregation truly edifying. In the following weeks, he administered Confirmation in Torbay, Portugal Cove and Petty
Harbour. In each place, there were more that 400 candidates.

Following this, on Friday, May 27, he set out for a whirlwind tour of Conception Bay. His first stop was to be Brigus
to bless the new church there, but in attempting to reach it,
he got more than he had bargained for. With Father Troy
and two or three laymen, he left St. John's in early morning,
intending to breakfast at Portugal Cove. But when they
reached the Cove, they discovered the winds were so

favourable that they decided to set out immediately without eating. Soon, however, the wind died down and then rose strongly again from the opposite direction. All that day and the following night they were buffeted by the capricious winds and driven here and there around Conception Bay. The result was that they did not reach their destination until 11 a.m. on Sunday, exhausted and famished, there to be welcomed by Father Mackin, the pastor. When they had eaten and recovered somewhat from their ordeal, the Bishop solemnly blessed the church in the presence of a large congregation which had gathered from the most distant parts of the bay.

Once more the winds made a mockery of their plans and they were forced to remain in Brigus for some days until favorable winds permitted them to return to Torbay where the Bishop consecrated another new church, one erected by Father Troy. On Tuesday, June 9, he and Father Troy set sail for Carbonear. Next day, the Bishop confirmed 600 people in Harbour Grace, including many converts, and on Friday another 700 in Carbonear. Immediately after the latter ceremony, they set sail again for St. John's where, unusually, they arrived without incident. On the following Monday, the day after Pentecost, he confirmed, in St. John's itself, another 400 who had not been sufficiently prepared on the previous occasion. Altogether during these months he had confirmed 3,260 people among whom were 314 converts. He had not been exactly idle.

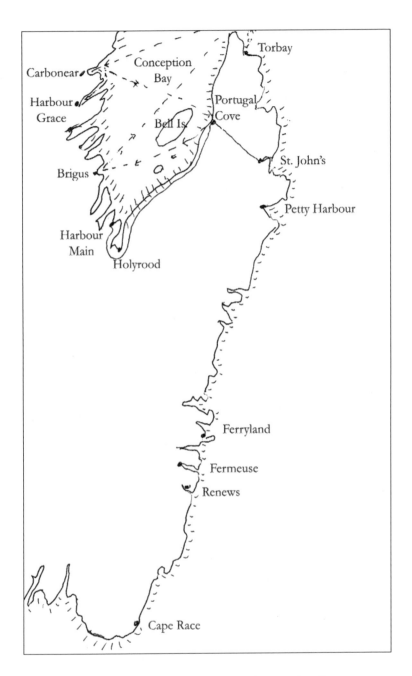

Bishop Fleming's Journey into Conception Bay

CHAPTER THIRTEEN
KNIGHTS VS. BISHOPS

No man has been worse used than the very exemplary prelate—
Doctor Fleming.

-Daniel O'Connell

ince the next few years were to be dominated by
an unending flow of accusations against Bishop
Fleming and his rather desperate efforts to
defend himself against them, perhaps it is time
to examine this situation more closely. These accusations go
back to 1834, when Governor Cochrane sued Father Troy,
Bishop Fleming's second in command, over letters the latter
had written attacking his administration. He accused
Bishop Fleming and his clergy of encouraging their follow-
ers—a naturally quiet and well-disposed people—to violence
and disorder. This accusation became the theme of a constant stream of communications between Newfoundland
and the Colonial Office and was the cause of the British
Government's increasingly hostile attitude towards the
Bishop. When Cochrane's successor, Governor Prescott,
arrived in November 1834, his initially favourable attitude
soon began to deteriorate. He became aware of the unpleasant incidents surrounding Cochrane's departure, of the part
which the Catholic clergy were believed to have played in
this unhappy event, and the danger it represented to his
own authority. He was undoubtedly influenced by the hostile propaganda constantly poured into his ears by the
Bishop's enemies who had ready access to him. Cochrane's

pejorative expressions were soon echoed by Prescott. Thus Cochrane's claims that "the ignorance of the Bishop and himself (Father Troy) are too well known," and "so long as Bishop Fleming and Mr. Troy are allowed to remain in Newfoundland there can be no peace for them," were soon echoed by Prescott's: "We have unfortunately an illiterate and vulgar RC bishop whose dependent clergy . . . too closely resemble him in character," and "the best remedy for Newfoundland would be removal of Bishop Fleming." Both of these expressions were used by Governor Prescott in the months immediately following his arrival.

In this strategy of prejudicing the Governor against the Bishop, two groups played the major part, the political establishment and the disaffected Catholics. Later in an official report to Rome, Bishop Fleming was to explain the reasons for their animosity: "The former (*politicians*) hate me," he wrote, "principally for political motives though their religious sentiments urges them to do so as a secondary cause; and the latter (*disaffected Catholics*) principally for religious motives although political prejudices are not lacking also to inspire their hatred." The important point to note here is the use the Bishop made, in a formal report to the Roman authorities, of the word "hate" and "hatred" to describe their attitude towards him, strong words indeed to use in an official statement.

Among the politicians who were working against Bishop Fleming, the Chief Justice, Judge Boulton; the Attorney General, James Simms; and John Sinclair, a member of the Executive Council and a leading member of the Orange Lodge, played a prominent part. Among the disaffected Catholics who were engaged in the campaign to undermine the Bishop's authority were: Judge Boulton's wife, Eliza; and Patrick Kough, a member of the Assembly and the superintendent of public buildings. As the wife of the Chief Justice, who was also President of the Executive Council, Mrs. Boulton was a frequent guest at Government House and had ample opportunity to spread her venom. In his testimony before the Select Committee in 1841, Captain Geary stated that she was "diametrically opposed to the bishop." He described the tactics she used to influence him when he first arrived in St. John's in 1835. Geary had bought a house from Patrick Kough, and Mrs. Boulton told him that he would have to give it up because of the Bishop's disapproval of Kough. When told that the Bishop himself had recommended the house, she replied: "Oh, indeed, you are finely taken in!"

Another of the tactics used by the alienated Catholics to discredit the Bishop and his priests was to take note of their sermons and then relay distorted résumés of them to the Governor and to the editor of the *Ledger*. The latter delighted in publishing these garbled accounts. These published articles were then forwarded to the Colonial Office by the Governor as if they were verbatim records of what had been said. Captain Geary, in his testimony before the Committee, listed several such cases of which he was personally aware. Perhaps the most glaring was the case of the Bishop's address to the sealers in mid-March of 1836 in which, as reported in the *Ledger*, he is supposed to have urged them strongly to boycott those Catholic merchants who opposed him. But Captain Geary, who was present at the sermon, declared that the Bishop "did not say that at all," and that he, Geary, had objected at the time to the editor about his mis-reporting. Nevertheless, Governor Prescott forwarded a copy of the article to the Colonial Office, affirming that it was substantially correct.

Not only had the authorities in Newfoundland convinced themselves that the Bishop was the evil genius behind every act of violence or unrest in the island, but they had largely succeeded in convincing the British Government of this as well. For instance, writing to Lord Palmerston, the Foreign Secretary, early in 1836, Lord Glenelg, the Secretary for the Colonies, bemoaned the situation in Newfoundland:

> The island is tormented, and the Catholic
> Population driven to the most atrocious extreme
> by the conduct and language of the Bishop
> Fletcher (*sic*), and still more of a priest Troy. Is it
> possible to get either of these removed from the
> Island and sent elsewhere? You did write about
> Fletcher, and he received admonition from Rome,
> but nothing will do, so long as he is there, and
> Troy with him. Troy especially ought to be
> removed. There is no peace and little safety while
> they are both there.

The "atrocious" conduct was, no doubt, the mutilation
of Winton's ears which was attributed to the Bishop's influence rather than to the provocative diatribes which Winton
poured forth in *The Ledger*; while the "language" in question was the garbled accounts of various sermons. On such
"evidence" was Government policy made!

Palmerston acceded to Glenelg's request and soon initi-
ated a determined effort to get rid of the Bishop. He saw to
it that Aubin, the British agent in Rome, received copies of
complaints about Bishop Fleming's conduct and proceedings, including a dispatch from Governor Prescott that cited
numerous acts of violence, such as the mutilation of
Winton's ears, and a copy of McLean Little's complaint.
Aubin was instructed to present to the appropriate Vatican
authorities this "evidence" of the Bishop's subversive efforts
to undermine the peace and tranquillity of the Colony and
to press for a powerful and authoritative reprimand to the
Bishop since earlier efforts to change his behaviour had had
no effect.

The complaints against the Bishop reached the desk of
Cardinal Fransoni, Prefect of Propaganda Fide through
Cardinal Lambruschini,* Secretary of State, but
Fransoni was by no means convinced of their truth. When

returning the documents to Lambruschini, he pointed out that Bishop Fleming was justly respected as one of the most distinguished Vicars Apostolic in the Church, outstanding for virtue and missionary zeal. He referred Lambruschini to the Bishop's recent *Relaztio*. Nevertheless he recognized that the complaints of the British Government required some recognition. Consequently he wrote Bishop Fleming in gentle and diplomatic language, urging the Vicar Apostolic and his clergy to refrain in future from meddling in political affairs. The Cardinal's letter did not at all satisfy the Colonial Office whose officials considered it weak and ineffectual, a mere slap on the wrist. They believed that the Bishop's high reputation in Rome prevented his being called to a stricter accounting for his actions.

Even so, Bishop Fleming had not yet received this gentle reprimand when events at home caused his relations with the Governor to deteriorate even further. The first such happening was an apparently insignificant event, the funeral of a Catholic soldier, John Neaven. Neaven had been a resident of St. John's for ten or twelve years, had achieved the rank of sergeant in the army and was very popular with the local people. His wife was the housekeeper for the commanding officer, Colonel Sall. Neaven discovered that the Colonel had seduced his wife and wrote a letter in *The Patriot* publicly condemning the Colonel's conduct. Neaven was disciplined accordingly. Like many others in similar circumstances, he now took to drink. He was court-martialed and reduced to the ranks, but his excessive drinking continued and eventually resulted in his death on Saturday, February 6, 1836.

In view of the circumstances, the military authorities were naturally anxious to have his funeral conducted as quietly as possible. Normally such a military cortege would pass through the main street of the town (Water Street) with a full military band so that all might pay their respects, but, in this instance, it was decided to proceed along the back of the town by what would now probably be Military Road and accompanied by only a fife and drum instead of the usual band. A large crowd had collected at the end of the lane (now Forest Road) leading to the hospital to pay their respects to the deceased. When the coffin emerged from the lane, some of the onlookers asked to be permitted to help carry the coffin, and Lieutenant Grant, who was in charge, agreed. What followed now had a touch of comic opera. The procession formed with the Lieutenant and the soldiers in front followed by the coffin and then the general public. All went well until it came to a fork at King's Road when Grant and his soldiers turned right to avoid the town. Those carrying the coffin, however, instead of following the soldiers, turned left and, followed by the crowd, began to march into the town. After some time, Lieutenant Grant chanced to look back and found, to his surprise, that the coffin was no longer following him. Surprised or not, however, he took prompt action, ordering his troop to "fix bayonets." At which point those carrying the coffin promptly dropped it and retreated. A heated dispute followed and the Lieutenant—with the crowd tagging along—decided to take the coffin to the military headquarters at Fort Townshend to obtain further orders. Arriving at the Fort, the cortege was met by Major Law, the commanding officer, who, having ordered all the troops to assemble with loaded muskets, began to harangue the crowd. Fortunately at this point, a local curate, Father Murphy, arrived on the scene. It was he who had attended Neaven in his last hours and who had been invited by the Military to perform the funeral rites. Father Murphy persuaded the crowd to let the funeral continue to the burial site on Long's Hill and pledged to the Major that there would be no further trouble. So the funeral ended peacefully.

One of the newspapers was severely critical of the conduct of the Military during the affair, so Governor Prescott took it upon himself to issue a public commendation of

Major Law and Lieutenant Grant and, by implication, condemned the behaviour of the people and the clergy. This whole affair might have blown over as just "a tempest in a teapot" except that Bishop Fleming, perhaps hoping to open the Governor's eyes to the kind of information he was receiving from his advisers, decided to answer the Governor publicly, giving his own version of the affair and including some hard-hitting observations. He complained that, if the Governor were not surrounded by advisors determined to injure the reputation of the people and of the clergy, he would never have taken up the position he had done.

His old antagonist, Henry Winton, the Editor of *The Ledger*, took umbrage at Bishop Fleming's statement and did so in most insulting terms: "His Lordship," he stated, "is unhappily too far behind, both in liberality and intelligence, a considerable and an influential portion of his flock, from whom he has imprudently severed himself." Three days later he returned to the attack in equally uncomplimentary terms. The others involved joined in the fray. Lieutenant Grant and Major Law both published sworn statements defending their actions, Father Murphy came to the defence of the Bishop and contradicted the statements of Major Law and Lieutenant Grant on several points. After occupying the press for an entire month, public interest gradually subsided and poor ex-Sergeant Neaven was allowed to rest in peace. However, the affair had disturbed Governor Prescott greatly, and in March, he wrote to the Colonial Secretary, Lord Glenelg, that "the course pursued by Doctor Fleming is deeply to be regretted, and the more that it seems to be beyond all hope of remedy."

CHAPTER FOURTEEN
BOULTON VS. DUFFY

*Really what we have here is only the tragic caricature of legality;
the democratic ideal . . . **is betrayed in its very foundations.***

- Pope John Paul II, *The Gospel of Life*, #20

he Neaven case was farcical enough, but its
absurdity was eclipsed by another affair, much
more serious and with consequences longer lasting. It involved one of the priests of the
Vicariate, Father James Duffy, parish priest of St. Mary's in
St. Mary's Bay. This second case caused the relations
between Bishop Fleming and the Government to deteriorate
radically. Once more the *bête noire* was the Bishop's main
antagonist, Judge Boulton.

Father James Duffy, a native of County Monaghan,
Ireland, was one of the clerics brought to Newfoundland by
Bishop Fleming in 1833 with the Presentation Sisters. After
being stationed for a short time in St. John's to acquire
some experience of the country, he was assigned as curate in
Ferryland and a large section of the parish placed under his
care. He soon proved his worth and after little more than a
year was made the first Parish Priest of St. Mary's, St.
Mary's Bay, a community of about 500 persons, all Catholics
except for the local agent for the firm of Slade & Elson, &
Co. and his assistants. This agent, John Wills Martin, was
also the local magistrate and a member of the House of
Assembly.

One of Father Duffy's first acts was to build a church on a patch of high ground. The church blew down! He built another on a similar spot. It also collapsed! Admitting defeat, he chose a sheltered spot near the beach and applied to the local magistrate, John Wills Martin, for approval to build there.

Martin objected to Father Duffy's request because the property was near the Company premises and suggested an alternate site. Father Duffy found this alternative unacceptable—it was boggy and inconvenient, and he went ahead with his original plans. Meanwhile, a fisherman named Fewer erected a fish flake on part of the beach, which, like all Newfoundland beaches, was considered public property. Martin immediately declared that this structure was illegal and, before dawn the next morning, he brought a crew and cut it down. Audaciously, to assert the Company's right to the entire beach, he then proceeded to run a new flake the full length of the beach. By doing this, he cut off access to the church site and to the cemetery, deprived the people of the only place on which they could haul up their boats in the winter and blocked the road to neighbouring settlements. Using Martin's own action against Fewer as a precedent, the people, doubtless under Father Duffy's leadership, cut the flake at the Company boundary so as to have access to the church, and notified Martin that they would destroy the rest of the flake if it was not removed. In retaliation, Martin, who was about to leave for St. John's for a session of the Assembly, instructed his clerk not to provide Father Duffy with any further supplies. After waiting several weeks without response from Martin, the people, at Father Duffy's direction, after Mass on Sunday, January 11, 1835, destroyed the flake except the section on Company property. Martin now instituted proceedings against Father Duffy and nine others involved. Although throughout that summer the circuit court sat at St. Mary's on the very spot of the controversy, no action was taken, nor evidence submitted.

Meanwhile, Judge Boulton left for England at the beginning of June 1835, to defend himself against a petition sent to the British Parliament for his removal. When he returned four months later, he issued, at the request of the Attorney General, a warrant against Father Duffy and his nine codefendants. The warrant read: "He, James Duffy and (listing nine others involved) being rioters and routers[1], did, at St. Mary's riotously and routously assemble, and then and there, and with force and arms demolish and destroy certain fish-flakes and erections, the property of Slade, Elson & Co." This was a very partisan wording of the indictment, and was not unintentional, for Judge Boulton was clearly after larger game. He wrote to Martin, that it was "certain now that Duffy and the whole rabble will be brought to heel, and with them the Irish faction of the House of Assembly and Bishop Fleming as well." It would be difficult to imagine a more outrageous perversion of the judicial system.

As this was happening, Bishop Fleming was on his way back from the visitation along the South Coast which we have described earlier. When he arrived at St. Mary's on September 8, therefore, he held a "rigid enquiry" and through it became convinced of the innocence of those accused.

At the same time, on the issuing of the writ, two constables were dispatched on the Colonial Brig *Maria* to apprehend the "culprits." They found Father Duffy at Fermeuse, arrested him and brought him to Ferryland where he was arraigned before a magistrate. There he gave recognizance for his appearance before the court in St. John's. The two constables now proceeded to St. Mary's but were blocked by the inhabitants with guns and sticks, while the accused fled into the woods. This was an understandable reaction since, if these men were imprisoned, they would lose the whole fishing season and they and their families would starve during the winter—a severe punishment for a misdemeanour, and a further example of the callousness of the establish-

ment towards the "rabble!" After three days of fruitless
search, the constables admitted defeat and returned to St.
John's.

For Father Duffy, having to appear before the court in
St. John's was a real injustice. Besides the hardship to himself of being forced to walk a hundred miles through track-
less country in the middle of winter, it would be almost
impossible for him to obtain needed witnesses since they
would also have to walk to St. John's, and this at a time
when small-pox was raging in the town.

John Bowen, another of the accused, was apprehended
in St. John's. He and Father Duffy were to appear in court
on December 29, 1835. For some time there had been agitation among the Catholic population for the right to be represented by lawyers of their own faith—none such had as
yet been accepted into the Bar. The need in this case was
obvious. A Catholic priest was to appear before such a prej-
udiced person as Judge Boulton and distrust of Protestant
representation was prevalent. Consequently agitation for
this right increased dramatically. A petition signed by 600
inhabitants of Harbour Grace, including the parish priest,
Father Charles Dalton, protested: "a Catholic Priest is to be
as arraigned before an exclusively Protestant Tribunal—his
Jury to be empaneled by a Protestant Sheriff," and it was
not right "to compel him to commit his defence to a
Protestant Barrister in whom he cannot sufficiently con-
fide." This petition was presented to the Court by three
highly respected citizens, John Dunscomb, William Thomas
and Patrick Morris—Dunscomb and Thomas being
Protestants and members of the Governor's Council. Judge
Boulton refused to receive the petition, saying, among other
things, that it was being returned to the presenters "as
being... of a character highly unbecoming..." Needless to say,
the presenters were rightly indignant and protested to
Governor Prescott at this insult to their person and their
position. The Governor, no matter what his private senti-

ments might be, could but answer that he had no power to
intervene in the dispute.

On Tuesday, December 29, 1835, the case opened with
Father Duffy the lone defendant present. John Bowen was
also supposed to be there, having been in attendance for the
past fortnight. Unfortunately, he became ill and could not be
found. Father Duffy's lawyer was Bryan Robinson, a distinguished lawyer. However, as the case opened, Robinson
stood up and, possibly because of the slur on the integrity of
Protestant lawyers who defended a Catholic priest, angrily
withdrew from the case. He may have particularly resented
the insult because he had been a close friend of Bishop
Scallan and, in fact, executor of his will. Another lawyer,
Hugh Emerson, then revealed that he had taken on this
responsibility, but asked for a day's postponement as he was
expecting three additional witnesses. So the case was postponed until Thursday morning.

When the Court reopened on Thursday morning, with
both Father Duffy and John Bowen in attendance, the
Attorney General announced that the Crown was not prepared to proceed because their witnesses, John Martin and
William Lush, his assistant, had not appeared. Instead of
the case being dismissed, it was then postponed until the
next term of the Court. The onlookers were indignant, for it
was obvious that the Crown had known from the beginning
of the session that Martin and Lush would not appear, but,
nevertheless, had kept Father Duffy and Bowen in attendance. So the defendants, having posted bail to the amount
of £100 each, had to trudge back to St. Mary's again without
having had the opportunity of clearing their names. The
supreme irony of the situation was that the case, being only
a misdemeanor, should not have appeared before the
Supreme Court at all.

From then on the whole affair descended into farce. It
centred on Governor Prescott's determination to bring
these 'rioters' to justice at all costs. He wrote to Lord

Glenelg, the Secretary of State for the Colonies. After describing the Catholics of St. Mary's as "of a quiet and inoffensive character," he called Father Duffy "an ignorant and bigoted priest" who had been stirring up trouble among them. He pointed out that, now that the colonial brig had been decommissioned through lack of finances, he had no means of sending a military detachment to St. Mary's. However, he suggested that the appearance of a Man of War would be helpful. He asked that a frigate be sent to St. John's where it would be manned by twenty to thirty soldiers, an intelligent magistrate, a law officer and some trustworthy constables and would then proceed to St. Mary's. He believed that such a demonstration of force would induce the offenders and witnesses to come forward and yield to the law. If they did not appear, he wanted the ship and troops to remain in the settlement until the offenders had complied. There was a large, empty house belonging to Slade & Co. in the settlement and this house would be able to accommodate the military detachment. Furthermore, there was no lack of supplies at the Company premises.

The Colonial Secretary acceded to his request, but it was May 1836, when the frigate arrived in St. John's. Before the ship could be sent to St. Mary's, Bishop Fleming addressed a pastoral letter to the people there. He warned them that of all their duties, none was more imperative than obedience to the laws of their country and respect for those in authority. Having said that, he turned on the authorities and severely criticized their actions, stating that their purpose was evidently to label the people of Newfoundland as turbulent, in order to prove the value to the Government of individuals in positions of authority who would be prepared to disregard the law in order to coerce the people. He warned the people of the danger of having soldiers stationed among their wives and daughters at a time when the men would necessarily be absent on the fishing grounds. To avoid this catastrophe, he urged all those named in the indictment to proceed to St.

John's and give bail for their appearance. He concluded with a high compliment to the Governor, unexpected in view of the relations between them, and possibly intended to heal the rift between them. He declared that the Governor was the only official in the country who was not directly opposed to the principles of the British Government and that he, the Governor, would be the people's refuge against the evil machinations of the real disturbers of the peace.

Thus given a graceful way out, and assured by the Bishop of the Governor's protection, the accused reported to St. John's in mid-July and posted bail. The case was then postponed until December. When December came, so did the defendants, but the trial was once more put off, because Lush, the principal witness for the prosecution, did not appear. One of Father Duffy's friends calculated that by now he had travelled 1379 miles in pursuit of justice and still hadn't obtained it. In May 1837, the case was finally disposed of. Martin's story was shown to be full of exaggerations and misrepresentations; his clerk, Lush, the chief witness, once more failed to appear, and the Jury necessarily returned a verdict of "Not Guilty." So ended a saga which had begun in December 1835 and which, as the quotation at the head of this Chapter states, "was a tragic caricature of legality." After continuing to serve St. Mary's faithfully for 16 years, Father Duffy left Newfoundland. He died in Charlottetown, Prince Edward Island, in December 1860 so renowned for holiness that his cause for canonization is now under consideration.[2]

This incident has been treated at length because it illustrates some of the outstanding qualities of Bishop Fleming. When this affair broke first, he was quite prepared to believe that Father Duffy and the people of St. Mary's were guilty. But having investigated, he realized his error. When convinced, he supported the people strongly in their struggles to claim their rights; in this case a right which had existed from time immemorial and which was essential to their survival—access to the beaches. At the same time, knowing, from his Irish experience, how easily uneducated people could become inflamed and take the law into their own hands, he was prepared to assert all his spiritual and moral authority to urge that they respect the law of the land. In this respect he was a true follower of Daniel O'Connell, his friend and mentor.

On the other hand, one would find it hard to believe that his opponents could have acted as ruthlessly as he frequently claimed they did—determined at all costs to preserve their own inherited privileges to the exclusion of the common people, exhibiting (or barely concealing) their hatred of the Catholic priesthood, which was leading and supporting the "lower orders" in their search for their rights—until one hears from their own lips the confirmation of this charge. When one finds the Chief Judge of the Supreme Court openly avowing his determination to bring "the rabble" and the priesthood, and even the Catholic elements in the House of Assembly "to heel", one can but shake one's head in disbelief. Charges of "ignorance" and "bigotry" are flung right and left at the priests and even at Bishop Fleming himself, and not just in private but in official dispatches to the British Government.

We thus have compelling reasons, based on documentary evidence, to treat with great scepticism the many other charges made against Bishop Fleming to the British Government and to Rome in order to destroy his influence and to get him discharged from his position. It was the old order fighting against the new, and the former recognized in this dauntless prelate the spearhead which would drive a wedge into their entrenched position and overturn the established order in which their privileges were enshrined. He had to be destroyed at all costs.

CHAPTER FIFTEEN
TRIUMPH....

"... in the presence of Cardinals, Bishops of all ranks,
Kings and Princes, Priests and people."

-Fleming to Troy, May 29, 1837

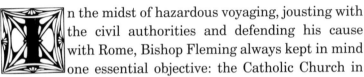n the midst of hazardous voyaging, jousting with the civil authorities and defending his cause with Rome, Bishop Fleming always kept in mind one essential objective: the Catholic Church in Newfoundland must have a Cathedral worthy of the name and capable of providing adequately for the people. The miserable church on Henry Street was hopelessly deficient. Forty years old, it was in poor repair and built on grounds rented at the exorbitant rate of $400 a year. Even with three or four Masses each Sunday, many of the men had to remain outside no matter what the weather, kneeling on the wet ground or in the snow, their bare heads exposed to the piercing winds.

It was not easy to obtain in the vicinity of St. John's a block of land large enough for the Bishop's ambitious program since, besides the Cathedral, he envisaged a priests' house, convents and schools and even a cemetery.[1] There were, in fact, only two such lots. One was the Williams' estate located towards the west of the town, but to buy this would take all his available capital. The other was the woodlot connected with Fort Townshend. As part of the economizing effort of the British Government after the Napoleonic Wars, the artillery stationed at Fort Townshend was consolidated with the infantry at Fort William, at the east end of the town. Consequently this woodlot was no longer required. It was perfect for his purpose. Almost ten acres in extent, it was situated on the well-maintained road connecting Fort Townshend with Fort William. A cathedral built on top of such an imposing hill would inevitably dominate the entire landscape. And if he could get it as a grant, so much the better.

Bishop Fleming's first attempt in 1834 to obtain this land had failed. Believing that Governor Cochrane would not be sympathetic to his request and knowing nothing of the new Governor, he had made his request between Governor Cochrane's departure and Governor Prescott's arrival. One is tempted to think that he hoped his request would "slide through the cracks," in the confusion surrounding the takeover. But he had been too clever. His manoeuvre was detected, and he was told to use proper channels and to apply through the Governor. Therefore, in 1836, he wrote Governor Prescott, asking him to forward his petition to the Colonial Office. The Liberals (Whigs) under Lord Melbourne had returned to office in April 1835, so a more sympathetic response could be expected from the new Secretary, Lord Glenelg, than from his Tory predecessor, Spring Rice. In his letter to the Governor, Bishop Fleming specified the land he required: "the vacant land in the Barrens near Fort Townshend in which the old Wood Yard stands." Unfortunately, in his petition to Lord Glenelg he was not so specific, merely asking for "the grant of waste land near Fort Townshend, now occupied by the Honourable the Board of Ordnance."

With the unpleasantness of the Neavin affair still rankling and with Father Duffy's trial and the controversy over Judge Boulton very much centre stage, Governor Prescott had no intention of releasing such a prime property to his nemesis, the Catholic Bishop. Yet he could not refuse him outright. He directed his secretary, Mr.

Templeman, to inform the Bishop that while he was prepared to support the grant of another piece of land larger
than the one he requested but on the other side of the fort,
the ground in question was reserved for a proposed jail. The
Bishop at once pointed out that the jail could without incon-
venience be moved to the other side of the fort, while access
to the main road was essential for his own purpose. The
Governor rejected this alternative out of hand, but replied
that he would transmit the Bishop's petition to Lord
Glenelg without delay and would place no obstacle in the
way of the Bishop's obtaining a grant elsewhere. In his covering letter to Lord Glenelg, the Governor declared that
some of the passages in the Bishop's Memorial, as in most of
his writings, were very objectionable. Nevertheless, he
would support a grant that would not interfere with the
intended site of the proposed jail and penitentiary.

The Bishop soon came to believe that the Governor was
deliberately blocking his project. Not without reason, for
Prescott admitted to Lord Glenelg that the construction of a
jail was not in his power, but in that of the Assembly. He further acknowledged that it was unlikely one would be built in
the near future and that, if it were, it would probably be
built elsewhere than on the woodlot.

The Bishop decided that if he were to have any chance of
obtaining this land, he must go over the head of the
Governor and, with the help of his friends in the Parliament,
plead his cause in person with the British Government.
Therefore, having appointed Father Troy as his Vicar
General during his absence, he set out for England early in
July 1836 on the brig *Irish Lass*. The Governor meanwhile
had warned Lord Glenelg of his coming.

Bishop Fleming's departure was subject to the petty
annoyance which he had become accustomed to endure. He
had been told that the vessel would sail at 9:30 a.m, but, as
he reached the wharf, he discovered that it had actually
sailed an hour before and was now a considerable distance

off. His trunks had been put on board earlier in the morning, so, snatching his hat, he boarded a small boat and reached the *Irish Lass* with considerable difficulty. No sooner was he on board, however, than the vessel turned about and returned to the town to pick up a military officer who had also booked passage.

While Bishop Fleming was *en route* to England, Bishop Brampston died—perhaps fortunately for him since Bishop Fleming would undoubtedly have called him to account for his interference in Newfoundland affairs. The voyage must have been a stormy one since, informing Father Troy of his arrival, Bishop Fleming wrote that he was "not able to hold a pen, for indeed I have not the use of my fingers no more than my feet."

When he reached London, he was dismayed to discover that Parliament was winding up and that most of its members had left town. However, he informed Father Troy, "I do not despair of success although the most nefarious means have been used to blast my projects and my character also." He attempted to obtain an interview with Lord Glenelg, but failed in spite of a strong endorsement from Daniel O'Connell.

By now, the Bishop had obtained some inkling that serious charges were being renewed against him by McLean Little. He requested the opportunity to refute these charges, and Lord Glenelg felt compelled to accede to his demands. The Bishop was shown a list of the charges and given the opportunity of responding. He wrote a lengthy and spirited defence of his conduct, using the opportunity also to state in stark terms what he considered the fundamental causes of the disturbed state of Newfoundland society.

The Government, he wrote, was in the hands of a party which administered it for the benefit of the rich and to the injury of the fishermen. Confidence in the administration of justice did not exist. Religious and political jealousy embittered not only private life, but poisoned justice at its source.

Unfortunately the Governor and his Council were embroiled in this distrust and unpopularity since they were seen to support the oppressors. As for the press, with one exception, *The Patriot,* it was involved in propaganda against the Catholic Church and its ministers, but still enjoyed the Government's patronage from which *The Patriot* was excluded. Moreover, an essential prerequisite for a Catholic or a liberal Protestant to enjoy Government favour was that he or she engage in abuse of Bishop Fleming or his clergy. The Bishop concluded with a dire warning of the possible political implications. He pointed out that because of this ill-treatment, 3000 seamen had left the colony during the past two years. Most of these had migrated to the United States and, in the event of war, these expert sailors would be at the service of England's enemies.

Both Governor Prescott and former Governor Cochrane were given copies of the Bishop's defence and asked to respond to it. Lord Grey's comment to Cochrane shows the prejudice existing in the Colonial Office: "His Lordship (*Lord Glenelg*) gives you ample opportunity to correct Bishop Fleming's vindication."

In the midst of these concerns, Bishop Fleming did not forget his people at home. In September he wrote Father Troy, telling him of his great disappointment at not receiving a single line from Newfoundland since he had left St. John's. Being so far removed from his people, he said, his anxiety of mind was great indeed. He complained that he had not had a moment's respite since his arrival in London, writing letters by night and endeavoring to press their consideration by day on the "heartless few about the seat of government."

A shrewd Irish farmer could not have bettered his next move. Deciding that he must be prepared for the worst as far as the field he wanted was concerned, he determined to get an option on the other large piece of land in St. John's, the Williams' Plantation[2], which apparently was up for sale.

He instructed Father Troy to use Mr. Wakeham, a close friend of the Bishop, as confidential agent to purchase the site, raising the money, if necessary, by mortgaging his farm and any other property he had. He was to keep the matter strictly confidential except that on the day of sale he was to get a trustworthy friend to make an offer for it in order to throw the enemy off his guard. He was also to make sure that the new Petty Harbour graveyard was cleared and that the people there had their pickets prepared for fencing, but they were not to attempt to put them up until the Bishop got home.

In October, the Bishop was in Dublin and addressed the Catholic Book Society to which he gave a lengthy account of the trials of his episcopacy. No doubt his audience contributed substantially as a result of his lecture. A comment by Dean Burke of the Galway diocese in his vote of thanks might help explain the Bishop's disinterest in local vocations. The Dean mentioned that the late Bishop Kelly of Galway had resolved to educate and ordain priests specially for the Newfoundland mission. The Dean added that he entertained ardent hopes that his illustrious successor, Doctor MacHale, would fulfill the intention which Bishop Brown's death left incomplete.

With a long, dreary winter before him and no prospect of returning to Newfoundland before spring, Bishop Fleming decided to visit Rome to receive the Pontifical benediction. However, he traveled slowly and did not reach Rome until March 12. He quickly regretted his tardiness since he found he was too late to fulfill the formalities necessary for participation in the Easter ceremonies at St. Peter's. Moreover, he did not have with him the vestments that would be needed to take part in the Easter ceremonies.

Now occurred an extraordinary event which not only made up for all the disappointments of the recent past but clearly revealed the esteem in which he was held in Rome. As he sat in his room in the Franciscan College of St. Isidore

brooding over his ill-fortune, he perceived a dragoon gallop-
ing up towards the College. The dragoon bore the news that
the Holy Father, having learned of his disappointment, had
waved all the normal requirements and desired that he take
his place among the bishops on the following day. This privilege was unprecedented. To add to his good fortune, the
Bishop discovered that a Franciscan archbishop had left his
robes behind him in the College, and so he was able to be
suitably attired for the ceremonies on Palm Sunday (March
18) and the following week. An even more extraordinary
privilege was to follow. On Tuesday of Holy Week, as he sat
among the bishops in St. Peter's, he was summoned from his
place and installed as one of the assistant prelates to the
Pope. He was simply overwhelmed. As he wrote, "that really was too much for a poor insignificant mortal like me conducted as it was in presence of Cardinals, Bishops of all
ranks, Kings and Princes, Priests and people." The ceremonies, too, left him in awe. They exceeded in splendor anything that can be conceived or imagined. He could not but
reflect that he would hardly have received these marked
attentions had not his name attracted the attention of the
Court of Rome through the medium of his enemies.

He planned to stay in Rome until the Feast of Saints
Peter and Paul on June 29, which marked the end of the
business year at the Vatican. When he was reminded by
Cardinal Mai, Secretary of Propaganda Fide, that he was
expected to submit a detailed report on his Vicariate[3] to the
Holy Father, he was taken aback since he had few particulars of the Vicariate with him and he had to rely on his memory. Nevertheless, he set to work and produced a document
which, in the Italian version, runs to eighty-six typewritten
pages. He submitted a draft to Cardinal Mai and was
advised to tone down some of his criticism of his predecessor, Bishop Scallan. He followed this advice and on May 6
wrote the Cardinal again asking him to expedite the print-
ing of the *Relatio* so that he could get back quickly to

Newfoundland and also so that copies could be distributed among "the principal and leading Romans...so that the piety and charity of the same may be aroused to lavish something towards the sustenance of my mission." On May 18, he was cordially received in audience by the Holy Father and presented his *Relatio*. It was for him a very emotional and reassuring occasion. Later that day, writing to Cardinal Mai to thank him for his help he exclaimed:

> Today a little before midday I had the singular honour of waiting upon His Holiness, the Supreme Pontiff, at whose feet I most humbly placed my Report on the Catholic Mission of Newfoundland. While life remains I will remember the most benevolent and paternal manner with which the Supreme Pontiff deigned to welcome and receive me—even the highest king would be honoured by such a reception and then his unhoped for benevolence, with which he embraced me, his unworthy servant and adding to these great honours, his approbation of my character and of my work in the kindest words. This is sufficient recompense to me for all my labours, trials, and difficulties, which I have undertaken as much for the defence as for the propagation of our common religion. This also, (as I hope) will be more and more a stimulus to new work in so far as it lies in me to promote the glory of God without any murmuring. ...
>
> Your kindness leaves a most grateful impression in my heart, which I will celebrate until the last and final breath of my life.

Cardinal Mai did more than facilitate his access to the Holy Father. He also presented him with a substantial supply of vestments, chalices and other church requisites, together with a collection of splendid paintings for his

Churches. In turn, Bishop Fleming took advantage of the favorable political climate to suggest that his Franciscan colleague, Father John Mullock, O.F.M., Parish Priest of Adam and Eve parish in Dublin, would be a fit candidate for the vacant Bishopric of Jamaica. He recommended Father Mullock as being "healthy and robust, a British subject, speaks and writes English, Spanish, Italian and French; he is prudent, humble, pious and never involved in politics." Father Mullock did not receive this appointment but was eventually to succeed Bishop Fleming as Bishop of Newfoundland.

Bishop Fleming was finding residence in Rome a rather expensive and pompous affair. "The expenses of a Bishop here," he wrote, "are enormous—my dress cost 200 dollars—and then every Bishop must keep a servant in livery with an enormous cocked hat going in his wake wherever he goes—then the carriages, etc., that I am ruined by it. But," he added hopefully, "I expect the Cardinal Prefect will pay my Bill."

To add to his triumph, on March 25, he received word from Lord Grey that the Governor of Newfoundland would be instructed to grant him as much of the land in question as might be necessary for the ecclesiastical buildings which he intended to erect. His voyage home must have been a very happy one.

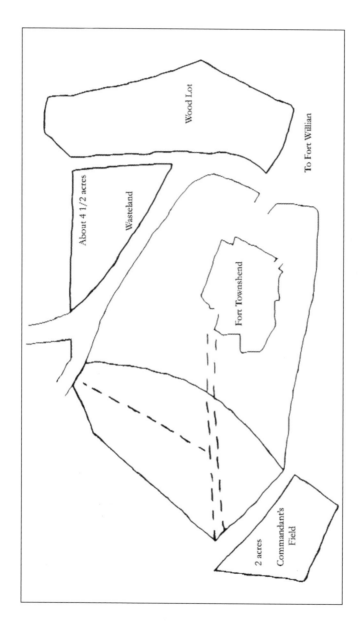

Wood Lot

About 4 1/2 acres

Wasteland

To Fort Willian

Fort Townshend

2 acres

Commandant's Field

Rough map of Fort Townshend area showing land Bishop Fleming wanted and which Ordinance wanted to give him.
Provincial Archives of Newfoundland and Labrador GN 1/1 1836 "68, October 14, 1836

CHAPTER SIXTEEN
...AND DISASTER

The opinion and the disgust of the people have
reached their utmost limits.

- Cardinal Lambruschini to Pope Gregory XVI

hese moments of glory, however, soon began to fade. If the Bishop had examined carefully the description of the field he was offered, he would have noted that there was considerable confusion about which of several lots of land in the area he was to receive. Lord Glenelg seemed to believe that it referred to the 4½ acre plot to the north. The Governor, who knew very well which property the Bishop wanted, wrote to Lord Glenelg that the Bishop would probably reject the 4½ acre section because of its proximity to the Fort, and recommended instead the 2 acre Commandant's Field to the south of the Fort as admirably suited for the purpose, remarking that such a grant should excite the gratitude of the Bishop and the Catholics generally — a statement which he must have made with tongue in cheek! He also attempted to make its acquisition more difficult by suggesting that it need not be deeded over until the Bishop was prepared to proceed with his work and that the transfer should be made subject to certain conditions, such as the buildings being completed within a fixed period, which would be very difficult for the Bishop to do.

Three months later, in July, Governor Prescott still procrastinating, wrote to Lord Glenelg that he would not proceed any further until he knew whether he might give the Bishop his choice between the 4½ acre field and the two acre one. When Lord Glenelg received this last communication, he was not amused. He fumed that Prescott already had that permission and added that, considering the length to which the correspondence on this subject had already been carried, and the consequent delay in deciding upon it, he would very much regret any further postponement which was not absolutely necessary. He requested, therefore, that on Bishop Fleming's return to Newfoundland, the Governor should take the earliest opportunity of bringing the matter to a final settlement. In none of those letters is there any mention of the 9½ acre woodlot which the Bishop had set his heart on. He was not to discover this until he returned to Newfoundland to claim it.

He had an even greater cause for concern. McLean Little had continued his barrage of affidavits derogatory of the Bishop and his clergy, affidavits which, as before, Prescott promptly dispatched to the Colonial Office. Other English officials joined in the attack. In January 1837, Aubin, the British agent in Rome, wrote to the Foreign Office to say that he had shown Monsignor Capaccini a copy of a sermon supposed to have been given by Father Troy during the recent elections in Newfoundland, and that Capaccini had agreed to alert the Pope. Aubin added: "I hope the Rev. Bishop will have no motive for congratulating himself upon the greeting he receives at Rome." He noted that Capaccini's letter to the Bishop, although not written in the strongest terms, was nevertheless sufficiently forceful to have deterred that Prelate from his unjustifiable course were he not a headstrong and turbulent character. In July, Prescott forwarded further complaints from Catholics in St. John's, mainly about the conduct of Father Troy. McLean wrote again, this time to Cardinal Fransoni, with a similar complaint. Other complaints were received from Patrick Kough and Robert Job.

Even though many of these complaints were made under oath, it is difficult to assess their reliability since in most cases the reply to them is not available. In one case, fortunately, we do have such a reply, and it may, perhaps, help evaluate similar complaints. Bishop Fleming was accused of falsifying a will made by Daniel Brophy, a resident of St. John's. As part of a general defence of his actions to Rome against the accusations of Father Browne, the Bishop testified as to what actually happened on this occasion, and thereby further illustrated the extraordinary behavior of Judge Boulton.

Daniel Brophy was, according to the Bishop, a good Catholic of moderate means, married to a fine Catholic woman but with no children except an illegitimate son whom he had fathered while still single and before coming to Newfoundland. This child had remained in Ireland and had been well provided for by Mr. Brophy. In 1837, Dan Brophy fell seriously ill and decided to make his will while still of sound mind. In this will, he left half his estate to his wife and half for the upkeep of the Presentation Sisters. His wife was present and concurred with his wishes.

When Brophy died, Judge Boulton called his widow into court to remonstrate with her against the "injustice" of the will. She explained the situation, but the Judge refused to listen to her or to let her be sworn. He examined one of the two witnesses to the will, who agreed with the widow's statement. The Judge again refused to listen to him or to have him sworn, and sent for the second witness. This man was a cousin of Father Browne. He was sworn in and testified that the will had been made two years earlier. In spite of the fact that the widow and the other witness were prepared to swear that it was indeed signed on the day written in the will, the Judge thereupon declared the will invalid.

Even so, the intention of Mr. Brophy would have been carried out since all the estate would now descend to the widow, and she was prepared to carry out the original

design. To forestall this, Judge Boulton sent for the illegitimate son from Ireland, refused to allow his legitimacy to be
questioned (an illegitimate child could not inherit) and
awarded him the half of the estate intended for the
Presentation Sisters. So much for the value of this charge
against the Bishop.

Nevertheless, the very volume of these complaints
forced the Roman authorities to take them seriously. Bishop
Fleming and his clergy became the subject of an exchange of
letters between Cardinal Lambruschini, Secretary of State,
and Cardinal Fransoni, Prefect of Propaganda Fide, as a
result of which Cardinal Lambruschini made a detailed
report of the entire affair to Pope Gregory and suggested
that the Pope write another and stronger letter to the
Bishop admonishing him for his conduct and that of his
clergy with the hope that the Bishop would act more pru-
dently on his return to Newfoundland. As for Father Troy,
he warned that the British government would probably take
severe measures against him unless His Holiness acted first.

For the moment, Bishop Fleming, still in Ireland, was
happily unaware of this turn of events. There were rumors
that he was to be appointed to the See of Waterford or to
some position in Rome. In writing to Father Troy of these
rumors, the Bishop revealed how deeply he had taken the
people of Newfoundland to his heart: "But solemnly before
Heaven I declare there is not a situation in the Catholic
church I would accept this very moment if that situation
was to keep me from Newfoundland." He was anxious to get
back to his Vicariate, and left Rome in late July or early
August. He passed through Lyons where he collected 10,100
francs from the Society for the Propagation of the Faith,
then traveled to Ireland to look for more priests for his mission. In early September, he landed in Newfoundland.

What had happened in Newfoundland during his fourteen months absence? The political and social scene had
erupted in frenzy. The mandate of the House of Assembly

having expired in 1836, new elections had been called. These elections were very hotly contested, the reformers realizing that if ever they were to obtain control of the Assembly and thus forward their plans for the improvement of the island, the time was now. Various historians have given much attention to the disturbances caused by the reform party during this campaign, but little to the reasons behind them. (Once more, it is important to remember that there was no secret ballot.) A newspaper of the time exposed the problem clearly. It maintained that those working in the merchants' stores or on their wharves were forced by their employers to vote for their oppressors or be dismissed. Debtors were threatened with jail unless they voted as their creditors desired. Captains of fishing vessels and shipbuilders were discharged if they voted against their employer's nominees as were all workers dependent on the merchants' for employment or subsistence. Besides this, many votes were bought by gifts of barrels of pork, flour or butter either to the voters themselves or to their wives.

While it is not intended to give a detailed account of events leading up to the election, one in particular deserves attention as illustrating the actual relations between Bishop Fleming and his priests. On Saturday, October 22, to bolster the confidence of their supporters, about 300 supporters of the establishment's candidates paraded through the town yelling and shouting insults to their opponents as was usual on such occasions. The following day, though a Sunday, the reformers determined on a like parade. This parade started at about 2 p.m. and marched to the "hustings" (a field in the west of the town where political meetings were held and where the voting was to take place). There they were addressed by the candidates, and then the parade, led by the candidates, returned to the town. Several priests on horseback also led the procession although the Bishop had written Father Troy expressly forbidding their participation. The procession became quite boisterous, and as a result sev-

eral of the leaders were indicted for unlawful assembly
although, as Prowse states, "there was not a tittle of evidence to sustain the charges against the members." All but
one were eventually acquitted, the one exception being a
man who put his face up to that of a member of the opposition and yelled "bah," for which grave offence he was fined
£25 with sureties of £100 to keep the peace for twelve
months! The point of mentioning this event is that, far from
being the subservient tools of the Bishop, as was maintained, the priests, led by the Vicar General, Father Troy,
were quite capable of disregarding his express commands.

The result of the election was a resounding victory for
the reformers who won eleven of the fifteen seats, the mercantile party returning only four. Commenting on the
results, *The Ledger*, in time honoured fashion, bemoaned
the wide nature of the franchise and declared that "the same
evils will abound so long as we have for the most part a
Catholic population controlled in their every movement by
an ignorant, a vicious, and a political priesthood." However,
the victors did not even have time to celebrate their triumph
before it was overturned. Judge Boulton discovered that the
writ authorizing the election in Conception Bay did not bear
the great seal, and therefore declared the election there was
invalid. Subsequent inquiries revealed that none of the
writs had the seal affixed to them. The Judge thereupon
pronounced the entire election process illegal and called for
a new election, thereby, as Lord Glenelg succinctly described
it, erecting "a minor error into a major difficulty."

This second election took place in June 1837 while
Bishop Fleming was still in Rome. Anticipating serious violence, the Governor requested an increase in troops and
another naval vessel. His request was denied but he was told
that he could call upon the forces in Halifax if this became
absolutely necessary. In the event, the proceedings this time
were very subdued, the merchants having abandoned the
field in despair. Hoping to discredit the Assembly, they nom-

inated candidates who were obviously unsuitable, one of them, for instance, could neither read nor write. The reformers swept the field. Only two conservatives, Hugh Emerson and William B. Row, were returned and, of them, Row refused to take his seat, not wishing to be associated with such a group.

The new Assembly quickly took advantage of its unity. It began to investigate the many cases of injustice or impropriety it believed to have happened under the previous Assembly. It agitated for the right to appoint its own clerk and other officials who up to then had been appointed by the Governor. Between it and the Legislative Council there was soon bitter warfare. As fast as the Assembly passed measures, the Legislative Council rejected them. Meanwhile, marking the change from one era to another, King William IV died and the youthful Victoria became queen.

It was in the midst of this political uproar, that Bishop Fleming arrived home. Receiving a hero's welcome, he was paraded through the streets to the Church while the House of Assembly adjourned to welcome him. Later, he entertained the members of the Assembly at dinner and expressed his joy at being once more in the midst of his real friends. He spoke of his satisfaction at finding "the spirit of the people unbroken, to find that they had snapped the chains that had fettered them, that they had achieved a happy and peaceful revolution."

His first order of business was to obtain from Governor Prescott the deed for the land for the Cathedral. He was soon disillusioned. When he met the Governor, the latter insisted that the choice must be made between the Commandant's Field and the 4½ acre lot. Moreover, he added the proviso that the Bishop must spend annually on the project a sum which would eventually amount to £20,000.

The Bishop realized that the Governor was immovable and so very reluctantly decided that he had no other choice but to return yet again to England to press his claim to the ground he wanted. Before leaving, he announced that the Holy Father had granted a Jubilee Year for the Vicariate. Even in the solemn pronouncement proclaiming this Jubilee, he could not restrain from complaining about the treatment he was receiving from the civil authorities, of the "artifices of the enemy" by which his hopes had been frustrated.

He set sail in the *Alamode* for England on December 30. His departure caused him to miss the threatened communications from Rome, one from Pope Gregory XVI himself, and the other from Cardinal Fransoni, both containing severe reprimands concerning the behaviour of Father Troy and warning the Bishop to keep a tighter rein on his clergy. Fransoni, indeed, went further and ordered the Bishop to remove Father Troy "from all duties of the Sacred Ministry." It was fortunate that the Bishop did miss these letters since otherwise he could hardly have left Father Troy in charge of the Vicariate and might have had to remain at home. By coincidence, his sailing had been preceded by a similar departure for England of two representatives of the Assembly, Doctor Carson and Valentine Nugent, who had been delegated by the Assembly to plead with the British Parliament for the dismissal of Judge Boulton. On January 5, 1838, the Judge himself set out for England to defend himself. Thus was set the final confrontation between these old protagonists.

CHAPTER SEVENTEEN
A TRAITOR IN THE RANKS

A man's enemies shall be those of his own household.

- Micah 6:7

ne of Bishop Fleming's priests, Father Timothy Browne, O.S.A., has already received passing mention in this narrative. He now moved centre stage as one of the Bishop's most effective antagonists. A few days before leaving Newfoundland in December 1837, Bishop Fleming had removed Father Browne from his position as Parish Priest of Ferryland and suspended him from all priestly activities except for the privilege of saying Mass privately. By doing so, he created a very dangerous enemy.

The animosity between them had been growing for a long time. They had first come into conflict after the Bishop's consecration in December 1829. This consecration itself was a galling disappointment for Father Browne. He had been one of the three "names" submitted to Propaganda Fide to succeed Bishop Lambert [*Church Law required the diocesan synod to nominate three persons whom it considered suitable for the position.*] He was again one the three priests nominated as Bishop Scallan's successor. He was considerably senior to Father Fleming and had been far longer in the Vicariate. Moreover—and though this may seem a trivial matter at the present day, it was a crucial point at the time, for there was bitter rivalry between the two Irish counties—Father Browne was from County

Wexford, as had been all the previous Bishops, while Father Fleming was from County Waterford.

The story of Father Browne is the sad one of a good man gradually succumbing to his weaknesses until he seemed to lose all sense of loyalty or responsibility and became the willing tool of those who would exploit him. Born in 1775 near New Ross in County Wexford, Timothy Browne was ordained as an Augustinian Friar in 1810 and came to Newfoundland in the following year at the invitation of Bishop Lambert. Some years later, he was assigned to the parish of Ferryland. At first he made a fine impression. When, in 1820, Father Browne's Superior in Ireland wanted to recall him, Bishop Scallan protested to Propaganda Fide, and the Superior was informed by Rome that Father Browne should remain in Newfoundland because of his outstanding service to the Vicariate. We find, in the 1821 list of Vicariates prepared by Propaganda Fide, the statement concerning Newfoundland: "Ten missionaries, the best is T. Browne, O.S.A."

However, this good beginning did not last and in 1822, Bishop Scallan, in his report to Propaganda Fide, said of Browne that he was "of good character and an excellent preacher, but recently lazy and financially unreliable." Apparently, he continued to deteriorate spiritually, for in 1824, a year after Father Fleming had arrived on the scene, Bishop Scallan wrote to Father Richard Walsh, the Superior of the Franciscan monastery in Wexford, that he found himself in an embarrassing situation. Father Fleming's Superior had asked for his return to Ireland but the Bishop wanted to retain his services because he "is a real treasure to me." However, he hesitated to write Propaganda Fide again as he had done for Father Browne "whom I would have no objection to part with now," and asked Father Walsh to intercede for him. He even introduced a little financial blackmail, noting that he had made his will. "However, the fulfillment of this must depend on the manner I will be treated by the Order." Later, Bishop Fleming was to describe the course of Father Browne's downfall. He characterized him as a person of moderate intelligence and limited education, but still one of the most respected priests in the Vicariate. However, soon after his appointment to Ferryland, the people there began to complain seriously about his neglect particularly of the dying whom he let die without the Sacraments even when he could easily have administered them. One of the most serious complaints was that, at times, when the congregation was assembled for Sunday Mass, he would send word that he was ill and unable to celebrate. As the people were leaving the Church, they would see him setting out with his Protestant friends on a hunting expedition. Possessed of a pleasant, light-hearted manner and fond of lay society, he formed a warm friendship with two or three prominent non-Catholic families in the district, and their homes were the only ones in the district to be honoured by his visits.

Shortly after Bishop Fleming's consecration, he was deputed by Bishop Scallan to make a visitation of Father Browne's district. When he returned, he submitted a devastating report of the abuses which he had discovered. In brief the report stated that a more neglected people were not to be found in the island, that any semblance of religion was preserved by a few older people who assembled their neighbours for the Rosary. None of the people had been prepared for Confirmation, the children were left without any religious instruction whatever. Confessions were almost totally neglected; not more than half a dozen people had been to Confession for the past five to fourteen years. The sick were permitted to die without the sacraments and to be buried without the rites of Religion. The cup used by Father Browne for Mass was unsuitable and was, moreover, used by him at his table entertaining his Protestant friends. He never said the Divine Office [*Priests were required under pain of serious sin to say the Breviary daily*]. On receiving his report, Bishop Scallan must have been shattered. He wrote to the representative of the Augustinian Order in Rome, Father John Rice, asking that Father Browne be recalled to Ireland. However, his rapidly declining health and his death on May 29, 1830, precluded any further action.

The newly consecrated Bishop Fleming now found himself in a very difficult position. Flattered by the acceptance of prominent Protestants and dissident Catholics, Father Browne had readily fallen in with their complaints against the strict discipline which the Bishop had introduced. Their main objection was that the Bishop was creating divisions in the community by forbidding Catholics to join in Protestant religious services as they had been accustomed to do under the previous regime. In spite of this edict, Father Browne openly took part in Protestant services. Nevertheless the Bishop sought reconciliation and Father Browne promised amendment. However, the same disregard of his duties continued, and, after a further four year test, the Bishop once more determined to remove him. But again, Father Browne promised amendment and the Bishop agreed on a further trial; once more to no effect. Another four years passed and so notorious had his conduct become that the Bishop's opponents embraced him openly, calculating that they would be able to obtain Bishop Fleming's removal now that they had obtained the support of a senior priest.

Father Browne now took up temporary residence in St. John's with one of the Bishop's principal enemies, a prominent Protestant, John Sinclair, a member of the Executive Council. While there, he also acted as unofficial chaplain to the wife of the Chief Justice, Mrs. Boulton, who had ceased to attend Church services. Here he spent five weeks, giving great scandal by his dissipation and leaving his Congregation without Mass or the Sacraments. One night, after a round of partying, he fell over a cliff and broke his leg. Though for a while his life was in danger, he made no attempt to make contact with the Bishop or one of the other priests.

He began to show the vindictive side of his nature by taking an active part in the furtive schemes of the Bishop's opponents to prevent him from getting land for his proposed Cathedral. The Bishop noted a curious coincidence. When Father Browne would come to St. John's from Ferryland, there would be tremendous furtive activity. When he left again for Ferryland, all would become quiet. The Bishop complained to Propaganda that these conspirators had, through the Governor, secretly sent unfavorable reports about him to the British Government.

> Several meetings were held, and secret communications were made to the Government through Captain Prescott, the then Governor, for he too was leagued in this crusade against my obtaining the ground, and all these communications were calumniatory of me; but particularly were they active in procuring a person of the name of Michael McLean Little, a reputed Catholic, but one who was a notorious infidel, to act in this warfare. This man, conceiving that as the principal Merchants of the Town were interested and as a promise had been made to him of a situation under Government, he, as he was steeped in poverty, would be raising good friends by joining in their underhand efforts particularly as the whole was involved in the most profound secrecy, and it was generally understood that, as heretofore, everything in the Colonial Office would be treated confidentially.

McLean's complaints did not have much impact until he concocted a scheme, with the connivance of the above group, to persuade the Secretary of State for the Colonies that his representations deserved weight. He went from house to house to obtain signatures to his petitions, falsely telling the people that he was getting a small office under the Government and required testimonials to secure it. Even so, very few Catholics signed the supposed petition, but Father Browne, though fully aware of the scheme, publicly put his name to it.

Finally, as we have seen, Bishop Fleming's patience became exhausted and in December 1837, he dismissed Father Browne from his parish. The defrocked priest now took the active leadership in the group's malicious attacks on the Bishop. Perhaps the most outrageous of all his activities was his report to Governor Prescott on the condition of the Church in Newfoundland. It came about in the following manner.

While Father Browne was staying with his friend John Sinclair in 1837, the Governor, knowing his disaffection from the Church and seeing an opportunity of obtaining further ammunition against Bishop Fleming, requested Sinclair to have Father Browne send him a report on the condition of the Catholic Church in Newfoundland and on the character of its priests. Father Browne eagerly seized the opportunity, expressing the pious hope that the result will have the effect of "removing ... a most intolerable grievance, viz, ecclesiastical tyranny and misrule." Since the arrival of Bishop Fleming, he maintained, "Everything resembling kind, or Christian, or friendly feeling has ceased to exist . . . The poor have been taught from the temple of the living God to look upon the rich and wealthy . . . as their greatest enemies . . . In the same Sacred place . . . a mode of proceeding has been adopted well calculated to bring authority into contempt and disregard." All this, he maintained, "originated solely with and from Doctor Fleming, whose intolerance, bigotry, and prejudice this community is well acquainted with, whose ambition is such that he will not be content with anything less than absolute power, Civil and Ecclesiastical . . . ."

Having thus disposed of the Bishop, Father Browne turned his attention to the clergy, most of whom he claimed to be influenced by principles of action similar to the Bishop's. He excepted himself and one or two others as "the only scions of the old stock," while, on the contrary, he singled out Fathers Mackin and Ward as being "intolerant, ignorant bigots." He ended with the sweeping condemnation that in St. John's, "in place of instruction have been substituted base ribaldry, obscenity, gross calumny, cursing, blasphemy, censures and anathemas denounced against the innocent, the publication and preaching of a crusade to extort money from the poor in the name of the Lord."

Delighted with this response, Governor Prescott forwarded it the very next day to Lord Glenelg together with a covering letter whose contents make it difficult to excuse him from duplicity.

> Wishing to obtain, for Your Lordship's information, an exact account of the number of Roman Catholic Priests at present established here and what proportion of them had been in the Colony previously to Doctor Fleming's appointment as Bishop, I requested Mr. Sinclair (a Member of the Council) to apply to Father Browne for this intelligence. I enclose a communication made in consequence by the Rev. Gentleman. It goes beyond my object and expectation and is certainly written in an angry spirit, but the writer is a man of exemplary life and amiable character, and is, I really believe, inspired by an honest indignation at conduct on the part of his Brethren, which justly appears to him subversive of the interests of true Religion.

So, as Bishop Fleming sailed for England, while he could congratulate himself on the likelihood that, with the dismissal of Judge Boulton, he would no longer have to contend with one of his major enemies. Still, unbeknownst to him, he was acquiring another enemy, one all the more deadly since he could carry his twisted dream of ousting the Bishop into the heart of the Vatican itself.

CHAPTER EIGHTEEN
THE END OF THE BEGINNING

His Lordship [Lord Glenelg] has directed Captain Prescott...
to put you at once in possession of the Land to the Eastward of Fort
Townshend

- Lord Grey to Bishop Fleming

After an invigorating voyage, Bishop Fleming arrived in Falmouth on January 19, 1838. From there he escorted a fellow passenger, Mary Dillon, to the Waterford Steamer at Bristol and then continued on to London. In London, he found Doctor Carson and Valentine Nugent comfortably housed and decided to join them in order to show his solidarity with their petition against Judge Boulton. He wrote back to Father Troy on the thirtieth of the month that he wished to be identified with the delegation and with the people of Newfoundland, and that with them he would prosper or perish. He added that the winter voyage across the Atlantic had been tolerable enough and that he had never felt in better health in his life than after the voyage. His belongings, however, had not survived so well. A sea had broken over the vessel when it was lying to and ruined almost everything he had.

This letter to Father Troy is important as being, perhaps, the only one still extant in which he dealt extensively with various business and political affairs. He revealed his influence over the Assembly when, at the head of the letter he wrote: "PRIVATE. It would be most important that the members of the House of Assembly should peremptorily refuse to meet until the return of their Delegates." He then continued:

> I have had an interview with persons here high in authority and I can safely say, that the presence of the enemies of Newfoundland at the Colonial Office will not be very agreeable. That they have friends there I believe, but the days of despotism are passed away. Under the best and most amicable Sovereign in Europe and a wise and liberal government, the Colonies as well as the Home Departments will soon be cleansed from the bigots and tyrants whose only glory is to trample on the lives and liberties of the people.

He assured Father Troy that Judge Boulton would not be returning to Newfoundland and that he expected to hear shortly of a successor whose conduct would make up for all the injuries and heartaches that the Judge had inflicted on the people of Newfoundland. He reported that the reception of the delegates at the Colonial Office had been very warm, and he was confident that the wishes of the people for a radical change would be met. He added that Nugent had been indefatigable and recommended that, when he returned to Newfoundland, he should receive some "substantial return for his inestimable services."

The turmoil which Newfoundland had experienced in recent years had been reflected in Quebec which, after the failed rebellion of Papineau, was likewise in turmoil. In order to calm the situation there, Earl Durham had been appointed Governor General with almost dictatorial powers. Bishop Fleming declared himself delighted at this news partly because Durham was to be accompanied by a personal friend of his [*we are not told whom this person was*], but principally because he had heard that Durham would be given similar powers over Newfoundland. [*This did not eventuate.*]

Then he turned to his own affairs. He assured Father Troy that, in spite of the obstacles thrown in his way in the most influential quarters, he was certain of getting the Government ground. However, he had not yet moved on the matter since he had been exerting all his efforts on behalf of the delegation. He was still torn between the Townshend site and the other possible site, Williams' plantation. The latter site offered all the advantages which he desired. The purchase papers were signed and he could take possession whenever he pleased, but he was alarmed at the prospect of having to lay out all his disposable funds to buy it. He was already short of funds and asked Father Troy to send what money he could spare. His final request was for the exact dimensions of the sanctuary rail of the Petty Harbour Church as well as the height and width of all its windows since he had lost this information with many other important documents in the storm mentioned above. He suggested that Father Troy publish this letter - with suitable emendations and omissions.

While he was thus engaged, however, his adversaries back home had been equally busy, attacking him and defending Judge Boulton. The Judge had received an imposing send off from his supporters in St. John's. *The Public Ledger*, making an obvious comparison with the Bishop's departure, declared: "No official personage—nor any other—has ever quitted these shores, with such powerful manifestations in his favour, as those which have accompanied the departure of Chief Justice Boulton." Even while both Bishop and Judge were on the high seas, the Chamber of Commerce, whose president was James Sinclair (the friend of Father Browne!), sent a formal petition to the Queen, a compendium of all the complaints that had been made against Bishop Fleming and his clergy, together with similar complaints against the House of Assembly, which the

Petition declared to be under the control of the clergy. The
Petition begged for the relief of the colony against "this
priestly tyranny." It also affirmed "our full confidence in the
integrity and ability of Mr. Boulton and our entire satisfaction with the firm, judicious and impartial manner in which
he has discharged his duties. . . .and we should lament as a
public calamity any circumstance that might cause his
removal or retirement from the Bench of this colony." This
Petition, however, did not go unchallenged. To counteract it,
the Assembly presented a powerful indictment of the Judge
which had been prepared by Patrick Morris.

The Colonial Office referred the case to the Privy
Council which brought down its verdict on July 5. Although
it did not find any ground for imputing to the Chief Justice
any corrupt motive or intentional deviation from his duty as
a Judge, it found "so much of indiscretion in the conduct of
the Chief Justice, and that he has permitted himself so
much to participate in the strong feelings which appear
unfortunately to have influenced the different parties in the
Colony . . . that we think it will be inexpedient that he
should be continued in the Office of Chief Justice of
Newfoundland." The Colonial Office had already decided, on
the recommendation of Governor Prescott, that, in future,
the Chief Justice would not be a member of the Executive
Council and thus the conflict of interests which the possession of the dual office had caused in the past would be avoided.

Bitterly disappointed at the decision, Judge Boulton
retired to private practice in Ontario. In his *History of
Newfoundland*, Prowse claims that the Judge was very
unfairly treated in this matter and made the scapegoat for
an unworkable political system. He argues that he should
have been pensioned, and not dismissed penniless after filling such a high office. Boulton was replaced by Judge John
G. Bourne, also a controversial character, who himself was

dismissed in 1844 for accusing Governor Harvey of making appointments because he owed money to the recipients.

While this decision of the Privy Council removed one of Bishop Fleming's most persistent enemies, other opponents were determined to continue their campaign against him. McLean Little and Father Browne, for example, through the willing agency of Governor Prescott, continued to deluge the Colonial Office with examples of the supposed wrong-doing of the Bishop and Catholic clergy. The Bishop's reply of January 1837 to the Colonial Office to the charges against him had provoked a flurry of angry responses and charges from those who had made the original complaints. To respond to these further charges, the Bishop wrote Lord Glenelg at the beginning of February asking for an interview. Lord Glenelg hedged, claiming that the correspondence was so bulky that it precluded a reply for some time. Alarmed, the Bishop requested copies of these later statements. The Colonial Office now found itself in a dilemma. It feared that to release these documents would add fuel to the divisions in Newfoundland society since they would make public the secret efforts of so many prominent citizens to have Bishop Fleming deposed, but how could it refuse the Bishop's request for them when it had already permitted Judge Boulton to see the documents he needed to defend himself! As one of their officials commented, their previous steps had led the Government into "as awkward a predicament as could well be imagined."

While the Colonial Office was pondering how to handle this touchy situation, the Bishop wrote Lord Grey, the Assistant Secretary of State, again urgently requesting the grant of land for his church and detailing the Governor's manoeuvres to block it. He even offered, if necessary, to purchase the property at its full value. Perhaps in the hope that satisfying the Bishop on this count would induce him to forego his request for the incriminating documents, and realizing that the Bishop was being trifled with in his request for land, Lord Glenelg decided that enough was enough, and that the matter should now be decided without further reference to the Colony. Consequently, on April 7, Lord Grey informed the Bishop that "His Lordship [*Lord Glenelg*] has directed Captain Prescott, if no insufferable objection should exist, to put you at once in possession of the Land to the Eastward of Fort Townshend." Now, at last, the Governor was defeated, and on June 30, the Deed for the land "*containing nine acres three rods and thirteen perches (more or less)*" was finally executed.

It would appear that the gift of land, so long sought after, did, indeed, induce the Bishop to relent in his persistent quest for justification. Noting this, Lord Glenelg, in May, wrote the Bishop that, for the sake of the peace of the island, he had decided to bring the controversy to a close and consequently would not release any further documentation. To his relief, the Bishop did not object but, instead, transferred his attention to the erection of his Cathedral.

In St. John's, the project was already in progress. Early in May, even before the Deed was signed, word of the victory reached the Island and, amidst general excitement, Father Troy, in his sermon on Sunday, May 13, outlined the program to be followed.

> You are all aware that I got the ground, I suppose, and I intend fencing it on Thursday, and I expect everyone will come and assist... I expect everyone will bring a longueur or postern-shore and the women too, I expect, will give assistance...Now I will want pick-axes, shovels and spades and crowbars. I expect it will be all done in half an hour... The bell of the Church will be rung on Thursday next at 10:00 p.m. as a signal for you to meet...

In the same article, *The Ledger*, with unaccustomed magnanimity, reported the actual fencing in:

> The whole was yesterday [*Thursday, May 17*]
> taken possession of and fenced in an incredibly
> short space of time by Father Troy and a very
> numerous assemblage of men, women and chil-
> dren congregated for that purpose. Of course the
> occasion was a joyous one and colors flying, the
> guns firing and booths erected, the men hur-
> rahing; and there was the white flag with the
> sacred emblem of the Cross upon it majestically
> waving over Gallows Hill [*the southern extremity
> of the hereafter-to-be- consecrated spot*]. The whole
> was a Gala Day and will, we don't doubt, long be
> remembered.

Bishop Howley, in his *History*, relates one amusing incident in connection with the fencing. A farmer was asked to
bring his horse and plough and trace out the boundaries
which had been laid out by the Government surveyors. But
when he came to the western portion, he noticed that the
stakes had been laid out in such a way that the property
would come to a point on the main road just where the
Bishop wanted his Cathedral to face. The farmer in question
was noted for always ploughing a straight furrow: but, on
this occasion, he turned the horse westward, cut a wide
curve, and thus preserved the square in front of the
Cathedral.

Now that the matter was finally settled, Bishop Fleming
made no delay in starting on the building itself. He visited
some of the main architects in England and Ireland. He
wrote from London to John Jones, an architect in Clonmel,
Ireland, on July 11, asking for plans and for estimates as to
the cost and quantity of stone for the ornamental work that
would be required. He also asked for instructions as to the
laying of the foundations which he hoped to lay as soon as
possible after his return to St. John's. He expected that the

proposed church would "rise a beauty alike credible to the Designer and an embellishment to the country."

He was in great need of funds to begin this work and, at his urging, Propaganda Fide wrote to the Apostolic Nuncio in Vienna asking that he request a substantial donation for the Bishop's work from the Associazione Leopoldina. Bishop Fleming also wrote the Committee for the Propagation of the Faith in Paris for the same purpose. In this latter letter, interestingly, he mentions the "hope to be able one day, with divine assistance, to send two zealous Priests to Labrador," the only reference the writer has been able to find in his writings to such a desire.

Not being able to obtain direct passage to Newfoundland, the Bishop was forced to travel via Hamburg where he was delayed for some weeks while the *Kingeloch*, the vessel he was to travel on, was being loaded. By a stroke of luck, while waiting, he met Mr. Schmidt, a Danish architect, and was so struck by the economy of his design and its suitability for the Newfoundland climate that he changed his mind about the style of the building and engaged Mr. Schmidt to prepare plans and to make a model for the work.

The vessel left Hamburg on August 28 with the Bishop and Valentine Nugent as passengers. Meeting atrocious storms on the river Elbe, in one of which they almost perished, they took an entire week to reach the coast at Cuxhaven. From there they sailed next day for the north of Scotland and again ran into such fierce storms that they barely escaped from being dashed on the coast of Aberdeen. Consequently they did not round the north of Scotland until September 21, almost a month after they had left Hamburg. Their course across the Atlantic was equally perilous, the vessel being driven many degrees north of its normal course. Finally, weak and ill, the Bishop *[we are not told how his companion Nugent fared]* arrived at St. John's at daybreak on October 18, thus completing his ninth and most perilous voyage across the Atlantic. Unfavourable winds prevented their sailing into the harbour, but their welcomers were not prepared to wait. Many boats came out to greet them, and towed them into safety.

Once landed, the Bishop was greeted by an enthusiastic crowd of all classes and persuasions. He was paraded through the streets to St. Mary's Church where he was the recipient of several formal Addresses to which he was expected to give an appropriate reply. That night, he collapsed in exhaustion and had to remain in bed some days to recover his strength.

CHAPTER NINETEEN
UNDER THE DISPLEASURE OF THE VATICAN

It cannot be tolerated without damage to religion that he
[Father Troy] *be retained in the exercise of the duties of the*
Sacred Ministry.

-Cardinal Fransoni

oubtlessly counseled by the officials at the Colonial Office, Bishop Fleming, as soon as he arrived back in St. John's, began to urge forgiveness of injuries and social harmony on the people of Newfoundland. When the citizens of Harbour Grace presented him with an Address of Welcome, he seized the opportunity to remind them of the great boon that the Church had received in obtaining the land for the Cathedral and to plead with them to show their gratitude by forgetting the wrongs they had suffered and seeking to make their enemies into friends.

The Address of Welcome itself revealed the true attitude of the ordinary Catholic people towards the Bishop. It read: "Yet are we compelled to admire your Lordship's leniency, wishing to win over and correct rather than condemn the few of your own flock, who have allied themselves with the persons at open war with Catholicity and its Ministers."

When the Bishop, in September of the previous year (1837), had returned to St. John's from his extended stay in Europe, the political scene had been in turmoil. Now, a year later, he found it a "theater of the absurd." To the despair of

the Colonial Office and the Governor, the Assembly and the
Executive Council were still at war, mainly over financial
affairs. Into this affray, a ridiculous element had intruded. It
began as a heated argument in public between John Kent,
the budding politician, and Doctor Kielly, Doctor Carson's
successor as Surgeon General, which mushroomed into a
formal confrontation between the Assembly and the
Judiciary, with both claiming precedence. What happened
next is difficult to believe. A judge of the Supreme Court
(Judge Lilly) and the High Sheriff, Benjamin Garrett, were
arrested by order of the Assembly and paraded through the
streets to jail. The Governor was forced to act. He promptly
released the prisoners and prorogued the Assembly for a
week to allow cooler heads to prevail. But the stalemate continued, and eventually the case had to be resolved by the
Privy Council in England which decided against the
Assembly. So, if it achieved nothing else, the case established
another precedent in English law.

However, none of this was the principal concern of the
Bishop who soon began his usual hectic round of activities,
organizing the affairs of his Vicariate and making practical
preparations for the commencement of his Cathedral. His
supply of priests was now sufficient for him to contemplate
setting up a separate parish for the people of Trinity Bay.
Consequently, on Thursday, October 25, just five days after
his arrival and having hardly recovered from the effects of
his difficult trans-Atlantic voyage, he set out for Trinity Bay
to make suitable preparations for the installation of a parish
priest. With him were Father Charles Dalton and Father
Thomas Waldron.

The Bishop had assumed that the trip would be reasonably straightforward since he could get the *St. Patrick
Packet* from Portugal Cove to Carbonear. From there a road,
he had been told, had recently been opened to Heart's
Content in Trinity Bay. On arrival at Carbonear, however,
they discovered that the "road" consisted of an opening

through the woods, made by cutting down the trees, leaving sharp stumps to threaten the travellers. The party set out on horseback, but soon Father Waldron's horse became lame and they had to walk the rest of the eighteen miles, much of it through bogs, with tree stumps endangering their every step. Though it was late in the evening when they reached Heart's Content, they immediately took sail for Trinity Harbour on the other side of the Bay.

Greeted on his arrival by a surprised and delighted congregation, the Bishop explained his intention to them. Happily, just as he was about to nominate one of their number to purchase a site for a new church and parochial residence, a Protestant lady sent word offering a piece of land ample for this purpose—an offer which the Bishop gratefully accepted.

The Bishop and his companions returned to Heart's Content that same evening. Next morning they again braved the hazards of the "road" and by evening had reached Carbonear, from where they walked to Harbour Grace. Here the Bishop was, once more, warmly welcomed. When about to leave in the early hours of the following morning, he learned that the people of the town intended to "parade" him back to Carbonear and, to avoid this, slipped away with his companions. But the people were not to be outwitted. The Bishop's party had not reached a mile from the town, when the whole town emerged from the trees with flags and bands and insisted on accompanying them to Carbonear. Here again he found the town gaily adorned with coloured banners. Before boarding the *St. Patrick Packet* once more for the return to St. John's, the Bishop addressed the crowd from the wharf "in brief but impassioned language, thanking them warmly for the compliments he had experienced at their hands, . . . imploring them to bury in the grave of oblivion all memory of wrong and all sense of injuries."

Father Dalton now returned to his parish of Harbour Grace while the Bishop and Father Waldron, on the *St. Patrick,* encountered severe weather. They beat against the winds all day long but made so little progress that they had only reached the eastward point of Bell Island before the coming of darkness compelled them to return to Carbonear. Next morning they tried again and this time reached St. John's safely much to the relief of the people who had been greatly concerned by their failure to arrive the previous evening.

Having thus set the Vicariate in order, the Bishop now busied himself with his plans for the Cathedral. He showed immediately that he intended to play a dominant role in its construction. He forwarded to Mr. Schmidt, the architect, 1,500 marks, which was half the agreed-upon price for the plans and model of the Cathedral, and promised the remainder as soon as the work was completed. The model was to be made on a scale of half an inch to a foot. Mr. Schmidt was "to be particularly careful to have the two fronts of the wings or arms of the cross executed in a handsome and striking manner," and the Bishop hinted that work on other churches would be forthcoming if he was pleased with the result.

On November 16, the Bishop wrote Michael McGrath, a builder in Waterford, with detailed instructions regarding the stone work for the Cathedral, enclosing plans for the exterior, side and floor plan and the architect's instruction regarding the stone work. The stone was to be obtained from the quarries near Waterford and should be of a quality able to bear the extremes of the climate to be endured in Newfoundland. He asked for an estimate of costs for the stone itself as well as for blocking and cutting, mentioning that the ornamental cutting was to be done in St. John's. Besides this he wanted an estimate of Mr. McGrath's charges for overseeing this work, forwarding the stone to St. John's and for coming himself to superintend its erection.

Finally McGrath was asked to find out the cost of buying and forwarding lime from Ireland to discover whether it was cheaper to buy the lime there or in St. John's. McGrath was assured that the Bishop would pay for advertising in *The Chronicle* for tenders for both stone and lime. Knowing how easily communications between Europe and Newfoundland could go astray, McGrath was asked to write in triplicate (forerunner of modern bureaucracy!); one letter by the vessel *Kingoloch* through Cork, another by post through Waterford, and a third through Graham & Taylor Merchants, Liverpool. On the same day the Bishop wrote Daniel Carrigan of Waterford asking for the cost of shipping a cargo of stone and lime in one of his large vessels. Carrigan was urged to reply (again in triplicate) as soon as possible so that the stone and lime could be brought out in the Spring.

In the midst of these activities, however, Bishop Fleming received a heart-rending blow. The long-delayed letter from His Holiness, Gregory XVI, finally arrived. It berated Father Troy for conduct prejudicial to good order and harmony in the Colony during the Bishop's absence. An accompanying letter from Cardinal Fransoni, Prefect of Propaganda Fide, stated that the Pope had ordered that Father Troy be suspended from "all duties of the Sacred Ministry."

The Bishop was shocked to receive such letters with their admonitions and directions for such severe action against the priest in his Vicariate in whom he placed most reliance. On November 24, he wrote a lengthy defense of Father Troy to the Pope, and three days later, a similar letter to Cardinal Fransoni. He related how on returning from England, flushed with his success in obtaining the land for his Cathedral, he had been plunged into the deepest sorrow on receiving the censure of His Holiness. His opponents, he declared, having failed in their attacks on himself, had decided to avenge themselves on the most useful and active of his priests.

He then proceeded to a spirited defence of the character and actions of Father Troy. He described the exemplary early career of the priest in Ireland and made a passionate plea for one "so valued by me, so loved by my People, so respected by all." He outlined the problems that the Pope's decision would cause him, particularly since he had relied on Father Troy to supervise the building of the Cathedral while he himself set about finding the needed funds for it. Now he must do both himself.

He hoped that his explanations would cause the Pope to revoke his decision. Nevertheless, while awaiting his response, he informed the Pontiff that he had consigned Father Troy to the remote District of Placentia nearly 300 miles by land from St. John's, "being one of the wildest and most difficult within my jurisdiction, there to await the further Orders of your Holiness."

Writing to Cardinal Fransoni three days later, the Bishop was even more forthright. After bemoaning the serious difficulties which the departure of Father Troy would cause him, he came to the heart of his complaint, referring to the injustice that was being done to him and his clergy in a passage that was probably as bold as any the authorities in Rome had ever received from one of their subordinates:

> I regret this circumstance the more from the precedent it would seem to establish, viz, that a Clergyman in Newfoundland may be censured by a Court so august as that of the Sacred City without knowing his accusers, without being heard in his defence, without a specification of the charges against him; that the influence of Laymen should prevail before an Ecclesiastical Tribunal over the Priesthood; and for this reason and lest it may open an avenue to the widest abuses, nay lest it prove subversive, utterly fatal to the Mission of this Country, I have kept the matter a profound Secret not communicating it to a single Individual

> even to the Priests who live under my roof lest by
> possibility it may be known why the Revd.
> Edward Troy has been sent from Saint John's....

He revealed his bitterness at the Holy See's action when
he concluded by saying that the ordinary management of his
Vicariate demanded every ounce of his mental energy and
almost superhuman physical powers. Consequently, he
wrote, if, upon the "fabricated tale of every idle slanderer,"
he was to be subjected to the necessity of preparing a
lengthy defense of his Vicariate, not only would it be impossible to obtain more priests, but the ones that he had would
become discontented and anxious to return to the peace of
the various Irish dioceses which they had left.

Rome must have accepted his defence and recognized its
own hastiness in condemning Father Troy without a hearing, because in March of the following year, Cardinal
Fransoni wrote a mollifying letter telling the Bishop that
both the Pope and the Sacred Congregation "desire most of
all that you should be of tranquil mind," and telling him
that, after the explanations he had given "concerning
Father Edward Troy, you may do whatever prudence and
conscience dictate you should do in the Lord." The Cardinal
concluded by hoping that this response would demonstrate
sufficiently that His Holiness and the Sacred Congregation
continued to hold him in as high regard as they had done
previously. In view of the difficulties which were still to
come, Bishop Fleming was very fortunate to have received
such a supportive letter from his Roman superiors.
Nevertheless, Father Troy spent nine years in the "wilder-
ness" of Placentia Bay before being transferred to Torbay,
near St. John's, where, as in Merasheen, he laboured hero-
ically until his death in 1872, having outlived his patron by
twenty-two years.

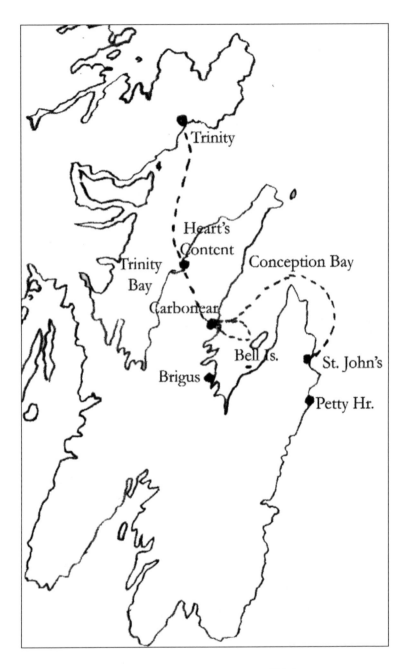

Bishop Fleming's Journey to Trinity

CHAPTER TWENTY
CREATING THE CATHEDRAL

A Man to whom everyone I have met attributes the improvement in architecture, and the new zeal for building churches, particularly amongst us Protestants.

> \- A visitor to St. John's
> speaking of Bishop Fleming

hen Bishop Fleming became responsible for the Catholic Church in Newfoundland, all the buildings in St. John's, with the exception of Government House, were simple, utilitarian structures without any pretension of elegance. His example of erecting more permanent and more dignified edifices soon stimulated the other denominations to emulate him. The quotation at the head of this Chapter was written in 1843, in which year the Anglican Cathedral was started, the Scotch Kirk was well under way, and the Benevolent Irish Society had added a handsome tower to its Hall.

His vision of the Cathedral he intended to build was one of supreme audacity. That he was conscious of what he was doing is evident when he wrote as early as 1834: "I am engaged in the construction of a cathedral on a scale of unusual elegance, extent and beauty." "Unusual extent" does not quite do justice to what was probably the largest church in North America at the time of its completion and is still considered a magnificent structure. It was to be 246 feet long, the transept 186 feet wide and the main body 55 feet wide, with ambulatories all around adding another 40 feet to the width. Its colossal size required an enormous quantity of building stone besides the marble and other materials needed for the altars and other accessories. Bishop Fleming himself calculated the amount of stone required as over 30,000 tons, the quantity of bricks as almost 500,000.

With the land at last securely in his possession, the Bishop devoted the two years, 1839 and 1840, to gathering the required materials and digging the foundations of the building. The logistics involved in this herculean project were mind-boggling. Of the thousands of tons of stone required, a large vessel could transport only about 800 tons per voyage. Consequently, many such ships had to be engaged. Corresponding amounts of lime and sand for mortar and of wood for scaffolding had also to be obtained. Some forty or fifty mason had to be imported from Ireland, since the trade was unknown in Newfoundland, and board and lodgings found for them. Many carpenters had to be engaged as well. Above all, the Bishop had to find the finances to pay for this. No wonder the few doubters criticized him for his impossible ambition: "(It) is condemned by every thinking man—it is not suited to our condition," was one complaint to the authorities in Rome.

But what to some was reckless imprudence, to Bishop Fleming was unbounded trust in God. As he confessed to Cardinal Fransoni, he knew very well that the project was beyond his means. But he was certain that, since God had brought him through all his other difficulties, He would provide the means to accomplish this one also. If want of means, he declared, had prevented him from attempting such projects, Newfoundland would still be as it was when he first saw it—without priests, without Churches, without education.

Fortunately he possessed a phenomenal ability to enthuse and organize the people. The visitor noted above, painted a picturesque panorama of his influence:

> At his nod a whole population rush into the
> forests—a distant [*sic*] of some twelve or thirteen
> miles—and bring £1,500 worth of timber for scaf-
> folds for his Cathedral; a word brings a second
> return for a convent; a beck and the immense
> foundation of his Cathedral and of his convent are
> excavated; and the expression of a wish places the
> mercantile marine, as it were, at his command for
> the gratuitous conveyance of stone for his build-
> ings some 100 or 120 miles; and when it is land-
> ed, no matter how valuable the time of the farmer
> or the mechanic, or even the most respectable
> shopkeeper—the carts of the former are con-
> tributed, the labor of the latter in conveying the
> stone, when landed, to the building site. This
> strange influence over the public mind appears,
> too, to have a sufficient cause.

This anonymous writer then went on to explain the reasons for Bishop Fleming's astonishing influence: out of his
own funds, he maintained four curates instead of the previous one; he made visitations that had never been attempted
before; he built chapels everywhere in his Vicariate. "The
simplicity of his life is such and his charity to the poor, that
he is very generally loved. He joins in these works like a
laboring man, and works as hard as any laborer."

This visitor met Bishop Fleming personally and his
meeting with the Bishop had a profound effect upon him. He
had been about two days in St. John's when curiosity caused
him to visit the site of the Cathedral. He met the overseer
who was dressed in a black vest and trousers, grey coat and
a very black ship hat, all pretty well daubed with mortar.
They fell into a conversation which caused the visitor to
believe him very little skilled in his trade. However, the
overseer took time away from his work to show the visitor
around the building and, discovering that he was a

Protestant, he explained carefully all the various parts of the building. He then excused himself as he had to leave the building. When the visitor inquired his name from one of the workmen, he was thunderstruck to discover that his host had been none other than Bishop Fleming himself.

In January 1839, the Bishop wrote a circular letter thanking the people for bringing out from the woods a "hawl" of scaffolding material for the erection of the Cathedral. While he thanked his own congregation, he paid special tribute to "the numerous and highly respectable Protestants" who had assisted. Such a "hawl of wood" was usually attended by a day of celebrations with bands playing brightly and flags flying briskly in the wind. On this occasion the military band had been in attendance. We can read between the lines when he expressed his gratitude for "the orderly and good humored demeanor which pervaded the vast assemblage." As for other materials, for sand he resorted to Trepassey, a port on the southeast tip of the Island; from the Estate of Robert Brine & Co., he purchased 800 tons of limestone.

However, Bishop Fleming was not satisfied to simply organize the project and do the paper work involved. The description of him, given above, as one who joined in the work of building the Cathedral like any laborer arouses our admiration. But, if fact, his personal physical involvement went much further than this, and his next undertaking reveals his almost incredible disregard of his own safety and comfort where the progress of his mission was concerned.

In Conception Bay, there is a small, uninhabited island, called Kelly's Island, which contains a substantial quarry (still in occasional use), of good building stone. The Bishop hired a team of workers and, as soon as weather conditions permitted, set up camp with them on this island. Here he lived in a primitive hut, a "lean-to" as it was called. To erect it, saplings were cut down and driven into the ground. Then boughs and the bark of birch trees were arranged upon them and the whole covered with canvas from an old sail for some defence against the uncertain weather. He slept on a bed, usually damp from the incessant rains, exposed to the capricious winds, the aroma of the boughs mingling with the acrid smell of the ancient canvas. He carried water from a spring in a little kettle and cooked his own food. His faithful dog kept away the maundering rats. While supervising the extraction of the stone, he worked in the quarry himself. From there the stone was conveyed to a temporary dock on the side of the island where the Bishop would often be up to his waist in water as he helped load the cumbersome stones onto the waiting vessels which would carry them to St. John's. There a military wharf had been loaned to the Bishop for his use. On this island he lived, five days a week, for months at a time, only returning to St. John's for the Sunday services. He continued to act in this manner for several years, and although he admitted that he suffered considerably, he claimed also that his health was not affected by this practice, another instance of his superb powers of endurance.

Early in 1839, he could report to his people that he had succeeded in raising from the quarries of Kelly's Island many thousand tons of building stone of a superior quality, of which a considerable quantity had been already landed in St. John's. J. B. Jukes, who had been commissioned by the Newfoundland Government to make a report on the physical geography and geology of the Island, observed in 1839:

> When I landed on Kelly's Island I found several workmen getting stone for the projected Catholic Cathedral in St. John's. The island is composed of shale with bands of hard fine-grained gritstone: a thick bed of the latter comes out in the cliff on the south-east side of the island, and, as the shale beneath and above it decomposed, it falls down and forms a considerable talus of fragments at the

cliff's foot. One or two schooners were carrying
away these loose blocks for building stones.

There are many stories connected with the project, some
funny, some daring, some tragic. The Bishop recounted one
such story about stone being brought in 1840 from Signal
Hill at the harbour entrance to St. John's. A great many
large granite blocks had been extracted from the hill by the
army for the purpose of fortifying it, but these had never
been used. They were lying scattered around and the Bishop
was given permission to take them. At his request, two thousand men collected these stones in a single pile in a few
hours during the autumn so that they could be more easily
transported when the snows of winter arrived. About six
weeks later at 9 a.m., they gathered again. At the Bishop's
suggestion, they divided themselves into various groups consisting of residents of the same street, different Societies,
and so forth, all with their sledges. There was tremendous
emulation as each group strove to prove that it could carry
the most and heaviest stones. Then came a dramatic event.
The sailors, who had the largest sledge, were also conveying
the largest stones. There was one huge rock of about ten
tons lying in a dangerous position on a steep slope. The
sailors began to try to move this hulk, but pretended to
abandon the attempt when the Bishop warned them against
it because of the danger involved. However, no sooner was
the Bishop's back turned than they returned to the challenge. With great effort, they succeeded in loosening the
huge mass, and it crashed down the hill to the bottom. It
took another hour for the sailors to lever it onto their sledge.
When finally they succeeded, they were presented with
another problem. In order to convey the rock to the town, it
had to be carried across a deep lake, and there was real danger that the weight of the stone together with that of 100
men who would be pulling it would cause the ice to collapse
and the men to be drowned. Ignoring the risk, they set off

and, pulling the rock across the ice at an incredible speed, reached the other side safely.

However, tragedy was always near. The crews bringing stone from Kelly's Island often ran into stormy weather and had to cut their cables to save themselves. One such vessel was cast ashore in a snow storm, and her captain, a Mr. Norris, was drowned.

By May 1840, the Bishop thought he had enough materials gathered to begin the actual building. Consequently, he sent out a call to the people to assist in the digging of the foundations. Two trenches—each eight feet deep by six feet wide and 600 feet long—were needed. Once more the response was extraordinary. "The result was, as he wrote elsewhere, that "in less than two days the foundations were excavated, containing 79,200 cubic feet, or 8,800 cubic yards." He described the bustling scene:

> Not only were all the laboring men and artisans employed but the independent Shopkeepers, Farmers, and Gentlemen at this laborious work, and even the women and children including those of the most respectable families, many of whom felt pride in being permitted to lend their feeble aid in removing the rubbish that had been dug up..... When amongst them all I beheld one old woman in her ninetieth year bent nearly double by the weight of time engaged carrying away the clay in her apron, I could not restrain my tears at an instance of devotion so touching.

Soon the whole venture began to resemble the communal building of a medieval Cathedral. A basic pattern emerged. During the autumn, the quantity of stone needed for the next year's operation was extracted from the quarry on Kelly's Island. In the following spring, after the sealers had unloaded their catch in St. John's, they would sail to the island and bring the stone to "the Bishop's Wharf." Next, the farmers would bring their carts to the wharf and convey the stone to the Cathedral grounds. Finally, each day a different Society would gather on these grounds and bring the stone required for that day's work to the building site. Even the women had their "ladies day"—Monday. Regular cargoes of cut stone arrived from Ireland and were treated similarly. Citizens of all persuasions responded to the Bishop's call for assistance and watched with pride the growth of the building.

Nevertheless, as time went on, it became apparent that Kelly's Island could not possibly supply the stone that was needed. The season was limited and transport by small fishing vessels was both sporadic and precarious. The Bishop found two other quarries near St. John's at Long Pond and at Mundy Pond but these also were insufficient. Eventually he realized that he would have to get most of the stone required from Ireland and England. Curiously, he also found that it was as cheap or cheaper to get stone from there as in Newfoundland, since wages were lower and the shipowners were willing to transport the stone in the springtime at a low price so as to use it for ballast.

So, towards the end of June 1840 he set sail across the Atlantic again. He arrived in Cork on July 16, and for the next six weeks was engaged in a frenzied round of activity, so much so that even though several times he passed within a few miles of his mother's home, he could not find time to visit her. He contracted with a master mason in Dublin for cut stone to the amount of £1,196 sterling, and hired a ship to transport this stone to Newfoundland for £270 sterling. He arranged with the builder, Michael McGrath of Waterford, to go to Newfoundland to superintend the building at a salary of £200 sterling. From a Mr. Graham in Hamburg he ordered 400,000 bricks to be delivered in Newfoundland at a cost of £200 sterling. He went to Liverpool and bought twelve tons of marble for the altars of the Cathedral which he forwarded to St. John's. He also received, at a cost of £100 sterling, the wooden model of the Cathedral he had requested from the architect, Mr. Schmidt in Hamburg.[1] To help raise the money for all of this, he traveled to Birmingham, had an engraving made of the proposed Cathedral and ordered 20,000 medals of it to be struck for the laying of the corner stone. These medals cost him 2d each, but he made a tidy profit by selling them for 3/6 each. [*Many of these medals are still in existence.*] In the midst of all this frenetic activity, he found time to visit the headquarters of the Sisters of Mercy in Baggot Street, Dublin, to pay for the support of a young lady, Mary Ann Creedon, whom he had entrusted to their care[2] to be trained as a Sister for a future foundation of their Order in Newfoundland. He visited Waterford, got three additional priests for his Mission, and arranged for their passage to Newfoundland. He returned to Liverpool where, as he wrote later, "now exhausted and subdued, my strength failed me and my shattered and harassed frame sank upon the bed of sickness where for the first time I arose only to step on board the vessel. . ." [*which was to take him back to Newfoundland.*] His exhaustion was not caused only by his physical labours. The day before he left, he received an intelligence which shattered him mentally and physically. Quite by accident, he learned that the British Government was pressing Rome to dismiss him from his position. What had led the British authorities to take such a drastic step?

CHAPTER TWENTY-ONE
THE FINAL CONFLICT—THE BEGINNING

". . .what measures could be taken at Rome for effecting the
removal of Doctor Fleming from the Colony."

- Colonial Office Dispatches, 1840

hen Bishop Fleming had returned to St. John's in the autumn of 1838, having at last obtained the grant of land for his Cathedral, he might have expected that his difficulties with his spiritual and political masters were over and that he could now devote his full time and energy to the building of his Cathedral. He had satisfied Rome of his integrity and had convinced Lord Glenelg that there was no point in pursuing the complaints against him any further. Indeed, when, early in February 1839, more of McLean's complaints were forwarded by Governor Prescott, Glenelg refused to accept them. To further reinforce the Bishop's position, in August of the same year, Prescott admitted to Lord John Russell, who had now succeeded Lord Glenelg as Secretary for the Colonies, that "the evils of clerical interference in politics had virtually ceased since the Bishop's return." For a brief while, therefore, it appeared that the Bishop's hopes for peace and quiet had been realized. But, in actuality, this tranquillity was only the calm in the eye of the storm.

Governor Prescott himself was becoming increasingly beleaguered. He was having difficulties with both the Executive Council and the Assembly. In the Council, he found that he could rely on only two members, the others having given their loyalty to the merchants. The Assembly was making charges of religious prejudice against him and the Governor had to defend himself to the Colonial Office against these accusations. His relations with Doctor Carson, now Speaker of the Assembly, were deplorable. He lamented to Lord Russell that Newfoundland had never had a governor as unpopular as himself and suggested that he be replaced by someone who could start his administration with a clean slate. In a moment of insight, he admitted that the political dissensions in Newfoundland might not, after all, arise from the activities of the Bishop as he had so often contended, but that they "proceed very much from the natural mortification which the richer and more intellectual part of the Community feel at being excluded from the influence which they should naturally possess and at finding themselves subjected in a certain degree to the control of People unfit for their station as legislators, and who certainly must be deemed in various particulars their Inferiors." Furthermore, he complained that it was impossible for him to improve relations with Bishop Fleming, as the Colonial Office had suggested. Although months had elapsed since the Bishop's return, he had never called at Government House, and consequently, there had been no opportunity of discussing their differences.

Bishop Fleming believed he had good reason for not calling on the Governor. He was convinced that the Governor was activated by "his hatred of everything Catholic" and of himself in particular. It would appear that Propaganda Fide had finally come to agree with him, for a note attached to one of its documents read: ". . .these complaints arise from the animus of the Governor." However, writing twenty years earlier, Anspach, in his *History of the island of Newfoundland*, seems to have had a more accurate view of the basis of the conflict between the Bishop and the Governor as, indeed, with Governor Cochrane before him. He wrote:

> As soon as a new Governor arrived, he was imme-
> diately surrounded by a number of individuals,
> who had preconcerted the impressions with which
> they hastened to prepossess his mind; while those
> who were capable of giving useful information
> were studiously kept at a distance from him by
> every art that ingenuity could devise.

The Governor had good cause to be discouraged, for the entire governmental process seemed to be falling apart. In 1838, the Council rejected ten of the twenty bills the Assembly submitted to it; in 1839, it treated nineteen of thirty bills in similar fashion; in 1840, an incredible thirty of forty were denied. Desperate to obtain some redress, in December of 1838, the Chamber of Commerce submitted a petition to Queen Victoria to abolish the Assembly entirely. In the following March, the merchants of Conception Bay made the same request, while in the autumn, the British merchants dealing with Newfoundland submitted a similar petition. In self-defense, the Assembly collected 3,000 signatures to a petition protesting against any such attempt to abolish it.

To understand the reason for the intensity with which the British Government reacted to subsequent events in Newfoundland, one must be aware of the series of international crises with which England was confronted. In 1839, England had become involved in war within Afghanistan; in 1840 against China; and, in 1845, in India. British armies were heavily involved in all of these conflicts. At home, Britain was being racked by dissension, riots, even armed rebellion, while being burdened with kings, George IV and William IV, who resisted every concession to the people's legitimate demands. One member of parliament, Lord Bougham, stated that England was "full of discontent and afflicted with distresses," while the Duke of Wellington, now

Prime Minister, mourned that "No man can satisfy himself of the safety either of the country or of himself."

But of all England's problems, Ireland was the most intractable. There, pitched battles were being fought by gangs of peasants with pikes and pitchforks against the armed constabulary. This was due in large measure to the resentment of the people at being forced to pay tithes for the support of the Anglican clergy. If they could not pay, their farm animals and household belongings were seized. In one such confrontation between the peasants and the police in 1831, thirteen peasants were killed; in 1832, a similar number suffered the same fate. In such an unequal contest, the Irish people, downtrodden and repressed, were in great need of inspired assistance. Fortunately, such assistance came to them through the genius of one man—Daniel O'Connell.

O'Connell with shrewd political insight, rejected an armed struggle which history had shown to be doomed to failure against such a powerful foe. Instead he turned England's own political institutions against themselves by founding a system of peaceful, persevering, popular agitation which kept strictly within the law—the first such popular movement in history. Its objectives were the emancipation of the Catholics and the repeal of the Union, i.e., the common parliament for Ireland and England which had been enacted on January 1, 1801. After a bitter political battle, emancipation of the Irish Catholics was won in 1829, earning O'Connell the title of Liberator. He then embarked on a campaign to increase pressure steadily on the British Parliament to repeal the Act of Union. The Irish peasants supported him *en masse*, and his control over them was so complete that one writer noted, "He was, indeed, becoming the uncrowned king of Ireland. Few crowned monarchs of that country had ever held such sway."

There can be little doubt that the English authorities regarded the turbulent situation in Newfoundland as an outgrowth of the unrest in Ireland and pictured Bishop

Fleming as the O'Connell of Newfoundland. The complaint of Lord Anglesey, Governor General of Ireland, that "the question is whether O'Connell or I shall govern Ireland," was echoed by Governor Cochrane's lament that Bishop Fleming's power was greater than his own. However, the mistake the British authorities made was to equate the Bishop's activities with those of O'Connell. While O'Connell was totally immersed in politics, John Greene, in his work, *Between Damnation and Starvation* (1999), is probably close to the truth when he claims that "Fleming himself, however, played no part in active politics after 1833 and instead immersed himself in church affairs."

As part of their campaign against O'Connell and his supporters, the English newspapers kept up a continual barrage of vicious comment on the supposed Catholic control of Newfoundland hoping thereby to block O'Connell's drive for Repeal of the Union in Ireland, the assumption being that, if he was successful, conditions in Ireland would become as chaotic—and as priest-run—as those in Newfoundland. The *London Record*, for instance, declared on September 20, 1838, that ". . .in Newfoundland, the Popish hierarchy are taking advantage of the present disposition of the O'Connell [*sic*] Government, and are doing all that in them lies to foment discontent, disorder, and ultimate rebellion."

In March 1840, an event occurred in St. John's which acted like a spark to a barrel of gunpowder. For some time, the Governor had been attempting to placate the Assembly by appointing one of their number to the Executive Council, and had been quietly negotiating with Patrick Morris for this purpose. In December 1839, the Colonial Treasurer, Newman Hoyles, died and, in March 1840, Morris was offered and accepted the post with its place on the Council. He tried stubbornly to maintain his place in the Assembly but was forced by the other members to withdraw and a by-election was called for May 1840.

In the by-election, the merchants refused to contest the seat: "Since the knaves have it, let them keep it," wrote Winton in *The Ledger.* Nevertheless, the election was not a formality. It took on the complexion of a modern election campaign with rival "reform" groups vying for the support of the electorate. Through a complicated series of political moves, the contest developed into a confrontation between Douglas, a liberal Scottish Protestant, and Laurence O'Brien, the leading Catholic businessman and a great friend and supporter of Bishop Fleming. The complications of the situation are underlined by the fact that Douglas was originally sponsored by the leading members of the Assembly—Nugent, Kent and O'Brien himself. The contest became a bitter Catholic-Protestant one and inevitably the priests were drawn in to support the Catholic cause. Eventually O'Brien was declared the victor, though his election was only made possible through the questionable tactics of the returning officer. Two very unfortunate results of this contest were the deep split in the ranks of the Reformers which it caused and the desertion of *The Patriot* from their camp—Parsons, the editor, being a friend and supporter of Douglas.

Bishop Fleming, who had warned from the very beginning that local government in a country such as Newfoundland would cause dissension and disorder, must by now have become thoroughly disillusioned with the whole process, but he was too much concerned with the progress of his Cathedral, the foundations of which were dug in May, to become actively involved. Once more, it is worth recording that it is inconceivable that he should have received the universal support which he did for the Cathedral project if he had been the source of all the dissension his enemies—especially Governor Prescott. Nevertheless, his opponents renewed their traditional mode of attack on him by listing and exaggerating the various incidents which took place during the elections, reporting them to the Colonial Office, and blaming them on Fleming.

In one such incident, a replay of the Winton affair, one of Winton's assistants also had his ears "clipped" on May 15 at about the same spot where Winton himself had been attacked. As early as January, Father Browne, with supreme audacity, had complained to Cardinal Fransoni that the Bishop was again disturbing the peace of the island. The Governor, he claimed, was a particular friend of his as of Catholics generally and was forwarding his letter. Further, he wrote that the Governor would complain to the English Government of the Bishop's shameful conduct, protesting that it was impossible for him to govern with Bishop Fleming inciting the people to revolt. Prescott himself had collected the accounts of the various incidents which had occurred during the elections and, in early June, forwarded them to Russell together with another packet of complaints from McLean. He commented that the Bishop, without the slightest reason, but apparently from a pure love of dissension, had again inflamed religious tensions. He was convinced, he stated, that no governor could obliterate religious jealousy while the Bishop remained on the island. It would seem that the Bishop was blamed no matter what he did. If he intervened, he was condemned for intruding in political affairs; if he kept aloof, he was equally censured for not using his influence to maintain the peace. One member of the Colonial Office noted that "the Governor lays the blame of all this on Doctor Fleming for not using his Episcopal influence to control the madness of the Catholic Population and on the sinister influence of the Priests."

Prescott's dispatches caused a flurry of activity between the Colonial Office and the Foreign Office. Until now it had been the Governor who had pressed for the Bishop's removal, while the Colonial Office, under Lord Glenelg, had simply acquiesced in this attempt. But Glenelg had been forced to resign, accused of being too soft on the "Papists," and his successor, Lord Russell, perhaps to prove that he was made of "sterner stuff" than Glenelg, now began to take the initiative in pressing for Bishop Fleming's dismissal. Russell wrote Palmerston, the Foreign Secretary "to beg what measures could be taken at Rome for effecting the removal of Doctor Fleming from the Colony," and suggesting that pressure be put on Rome by telling the authorities there that in future, the Colonial Office must "decline to accede to any applications for pecuniary grants, or salaries to Roman Catholic Bishops and Priests in the Colonies" unless this was done—diplomatic blackmail at its worst.

It was the news of this determined and totally unexpected effort on the part of the British Government to achieve his removal and thus destroy all his hopes for his Cathedral which had such a shattering effect on Bishop Fleming as he lay ill waiting for his vessel to leave for Newfoundland at the end of August 1840.

CHAPTER TWENTY-TWO
THE FINAL CONFLICT — THE GATHERING CLOUDS

Whatever will be the destiny that awaits me?
What will become of my honor, of the interests of the Mission?

- Bishop Fleming, August 28, 1840

s Bishop Fleming lay on his bed of sickness contemplating the shattering news of the British Government's demand for his dismissal, he was closer to despair than he had ever been before. The earlier news of the Pope's demand that he suspend Father Troy had been devastating enough, but it bore no comparison with the impact of this latest communication. In one stroke, he could see all his hopes for his mission destroyed, all his magnificent plans for his Cathedral vanishing into thin air, all his herculean efforts wasted, while he himself would be burdened with the crushing debts which he had recently contracted and which he would have no means of repaying.

Nevertheless, he did not completely lose hope but, trusting in the integrity of the Roman officials, he dragged himself to his writing desk to send Cardinal Fransoni a final appeal. "I write this present letter," he began, "finding myself tormented by the most grievous anguish. This morning the news was communicated to me of another secret plot organized by my implacable enemy Captain Prescott, Governor of Newfoundland, to disgrace me and to impede the completion of the splendid edifice undertaken by me for the glory of God and of our Holy Religion." He spoke of the "horror" he felt at the news of the charges against him and continued:

> I have not the courage to continue this letter. God has up till now blessed my labors; for eighteen years I have been engaged in this Mission. I have seen this Island, with the help of God, almost entirely Catholic; and being on the point of increasing the splendor of our Religion by building several sacred edifices, the open and the secret enemies of our faith have hurried to block my conceived hopes and to have me disgraced by taking from me the means of fulfilling the obligations annexed to the contract recently concluded. This is a new persecution which is tried against me. But I do not care in the least, while I can have the consolation to see my conduct approved by the Sacred Congregation of Propaganda as it is by my conscience.

He regretted being the innocent cause of so much annoyance to the Sacred Congregation. If, he declared, Lord Russell would grant him the right to defend himself, he would know how to deal with this new calumny as with so many others. But, if not, he concluded sadly, "whatever will be the destiny that awaits me? What will become of my honor, of the interests of the Mission?" One can almost hear the despair in his voice. No wonder, as he said, "exhausted and subdued," his strength failed him and his "shattered and harassed frame" sank upon the bed of sickness as he boarded his vessel for his return to Newfoundland.

An uneventful ocean trip back to St. John's, together with the Bishop's natural powers of recuperation, largely restored his health and spirits. On his arrival, without waiting for the results of his appeal to Rome, he set to work again on the construction of the Cathedral. Shortly after his return, he gave a report of his work from the altar, explain-

ing the preparations he had made so that that work on the
Cathedral could begin without further delay when the first
vessels arrived in the spring. He requested that the
schooner owners who had not brought stone from Kelly's
Island the previous spring would do so now. He himself soon
became so heavily involved in the many details that he hardly had time to carry out the correspondence his responsibilities demanded. Writing to Propaganda Fide concerning the
support at the College of Propaganda in Rome of a young
seminarian, John Dalton,[1] a nephew of Father Charles
Dalton, he complained that he was embarrassed by the burden of many workers and masons and had to suffer inter-
ruptions almost every moment even while trying to write
the Cardinal.

Just at this time, Bishop Fleming made a tactical error
which caused an open breach between himself and Patrick
Morris, one of his main supporters. When Morris received
the post of Colonial Secretary, he approached the Bishop to
be one of his sureties (a nominee, on receiving this position,
had to obtain backers who would accept financial responsibility in case of default). The Bishop had agreed while pointing out that he did so to show his support for the Governor's
action in appointing a Catholic but lacked the means to back
up his financial commitment if such should be demanded of
him. In November, however, the Bishop wrote Morris asking
to be relieved of this responsibility. He gave as his reason
that he had, in the meantime, incurred serious expenses in
connection with the building of the Cathedral. This was true
enough, but Morris suspected that the real reason was to
show displeasure at his clinging to office in the Assembly.
Morris thereupon wrote a scathing reply, and had both the
Bishop's letter and his own answer published in *The Patriot*.
He gave as a reason for accepting the office of Treasurer
that he held views very similar to those of the Governor and
had a profound respect for his private character—an opinion
not calculated to endear him with one who considered the

Governor his "implacable enemy!" Further, he accused the
Bishop of acting very inconsiderately, since the same conditions existed now as at the time he became surety, and he
feared that the public would consider the Bishop's action a
manifestation of his displeasure. Bishop Fleming replied
angrily, accusing Morris of unethically publicizing private
correspondence. He explained that he had taken on further
heavy financial responsibilities—the contracts he had
signed for huge quantities of brick and stone weighed heavily upon him. Unfortunately, he concluded with a nasty slur:
"his unwarrantable publication of my private note . . . convinced me that I had not acted improperly in withdrawing
my name as surety for one who could thus bring himself to
violate confidence." Yet one must have a certain sympathy
for Morris, for surely the Bishop should have realized that
his withdrawal of support would inevitably become public
knowledge. In any case, whatever one may think of the incident, it does demonstrate that the Bishop's hold over his
flock was less than absolute, especially in political affairs,
when perhaps its most prominent member could thus publicly upbraid him.

Unfortunately, the political situation continued to deteriorate. In fact, it might be said that society itself had begun
to break up. The Kent-Kielley confrontation in the spring
had produced an entirely new breach in the social structure.
It would appear that, for some time, resentment had been
growing among the native-born Newfoundlanders over the
dominance which expatriates from Ireland and England
exercised over the Assembly and the powerful Benevolent
Irish Society. When his row with Kent had subsided, Doctor
Kielley called a meeting of these "natives" and attracted a
large response. As a result, a "Native Society" was formed
with a constitution declaring that "this society shall be composed of the Natives of Newfoundland exclusively." In its
format and purpose, it was obviously intended to rival the
Benevolent Irish Society. Presbyterians formed a large part

of its membership with Doctor Kielley as President and Parsons, editor of the *Patriot,* as a member of the executive. Thus the divisions in society now included Catholic vs. Protestant, merchant vs. worker and Native vs. "Outsider."

This divisiveness soon began to threaten the very political structure of the Island. The heat of the by-election in the spring had hardly begun to die down when, in June, Anthony Godfrey, member for Conception Bay, died. Still another by-election now became necessary, even while the Assembly was still wrangling over Morris's attempt to maintain his position there. Two men put forward their candidacy for the Conception Bay seat. They were both Catholics, but one, James Prendergast, a Harbour Grace merchant, was an anti-clerical. The other was Edmund Hanrahan, the principal merchant of Carbonear, a ship's captain and a friend of Carson and Kent. While there was much heated language during the campaign, the voting passed off quietly enough in Harbour Grace where Prendergast emerged with a large majority. When the polls moved to Carbonear, however, the mood changed. As Prendergast's supporters from Harbour Grace approached the polls in Carbonear, they were attacked by a group supporting Hanrahan. When the crowd threatened a Prendergast supporter named Ash, he fired upon them, wounding several, and then fled into the woods. The crowd, infuriated, burned down his home. The returning officer forthwith called off the election. Troops were summoned but by the time they arrived everything was quiet.

Nevertheless, the officials sent a series of lurid reports to the Governor about the rioting, and he promptly forwarded them to the Colonial Office, declaring, "I hold the priests responsible." This in spite of the fact that Father Walsh,[2] parish priest of Harbour Grace, had insisted on remaining neutral and that he and the other priests had used their influence to quiet the disturbances. While officially accepting the Governor's version of the affair, the

Colonial Office apparently had doubts about its veracity for Stephen noted, "I see no proof of it, on the contrary, the Priests would seem to have acted well as far as they interfered openly." A public inquiry, held six months later, agreed with Stephen and concluded that the accounts of the riots had been greatly exaggerated. Chief Justice John G. Bourne, who conducted the inquiry, stated: "The troops . . . entered a peaceful town with a quiet people where the only sound or movement was that of a woman peering curiously out a window towards the embarrassed troops. For the soldiers, apparently, it all became a great joke." He concluded that the disturbances could be traced as much to local jealousy between Harbour Grace and Carbonear as to clerical involvement.

However, these disturbances were the last straw to the British government which was not willing to tolerate such nonsense any longer. Governor Prescott was ordered to dissolve the Legislature. This he did on April 26, 1841, expressing to the Assembly his regret that such a proceeding should have become indispensable to the tranquillity and security of the Colony. The Island now reverted to direct rule by the Governor. It was to remain in this condition for a year and a half.

Meanwhile the British Government's campaign against Bishop Fleming continued unabated. Earlier in the century, England had taken over the island of Corfu in Greece from the French, and in 1840, when Rome wished to appoint a Vicar Apostolic there, Russell seized the opportunity to apply further pressure on the Roman authorities by telling the Prefect of Propaganda Fide that approval for this appointment would depend on the dismissal of Bishop Fleming. At the time there was no diplomatic tie between Rome and England and, therefore, no direct communication possible (a "secret" agent, Thomas Aubin, was the English contact in Rome). Russell, consequently, had to take a torturous, circuitous route to convey his ultimatum: through

Lord Palmerston, the Foreign Secretary, to Prince
Metternich in Vienna, from him to the Papal Nuncio there,
from there to Cardinal Lambruschini, the Papal Secretary of
State, and finally to Cardinal Fransoni, Prefect of
Propaganda Fide, who was ultimately responsible for
Bishop Fleming.

Simultaneously, Thomas Aubin, poured a constant
stream of accusations into the hands of Monsignor
Capaccini regarding the supposed dire doings of the clergy
in Newfoundland. Although Capaccini had the reputation of
being one of the best diplomats of the age, he seems to have
accepted Aubin's reports without question and to have
passed them along uncritically to Cardinal Fransoni as well
as to Pope Gregory XVI with whom he had worked closely
before the latter was made Pope. So sure was Aubin of the
success of his mission that he reported to the British authorities, "His Excellency [*i.e., Bishop Fleming*] will find that
the matter was arranged before his arrival."

These damning reports from the British government so
displeased the Pope that he decided to summon Bishop
Fleming to Rome to answer for his conduct. Cardinal
Fransoni, in forwarding the Pope's directive to the Bishop,
diplomatically stated the reasons for the summons:

> It is not without great sadness of soul that I
> report to Your Grace, with these present, what
> His Holiness Pope Gregory XVI, with grief and
> sorrow, has conveyed to me, namely that the
> British Government has complained gravely and
> bitterly to the Holy See concerning you and your
> missionaries that you yourself, no less than them,
> continue to agitate. The matter has now pro-
> gressed so far that the aforesaid Government has
> declared that in future it will do nothing to
> advance the business of the Holy Apostolic See
> unless it be fully satisfied concerning your rea-
> sons for so acting. And hence that the Apostolic

Visitation of the Island of Corfu which was to be commenced, should be postponed.

Now from this you will easily grasp how much is to be feared from Your Grace's behavior, not listening to the repeated admonitions of this Sacred Congregation, nor indeed of the Holy Father himself, when indeed you may see from this that both the dignity of the Holy See and the good of the Catholic religion are brought into disrepute.

Further, this is the express wish of His Holiness Pope Gregory XVI that, leaving a Vicar General in your diocese with appropriate faculties, **you should proceed at once to Rome,**[3] and, if possible, travelling through London, where you yourself should meet with the British Government concerning all those things which you will judge necessary to remove every cause of conflict.

But the British Government was still not satisfied. It pressed for a categorical assent that the Bishop would be dismissed, but Rome resisted this demand for it could not understand the situation. The day after receiving the above communication, Cardinal Lambruschini wrote at length to Cardinal Fransoni expressing his puzzlement, ". . .it is incomprehensible that while in London he [*Bishop Fleming*] obtained copious subsidies and other signal favors from the British Government." Still, the Cardinal agreed that, in view of the British objections, it would be very difficult for the Holy See to let Bishop Fleming return to Newfoundland. Nevertheless, the Cardinal gave evidence of Rome's continued uncertainty when he noted his great hesitation in condemning a person before knowing what his defense might be. In response to the British demand, the Cardinal instead suggested that the British should admit the Vicar Apostolic to Corfu. This would enable the Holy See more easily to offer to the English Government, as a courtesy, the assurance that Bishop Fleming would not return to Newfoundland, unless his defense should completely refute the charges against him. With this the British Government had to be content.

There was still another avenue of attack against Bishop Fleming to be explored. The Newfoundland Chamber of Commerce, believing that Father Browne could be of great use in their campaign against the Bishop, decided to send him to Rome for the express purpose of defaming him. Father Browne left Newfoundland for Rome late in 1840, taking with him various sworn statements alleging misbehavior on the part of the Bishop and his priests towards their parishioners. He also brought a petition with 700 signatures from his former parish of Ferryland, appealing for his reinstatement. He brought as well a testimonial to himself presented by citizens of St. John's before his departure, and, rather surprisingly, a recommendation from Patrick Morris! In Rome, he began an intensive campaign to discredit Bishop Fleming. Later the Bishop explained to Cardinal Fransoni how this came about:

> It was quite notorious here that it was this latter body [*The Chamber of Commerce*] that sent the Rev. Mr. Brown to Rome to second their efforts for my removal. It was publicly known that large sums were contributed for this purpose by these Orange Merchants, but the Hon. Mr. Tobin[4] informed me subsequently to the departure of Rev. Mr. Brown of the arrival of a letter from Mr. Brooking accounting for the expenditure of this money which it now appears they feared to trust to the Rev. Gentleman himself, as it was given on the express condition that he should proceed to Rome. Hence when he went to London, where he was a few days in training with the Attorney General of this Island who was then in London, even there he was refused to be paid this money

and to render it impossible for him to betray his Orange Party or refrain from going, Mr. Brooking himself remitted the money to Rome....

Attacked by the British Government, by the Newfoundland establishment and by his own renegade clergy, Bishop Fleming's chances of maintaining his position appeared slight indeed. Nevertheless, he had no intention of conceding the contest.

CHAPTER TWENTY-THREE
COUNTERATTACK

His removal at this moment and in such circumstances from his
Vicariate would be to give victory to the Protestants and to place the
Catholic religion in that Island in grave danger of ruin.

- Abbè De Luca at Propaganda Fide, 1841

ow that the British Government had obtained
the cooperation, albeit reluctant, of the Vatican
against Bishop Fleming for his "turbulent and
unprecedented conduct," as Cardinal
Lambruschini described it in a letter to Cardinal Fransoni,
the officials at the Colonial Office must have felt assured
that the departure of "that incendiary priest" was just a
matter of time. If so, they had not reckoned with the tenac-
ity of their quarry who had no intention of quietly resigning
himself to his fate. He was determined to fight to clear himself, but to do this, it was essential that he obtain the particulars of the charges against him. How to obtain them?
Knowing that they had been sent to Rome, he asked his
friend and agent there, the Abbè De Luca, to inquire about
them, but to no avail. In November he demanded them
directly from Lord Russell, charging that the British
Government had "entertained charges against a British
subject in a British colony behind his back." In the following
month, December 27, he made a strategic move in his own
defense by writing an eloquent appeal to Cardinal Fransoni
who, it will be remembered, was his immediate superior. He

hoped, thereby, to discredit in the Cardinal's eyes the charges against him.

In this lengthy letter, he protested against the "veil of impenetrable secrecy which had been thrown over the proceedings." He delineated the history of the various social and political difficulties he had encountered throughout his episcopacy and charged that the real reason for the request for his dismissal was his success in fostering the Catholic religion which had made him obnoxious to "the High Church Party."[1] The British Government, he declared, had traditionally tried to obtain control over the Catholic Bishops at home and in the Colonies as witnessed by its attempt to obtain a veto over the appointment of the Irish Bishops. Unsuccessful in this attempt, the Government, despairing of being able to control the Catholic Religion in Ireland, turned their attention to the Catholic Church in the colonies. As long as the colonial Bishops were subservient, they were tolerated. But if any of them displayed apostolic zeal, they "should be cast off from their positions and consigned to ignominy"—and here he criticized his predecessors harshly for their subservient attitude to the Government. That attitude, he claimed, was responsible for the lack of progress of the Church in Newfoundland since its foundation by Bishop O'Donel forty-two years before.

He then brought up the case of Father Browne, who, since his suspension in 1837, had been obsessively engaged in organizing the malicious attacks of the Orange Party in Newfoundland upon him. He had heard that Father Browne had gone to Sicily, but suspected that he was in Rome though he found it hard to believe that, however inclined to give him annoyance at home, he could carry his malevolence so far as to slander him in the Eternal City. He concluded: "I cannot believe, may it please Your Eminence, that under such circumstances the secret slanderer would be listened to at the Court of Rome or be allowed to whisper away my name or rob me of the good opinion (to me above price) of the Holy Father or the numerous Dignitaries of Rome who have honoured me with their consideration."

On February 2, 1841, he received the awaited reply from Lord Russell who, according to the Bishop, gave "a peremptory, an offensive refusal" to supply the documents in question. The reason Russell gave for this refusal, with scant regard for the truth, was the Bishop's claim that he was not responsible to the British Government for any act that pertained to his office as Bishop. Therefore, said Russell, to request explanations from him about any of these acts would have been to provoke from him a protest that the Government was intruding in matters which do not properly belong to it. He ignored the fact that it was not a case of the Government seeking explanations but of the Bishop requesting the opportunity to provide them.

Before this response arrived, the Bishop had received another letter from the Abbè De Luca telling him about the unhappy decision of the Pope in his regard. He was distraught at the news that Rome was prepared to remove him in order to satisfy the British Government. In his lengthy reply to the Abbè, who was now a consultor with Propaganda Fide and could be expected to relay the information to Cardinal Fransoni, he declared that he had never received the order to proceed to London and Rome. "My heart was pierced by an indescribable pain at the mere thought that His Holiness may have been able to believe for a moment that I did not follow the instructions given me by the Sacred Congregation." If he had received them while in England, he declared, he would have gone immediately to the Colonial Office to justify himself, and he would not have spent, as he had just done, £2,000 on materials for his cathedral, which project would now have to be abandoned. He continued with a detailed account of the religious challenge in Newfoundland where an Anglican bishopric had recently been established and an Anglican seminary begun. He included various newspaper accounts attesting to the various intrigues intended to destroy the civil and religious rights of the Catholic population.

It would seem that this stirring appeal caused the tide of opinion at the Vatican to begin to turn in Bishop Fleming's favour, for a note written on this document by an official of Propaganda Fide reveals a change of attitude in that department and its desire to postpone a decision on the Bishop. This comment read, "From these facts, it is obvious that his removal at this moment and in such circumstances from his Vicariate would be to give victory to the Protestants and to place the Catholic religion in that Island in grave danger of ruin." Two reasons were given for suggesting a postponement of a decision: first, the imprisonment of Bishop Hughes, Vicar Apostolic of Gibraltar; second, the formation of a special Commission in the British Parliament to examine Newfoundland affairs. Both of these deserve fuller explanation.

As to the first of these reasons, while the British Government was thus pressuring Rome to dismiss Bishop Fleming, its actions in another Colony were arousing the suspicions of the Roman authorities about its real intentions. At the end of 1839, Bishop Henry Hughes, O.F.M., had arrived in Gibraltar from Ireland as Vicar Apostolic. There the Church was dominated by a "Junta" of laymen who had taken over control, collected the fees for baptisms and confirmations, and paid the clergy a salary. Bishop Hughes, when he realized the situation, refused to collect such fees, and told the people also to refuse to pay them. As a result, the Junta brought him before the civil court which found him guilty and had him imprisoned. It was only six months later, at the intervention of Daniel O'Connell, that he was released. Writing to Bishop Fleming, the Abbè De Luca commented that "The deplorable imprisonment of the Rt. Rev. Doctor Hughes by Gibraltar authorities has excited here in Rome a most painful feeling, and this coincidence contributes to unmask the hypocrisy of the present ministry towards the Catholic religion in the British Colonies."

The second matter, the proposal of a "Select Committee" to investigate the turmoil in Newfoundland, had been mooted in the British Parliament as early as 1839. Both Governor Prescott and Bishop Fleming looked forward to this Committee but for opposite reasons: the Governor hoped it would be the means of freeing him from this thorn in his side, while the Bishop anticipated that he would receive impartial justice therein. In preparation, the Governor forwarded to the Committee a constant stream of documents detailing the unrest in the Colony and the part the Catholic Bishop and clergy were said to be playing in it.

The Committee, when it met in May 1841, contained some of the most distinguished members of the British Parliament, including Mr. W. E. Gladstone, Daniel O'Connell, Lord John Russell, and Lord Stanley. Daniel O'Connell had not been named to the original Committee, but, discovering this, had asked that he or one of his colleagues be appointed. The Committee met on May 3, 6, 11, 14, 18 and 25. Unfortunately, as Gunn states in her *Political History of Newfoundland*, "the evidence taken was almost entirely *ex parte*," [i.e., from one side only]. The Newfoundland Assembly had sent over delegates, J. V. Nugent, Peter Brown and Laurence O'Brien, to give evidence, but the Committee did not wait for their arrival. Of the seven witnesses questioned, one was the former governor, Sir Thomas Cochrane, three others were English merchants. A fifth was Doctor Joseph Shea, a member of the prominent Shea family which owned the *Newfoundlander* newspaper. He was a Catholic but, unfortunately, at odds with the Bishop who considered him one of the dissident members of his flock. As might be expected, all of these witnesses reiterated the party line that all Newfoundland's troubles arose from the actions of Bishop Fleming and his clergy. The sixth witness was Captain Henry Geary, a

Captain in the artillery, a convert to Catholicism, who had been stationed in Newfoundland for some years. As we shall see later, he had a very different story to tell. Finally came Thomas Browning, a former clerk in a business house in Brigus, who spoke unfavorably of the merchants.

Since the stated purpose of the Committee was to examine the political situation in Newfoundland, it is remarkable how many of the questions revolved around Bishop Fleming and his clergy. One cannot but suspect that the undisclosed purpose of the government was to bolster further its claim that the Bishop should be dismissed. It took the adroit questioning of Daniel O'Connell and Mr. Langdale, another Catholic member of the Committee, to bring out the opposing point of view. There is little point in examining the findings of the Committee in detail since they were never formally submitted to Parliament. Still the answers of the various witnesses give an interesting insight into their own attitudes and the Newfoundland situation.

Sir Thomas Cochrane had retired in England. His opinion of Newfoundland was hardly a favorable one since he viewed the island as "nothing more than a great ship with stages lying round her, on which to carry on the fishery; and having made their fortunes, they (the merchants) are no further concerned as to what is in it. . . . A more desolate, unproductive, unmanageable country, except Labrador, does not, in my opinion, exist on the face of the earth." As for Newfoundland Catholics, they were "in a very low station... easily led wrong," with "very few respectable Roman-Catholics in the Colony." As for the clergy, "Whenever political power came into question, there seemed to be that desire on their part to possess political power which has induced them to take very improper means to influence the people... Under the priests, the population work as one man." Regarding the Bishop, he said that he had tried to keep on good terms with him because "his power was greater than mine."

Thomas Brooking, who appeared next, had been one of the leaders in the drive for representative government in Newfoundland. He now declared that the experiment had "significantly failed." He had high praise for Bishop Scallan "a most estimable man" for whose will he had been the sole executor. He had also had the privilege of forwarding to Rome the Bishop's nomination of Bishop Fleming as his coadjutor. Brooking claimed to have been on intimate terms of friendship with Bishop Fleming before returning to England, but that when he again went to Newfoundland in 1835 he found the country "perfectly distracted," that respectable Catholics shunned him in the streets. He condemned the Constitutional Society, which had been formed by Patrick Morris and his allies in opposition to the merchants, as conducive "to bring all law and order into contempt, and considered to be under the influence of the Bishop and his clergy."

When questioned by Mr. O'Connell, Brooking stated that the grievances in Newfoundland lay with those opposed to the Priests' party. "The Roman Catholic priest party wanted to get possession of the House of Assembly, and govern the island," he asserted, "and we wanted to prevent it." The clergy wanted people in the House of Assembly who would be perfect tools in their hands. As for the Council, he did not think a single Roman Catholic could be found fit to sit in it. (Later, he amended that statement to say that one, Mr. Sweetman, the principal merchant in Placentia, was suitable.) He stated his belief that the outrage on Henry Winton had been occasioned by the bold and fearless manner in which he expressed his political sentiments. The explosive article on the Nuns, he claimed, had been written four years before the attack. (Later he corrected this to "more than six months".) He blamed the religious discord in the country on the part the Catholic clergy had taken in political affairs. Father Browne, he claimed, was a very respectable person, discharging his duties in a proper manner.

In answering other questions, Brooking revealed his negative attitude towards the development of Newfoundland and his contempt for its people. He stated that the Assembly had squandered vast amounts of money on road-building, a project which the Assembly had undertaken to unite the various settlements. He claimed that it was not "quite congenial to the feelings of Englishmen to be governed by universal suffrage," and that William Rowe had refused to take his seat in the Assembly because he would not sit with fishermen. He admitted that the Catholic people were greatly attached to Bishop Fleming.

Captain Henry Geary, the next witness, had converted to Catholicism at Glasgow in 1831 or 1832, and had been stationed in St. John's from June 1835 to October 1840. He painted a very different picture from the other witnesses. When he arrived in St. John's, he said, he had been warned to be very careful of his politics lest he be excommunicated. Shortly afterwards he became acquainted with the Bishop and formed a very different opinion of him. He realized that what he had been told had no foundation in truth. When, for instance, he told the Bishop that he intended to buy a house from Mr. Kough, the Bishop had recommended it to him. He said that statements of the priests from the altar were "totally perverted in *The Ledger*." He also contradicted many statements of the other witnesses regarding unacceptable conduct on the part of the priests. He asserted that only a few Catholics opposed the Bishop and most of these never attended Mass.

Captain Geary spoke of the Bishop in the highest terms as "a most laborious man; he lives like the meanest curate in the place and devotes every farthing that he has in charity and in building churches and chapels, and so on. . . . He is one of the most laborious and one of the most virtuous men I ever met with." He stated that the Bishop was exceedingly loved by all the people except for a half dozen or so, and that the trouble really arose from transplanted inter-county rivalry between expatriates from Wexford and Waterford. He was equally high in his praise of Father Troy as "uncommonly well educated. . . . His moral conduct stands exceedingly high; he is adored among the people almost; they have almost as great a respect for him as they have for the bishop."

Last to be examined was Mr. Thomas Browning. From 1824 to 1836/7, he had been a resident in Brigus, Conception Bay, where he had served as a clerk in a business firm. His testimony dealt exclusively with the relations between the merchants and the planters. He was not very complimenta-ry to the merchants stating that "the planter always looks upon him [*the merchant*] as an oppressor; he always looks upon him as extortionate." Perhaps Browning's testimony gave a truer picture of the source of Newfoundland's trou-bles than that given by the merchants.

After Browning had completed his testimony, the Committee was adjourned. It never reconvened because of the fall of the government and the subsequent victory in the polls of the Conservatives—as the Tories had come to be called—under Sir Robert Peel. A considerable time elapsed before the Minutes were published. Revealingly, inside the cover of the copy in the Colonial Office archives there is a handwritten note reading: "This evidence has been pub-lished by order of the House of Commons. It was sup-pressed; and, in fact, hence never reported. This was done under the influence, and almost command of Mr. O'Connell. The evidence against the doings of Popery in Newfoundland was too strong." It would seem that at least some of the Colonial Office officials were not exactly impartial in this matter.

CHAPTER TWENTY-FOUR
WINTER MARTYRDOM—CORNER STONE LAYING

Never did I suffer so much as upon this day, nor has my health
been ever since thoroughly recruited.

- Bishop Fleming

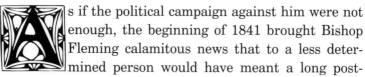s if the political campaign against him were not enough, the beginning of 1841 brought Bishop Fleming calamitous news that to a less determined person would have meant a long postponement or even an abandonment of his cherished plans. This news was the failure of Wright's Bank in England. In this bank, he had deposited all the monies he had collected for the building of the Cathedral as well as all the ordinary funds of the Vicariate. The loss to him was £4,700. But even this disaster he shrugged off. Reporting this loss to his people, he declared that he was aware that those who wanted to block the building of the Cathedral would be gratified at this devastating event, but that, as far as he was concerned he "cared not a straw for the loss—it should not interrupt him an hour."

Never was the Bishop's strength of character more in evidence than at this juncture of his fortunes. Attacked by the British Government, apparently deserted by his superiors in Rome, all the funds he had so painstakingly accumulated suddenly lost, his own future seemed in serious jeopardy, one would have expected that discouragement would at least have caused him to withdraw from his frenetic activities and reassess his plans for his future. Instead he set forth on what was to prove the most death-defying of all his hazardous adventures.

His previous visitations to the outlying districts had not been totally satisfactory, because they had taken place in summer when most of the men were absent at the fishery and consequently not available for the Sacrament of Confirmation. He now decided to make a winter visitation of St. Mary's Bay and Conception Bay when the men would be at home. In January 1841, when the weather had stabilized and seemed favorable enough, he booked passage on board a small fishing boat which was about to set sail for St. Mary's near the eastern tip of St. Mary's Bay. He arrived safely though not without being, on at least one occasion, in imminent danger of shipwreck. In St. Mary's, he spent three days preparing the candidates for Confirmation and administering the sacrament. In the midst of a howling storm, he then set out to walk along the coast to Salmonier, a distance of some twenty miles with no roads and so deeply covered in snow that he and his companions had to set their course by compass. Trudging through the snow, hour and hour, with heads bowed against the biting wind, they finally reached their destination. Exhausted and famished from their twelve-hour trek, they found shelter in a miserable hut whose poverty-stricken inhabitants welcomed them heartily but had no food to share with them. The Bishop and his companion would have gone to bed hungry except that he had brought a little bread and meat with him in his pocket. One wonders what kind of bed was provided for them.

The next day the inhabitants of the settlement were notified and he administered Confirmation to them. Afterwards, he would have then resumed his journey, but the still raging storm forced him to delay his departure. When the storm abated, he set out once more towards Conception Bay, a cross-country journey of almost thirty miles across uninhabited country whose rivers, bogs and thick forests would daunt even the hardiest traveler.

Usually, those attempting this hazardous trip remained overnight in a log hut that had been built along the route many years before for this very purpose. However, since the snow was now even deeper and he felt his strength weakening, the Bishop decided, if at all possible, to make the trip in one day. Consequently, taking with him a sturdy young man to lead the way, he left Salmonier some two or three hours before daybreak. They waded through snow several feet deep, sometimes plunging into holes where the snow covered them completely, at other times, crawling on their hands and knees for considerable distances because of the depth and softness of the snow. Their feet were frequently under water for the weather for the previous two weeks had been warm and the snow had begun to melt.

Midway through their journey, they encountered a deep, fast-flowing river. Though they succeeded in fording this, they received a good soaking in doing so, for the water came up to their waists. Wet and exhausted, they struggled on until, only about four miles from their destination, they encountered another river, not as wide as the previous one but much deeper and flowing very strongly. Night was now approaching and the Bishop was utterly fatigued. The angry waters daunted him but there was no alternative to attempting the crossing for the hut mentioned above had been passed some six or seven miles back on the other side of the first river. He did not have the strength to return to it nor, soaking wet as they were, could they remain where they were. He cut down a pole to assist him and then, commending himself to God, he waded into the torrent. He spied, near the middle of the river, a small rock about two feet below the surface. Cautiously he approached this, using the pole to brace himself against the current. Reaching the rock, he paused for a few moments to recover his breath and then renewed his efforts. The water now reached over his shoulders and, just as he was approaching the shore, the current proved too strong and began to sweep him away.

Fortunately his companion had reached shore before him and saw his danger. He reached out, caught the Bishop and dragged him to safety.

Soaked and faint with exhaustion, he sat down on the bank. Soon, however, realizing their predicament, he and his companion rose to their feet and pressed onward. Although so near to Holyrood, they lost their way in the darkness and it was midnight before they reached that settlement. Incredibly, finding himself once more in civilization, the Bishop's strength revived. Since all the houses were shut and their inhabitants asleep, he decided to continue to Harbour Main three miles further along the shore where lived the curate, Father O'Keefe. Reaching there at two o'clock in the morning, he was welcomed by the priest, and he and his companion were soon enjoying the comforts of a good bed. However, he never fully recovered from this ordeal. As he wrote later, "Never did I suffer so much as upon this day, nor has my health been ever since thoroughly recruited."

Still, he gave himself only three days to recover from this ordeal. Then, on Friday, he set out on a whirlwind tour of the area. All had to be done on foot since the weather was too stormy and cold for a horse. His first objective was Carbonear. On the way he paused at Brigus where the pastor, Father Mackin, decided to accompany him, and then continued to Harbour Grace where Father Dalton, the parish priest, had his residence. The following day, Sunday, he went to Carbonear, three miles away, and administered Confirmation to some 120 candidates, then returned to Harbour Grace to confirm a further 230 people there. On Monday, he went to Port de Grave, about nine miles past Brigus, confirmed 110 people on Tuesday morning and returned to Harbour Grace the same evening. Wednesday he journeyed back to Brigus and administered Confirmation to 170 individuals and in the afternoon set out for Harbour Main where he confirmed 192 candidates. On Friday morning he was in Holyrood again administering the Sacrament to over 500 persons.

By Friday, he was extremely tired. Nevertheless, he had agreed to bless the new Church in Carbonear on Sunday. So, at one o'clock on Friday afternoon, he set out on the twelve miles to Brigus. Once more he was beleaguered by the elements. He and his companions went on foot, battling against a strong northwest wind. After a few miles the wind rose to a furious gale and the blinding snow prevented them from seeing more than a very short distance ahead. Somehow they struggled onward but it was midnight before they reached Brigus in a state of absolute exhaustion.

Yet he could not rest, for the following morning he had to set out again for Harbour Grace and Carbonear. Fortunately the weather had improved, and the only difficulty he and his companions experienced was having to wade through mountains of new snow. In Carbonear on Sunday morning, he blessed the new church, dedicating it to St. Patrick, administered Confirmation and preached at both Mass and Vespers. The sermon at Mass was "particularly pointed to a numerous assemblage of highly respectable Protestants."

He rested on the following day, but on Tuesday, February 2, he went further along the coast to visit the parish of Northern Bay which he had set up two years previously. Accompanied by Father Duffy, the Parish Priest of Northern Bay, and Fathers Cummings and O'Keefe, the curates of Harbour Grace and Harbour Main respectively, he set out for Father Duffy's residence in Bay de Verde. Fortunately there had been a heavy frost for several days previously and they were able to ride horseback most of the twenty four miles to Northern Bay, arriving at 10 p.m. Here the Bishop remained for two days, preparing the people and administering Confirmation. He wanted to continue even farther along the coast but heavy drifts prevented them from doing so. So, on Friday he began his return journey.

His misfortunes, however, were not over. Two miles on the way, his horse fell and rolled on him in a deep pile of snow. He would have lost his life were it not that a number of residents of the settlement who had accompanied him were able to rescue him. Even so, his thigh was severely strained and he suffered much pain for many weeks afterwards. They continued their journey to Gusset's Cove only six miles away, but so difficult was the traveling that it took the entire day to reach there. Exhausted as he must have been, the Bishop did not rest but devoted three hours that evening to the instruction of the candidates for Confirmation. The following morning he administered the Sacrament, parted company with Father Duffy and set out once more for Carbonear where he arrived on Saturday night. He rested, more or less, for the next few days which he spent visiting Father Dalton at Harbour Grace and Father Mackin at Brigus.

The following Friday, he set out on the final stage of his return journey to St. John's. Arriving at Harbour Main he found a boat about to attempt to sail to Kelligrews, a dangerous experiment in those ice-filled waters. Still, since it would take fourteen miles from his journey, the Bishop decided to chance it. Soon after they had set out, a strong north-east wind caused the bay to become filled with pack ice. This so hindered them that they did not reach their destination until an hour after nightfall. Next morning he set out on foot from Kelligrews for St. John's, twelve miles away and arrived there at 3 p.m., "truly oppressed with fatigue"— and no wonder!

As often happens with those who expend such huge amounts of nervous and physical energy, the Bishop now fell prostrate and lay in bed for ten days, fretting over the amount of work which lay before him. During these ten days he received, as a bolt from the blue, the letter from the Abbè de Luca which has been discussed in the previous Chapter.

To offset this setback, on his recovery from his exhaustion, he rejoiced to experience one of the most magnificent fruits of the arrival of the Presentation Sisters eight years before. On Shrove Tuesday, February 23, the day before Ash Wednesday, he confirmed 500 girls whom he found well prepared by the Sisters for the Sacrament. With them were 800 boys who had been prepared by the curates of the parish assisted by the Christian Doctrine Society. There were as well eighty-nine converts. In the past, during the evenings of Lent, he had been accustomed to give a daily series of lectures. This year, after his recent exertions, he feared that his strength would not be equal to the challenge. However, as seems to have been usual with him, the act of preaching revitalized his energy and he was able to complete the series successfully without omitting a single day. He noted that the congregations had never been larger.

None of this detracted from his work on the Cathedral. On February 16, the very first day the Bishop left his house after his illness, he called for the "hawl" of stones from Signal Hill—an incident which has been described in an earlier chapter. During the spring, five cargoes of cut stone, which he had ordered while in Ireland the previous summer, arrived and were likewise brought to the Cathedral grounds. In the vessel which brought this cargo were also the masons from Ireland with whom he had contracted for the stone work of the Cathedral.

Believing that he now had sufficient materials and sufficient expertise to begin, and being urged by his advisers that a start would encourage the people to even greater efforts, the Bishop decided that the time to lay the corner stone for the building had come. During the month of May, the priests of the Vicariate normally came to St. John's to obtain the Holy Oils they needed for the administration of the various sacraments. Taking advantage of this assembly, the Bishop appointed Ascension Thursday, May 20, as the date for this decisive event. It was a gala day for the people of St. John's and its environs. Even the weather cooperated; the day broke fine and clear. From early morning, crowds of people, old and young, could be seen pouring into the city from the nearby outports. After last Mass, towards 12:30 p.m., a procession began to form. It wound its way from St. Mary's Church on Henry Street via Queen's Street and Water Street, thence up Cochrane Street and Military Road to the Cathedral site. So large was the crowd that it was an hour before the tail of the procession even began. A local newspaper estimated the numbers as being almost 20,000 though Bishop Fleming himself later gave the figure as being 9,000—an uncharacteristic understatement on his part. All classes and religions took part. It must have been a colourful affair. The Regimental Band and another unnamed band provided suitable music, the Societies paraded in their official regalia, the school girls in their white dresses. The *pièce de resistance* was undoubtedly the large model of the Cathedral which had arrived from Hamburg. It was carried by four strong men. Arriving at the proposed site of the main altar where a large cross had been erected, the Bishop, assisted by twelve priests, performed the blessing of the corner stone. This stone was a granite block weighing approximately two tons with a cavity in the centre where was deposited a copper box, lined with lead, into which suitable memorabilia[1] were placed. To conclude the proceedings, Bishop Fleming then preached a short but impressive sermon on the significance of what had been done that day.

Just as the ceremony ended, the Bishop received a welcome surprise. Mr. Laurence O'Brien stepped forward and placed £250 on the newly blessed corner stone. Immediately his example was followed by many others, both rich and poor, so that in half an hour, the Bishop had collected £2,500. "I saw," he wrote later, "poor sailors come to deposit in my hands their last crown, to pay with it their homage to God, and even humble laborers bestowed their only pound, which constituted all their property." God blessed their sacrifice, for the fishery that year was more productive than it had been for twenty years. What a great encouragement this event must have been for the Bishop after his recent financial losses and when his fate was being determined by the far-off British parliament!

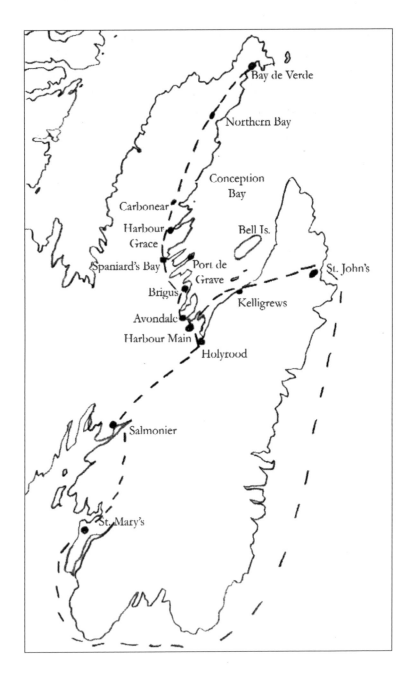

Bishop Fleming's excursion around the Avalon

CHAPTER TWENTY-FIVE
THE CLOUDS CLEAR

*I trust that the day star of happiness is dawning for the long
suffering though loyal people of Newfoundland.*

- Bishop Fleming

he Bishop received even greater encouragement
from the political developments around him. He
must have found it hard to believe how rapidly
his troubles were beginning to disappear. The
political turmoil in Newfoundland became muted, at least
temporarily, when Governor Prescott dissolved the
Assembly on April 26, 1841. Shortly afterwards, the
Governor, the Bishop's constant adversary, himself resigned
and returned to England. On May 25, the Select Committee
of the British Parliament adjourned without submitting a
formal report. And while from his residence in Rome, Father
Browne continued to issue his predictable, tiresome tirades
against Bishop Fleming, these allegations were now dismissed as frivolous by the officials of Propaganda Fide, particularly when he had the audacity to suggest to them that
his debts be absolved and that he be given financial support.
Clearly the clouds of suspicion about Bishop Fleming's
incendiary role in Newfoundland politics were beginning to
dissipate.

Although the proceedings of the Select Committee were
not published, Bishop Fleming obtained some extracts from
them through Daniel O'Connell, and wasted no time in forwarding a copy of Captain Geary's testimony to the Abbè de

Luca. This testimony further boosted his standing with Propaganda Fide and, together with the altered political situation, was probably responsible for his summons to Rome being quietly shelved, for we hear no more about it.

More good news followed. After the resignation of Governor Prescott, a very different type of person was appointed as his successor. The new Governor, Sir John Harvey, arrived in October 1841, and immediately brought about a dramatic change in the political climate of the Colony. For once the British Government had made an appointment which improved rather than exacerbated the local situation. A note appended by Lord Russell to one of Governor Harvey's letters stated: "Sir John Harvey undoubtedly possesses to a singular extent, some of the arts of conciliation, and is more likely than any man I know to allay the storms which have so long agitated Society in Newfoundland." As Governor of New Brunswick, Sir John had done much to promote harmony there and when he arrived in St. John's, his pacific influence was immediately felt. While his predecessors had retained the traditional autocratic mind set, Governor Harvey was of a new breed of administrators, able to accept the transition of society from autocracy to democracy. As Prowse comments: "The Governments of Captain Prescott and Sir John Harvey mark the parting of the ways."

Bishop Fleming was very happy with the appointment. He described the Governor as being "a British Soldier and honorable Gentleman, a man who by lengthened services has acquired a high and estimable character." Harvey himself believed that the underlying division in Newfoundland society was religious rather than political and that, in recent times at least, the Catholic clergy had been the main cause of this distrust. He recognized the pivotal role which Bishop Fleming must play in achieving social peace. Consequently, in his conversations with the Bishop, he quietly but firmly urged the necessity of his exercising firm control over the conduct of his priests as an essential condition for the return of Representative Government to the Island.

In other ways, Governor Harvey's attitude was also in marked contrast with that of his immediate predecessors. For instance, when, as in duty bound, he transmitted another petition from McLean Little containing more complaints about his treatment by the Catholic clergy, Harvey perceptively commented: ". . .in point of fact, I am assured that in a worldly point of view, Mr. Little has gained more by the countenance & patronage of one party that he ever lost by the persecution of the other." He respected the Catholic politicians. Reporting on John Kent and Patrick Morris, he reflected that Mr. Kent's presence in the Assembly had been marked by good sense and moderation, and that the colony did not contain a more staunch supporter of Her Majesty's Government or a more loyal subject than Mr. Morris.

Bishop Fleming quickly established friendly relations with the new Governor. He wrote to De Luca in April of the following year, "Peace and contentment reign among us. He [*Governor Harvey*] is our friend, he appreciates our loyalty and sincerity, he reposes in us all his trust, and he has depicted us with true colours to the ministers of our Sovereign. . . .he has demonstrated a particular friendship for me."

In this new and more congenial atmosphere, the Bishop could pursue with equanimity his plans for the betterment of his Vicariate. In October 1841, inspired by the success of Father Matthew's temperance movement in Ireland and with the assistance of Father Kieran Walsh who was becoming his right-hand man after the departure of Father Troy, he established a Total Abstinence Society which was to have a remarkable effect on the lives of his people.

After the laying of the corner stone of the Cathedral in May, the work of construction proceeded rapidly, perhaps too rapidly. To McGrath's frustration, the Bishop tended to take charge of the operation himself, consequently he and the Bishop soon quarreled and McGrath was dismissed. He sued the Bishop for breach of contract and was awarded £200. However, seeing the opportunities that were opening up in Newfoundland, he remained in St. John's and set up a successful construction business for himself. He was replaced by James Purcell, who was later to make his mark in Newfoundland architecture.

The change of builders did not effect the progress of the work on the Cathedral. By the end of July, the main walls had been raised to twelve feet above the foundations. By the end of November, they had reached twenty feet and the ambulatory walls had been completed. The edifice was fast becoming, as the Bishop boasted to De Luca, "the grandest Catholic Church that there is in the domain of Her British Majesty." But—and a large BUT it was—all the stone that had been so laboriously collected had now been exhausted, much of it swallowed up in the gaping foundations. The Bishop himself spent three weeks on Kelly's Island supervising the quarrying of more stone there. Enough was obtained for the following year but it had to be brought to St. John's, and the Bishop made tremendous efforts during the autumn of 1841 to persuade the ship owners to transport it.

Still far more stone was needed and he now decided that still another voyage to Europe was necessary to obtain it. He embarked on December 5 and reached Waterford on December 14 —a remarkably swift passage.

Even while he was away the work on the Cathedral continued. Enough stone had been accumulated at the Mundy Pond and Long Pond quarries to justify a major effort to transport it to the Cathedral site. So, in February 1842, with a good cushion of snow on the ground, the priests organized a massive "hawl," and in four days, 1,200 tons of good stone were placed on the site. During the same month, Father Walsh, now his main assistant in the project, emulated the Bishop's own example and lived on Kelly's Island for over two weeks enduring the bitter cold of an unusually severe winter while supervising the loading of stone on the sealing vessels.

In travelling to Ireland once more, Bishop Fleming had still another objective. While the poor Catholic girls of St. John's were being well cared for by the Presentation Sisters, the growing group of middle class Catholic girls were subjected to the temptation of aping the attitudes, the mores and even the religion of the wealthier class, and were in need of assistance. He had already made tentative arrangements with a suitable group of Sisters, the Sisters of Mercy, for this new educational initiative. In a letter to Cardinal Fransoni dated August 28, 1840, the Bishop had noted that, "I have paid to the Sisters of Charity[1] in Dublin the sum of £60 which is the stipend agreed on with them for the Novices whom I maintain in their convent, to come from there to Newfoundland where I have bought, at a cost of £600, a house which will serve as their dwelling, and for the school which will be opened as soon as they arrive."

The Sisters of Mercy were a new and daringly innovative Congregation of Religious Sisters founded by a wealthy young Irish lady, Catherine McAuley in 1831, just a year after the Bishop had himself taken over the Vicariate of Newfoundland. Their rule was based on that of the Presentation Order but—a first in the Catholic Church in post-Reformation times—the Sisters were not subject to enclosure as were the Presentation Sisters and, indeed, all religious Sisters of the time. Hence they received the popular name "walking nuns." As well as education, their apostolate included the care of the sick. It is a tribute to the farsightedness of Bishop Fleming that, at a time when many bishops in Ireland were objecting strongly to such an innovation, he encouraged this fledgling Congregation and chose it as the instrument of his plans. His relations with Mother McAuley were so friendly that she called him "my Bishop." The young lady, Mary Anne Creedon, whom he had entrusted to Mother McAulay's care three years previously, was now Sister Mary Francis, a fully fledged Religious Sister, ready to return to Newfoundland to initiate the Mercy Sisters' apostolate there. The Bishop had encouraged his own niece, Anne Fleming, to enter the Congregation, probably with the intention of having her join Sister Francis on the Mission. But this intention was not to be realized since Anne, who was of delicate health, died on December 10, while the Bishop was on his way to Ireland.

Unfortunately, Mother McAuley too had died during the previous month—November 11, and her successor, Mother Mary Magdalen de Pazzi Delany, was a very different type of person. Still, when Bishop Fleming arrived at Baggot Street to conclude the agreement which Mother McAuley had made with him, Mother de Pazzi, though not in favour of such ventures, rather reluctantly permitted two professed Sisters to accompany Sister Francis to Newfoundland. They were Sister M. Ursula Frayne and Sister M. Rose Lynch, both volunteers for the Mission.

The Bishop had hoped to return to Newfoundland in February but decided against it because the weather was so stormy and the prevalence of westerly winds promised a tedious and hazardous voyage. He was afraid such a difficult voyage would be too much for his delicate health. Besides by staying, he could make better arrangements for the preparation and shipping of the cut stone that he needed for the Cathedral. He would also have a greater opportunity to obtain the number of priests he needed. Eventually, having shipped two boat loads of stone to St. John's with another 800 tons being loaded, and having recruited several priests for the Vicariate, he booked passage for the Mercy Sisters on the *Sir Walter Scott*, which was to leave on May 4.

Impatient to return to renew the building of the Cathedral and especially to persuade the sealers to bring stone from Kelly's Island, for the sealing season would soon be over, he did not wait to return with the Sisters, but sailed in early April and arrived in St. John's late in the evening of Sunday, April 24. His arrival was quite a spectacular event, with many of the houses, both Catholic and Protestant being illuminated in honor of his arrival. A large crowd gathered to greet him. Extremely weary, after speaking briefly to the people, he sought refuge in a friend's house hoping the throng outside would disperse. But the crowd only increased and, after delaying for an hour, he finally had to submit to being escorted back to the Church on Henry Street. There prayers of thanksgiving were offered for his safe arrival and Addresses of Welcome given by the various societies. When eventually he was allowed to retire, he was confined to his room for several days recovering from the effects of his voyage.

CHAPTER TWENTY-SIX
THE DAY OF MERCY

The new style of religious women introduced to the Church in
Dublin, . . . they were called "walking nuns."

- Sister M. Williamina Hogan,
"The Pathways of Mercy"

ight days after the Bishop's arrival in St. John's, on May 2, 1842, the three pioneer Mercy Sisters, accompanied by three young ladies who were candidates for the religious life, left Dublin for Kingston Harbour (the present day Cobh) which was a principal setting off point in Ireland for trans-Atlantic voyages. The three candidates were Miss Maria Supple and Miss Catherine Waters from Dublin and Miss Catherine Phelan from New Ross. Two days later, the group embarked on the *Sir Walter Scott,* a large vessel which Bishop Fleming had chartered to convey them to St. John's. On board also were the five priests who had volunteered for the Newfoundland mission: Fathers John Regan and James Gleeson from Waterford, Fathers Matthew Scallan and John O'Neill from Cashel, and Father John Cullen from Wexford. The vessel also carried a cargo of granite destined for the Bishop's Cathedral. Unlike the trans-Atlantic voyage of the Presentation Sisters, this passage passed peacefully, and the passengers arrived at St. John's in the early morning of June 3 in remarkably good health. Unfavourable winds, however, made it impossible for the vessel to enter the harbour and, early in the afternoon, the Bishop became impatient with the delay and went out in a small boat to get them. The stormy conditions made the transfer of the Sisters and priests from the *Sir Walter Scott* hazardous but they succeeded in doing so without incident and reached shore safely.

Their arrival was greeted enthusiastically by the expectant people who thronged the neighbouring wharves. The Bishop then brought the new arrivals to the Presentation Convent where the candidates for that community were welcomed with open arms. The Mercy Sisters and the five priests now accompanied the Bishop to St. Mary's Church to offer prayers of thanksgiving for their safe arrival and to ask God's blessing on their mission. As he had done with the Presentation Sisters, the Bishop handed over his residence to the Mercy Sisters until their convent could be completed. This convent had already been started on Military Road immediately adjoining the Cathedral grounds. It was to be an elegant structure of an unusual architectural style. Built of wood, about sixty feet long and thirty feet wide, the convent featured on its west end a tower more that fifty feet high surmounted by a large gilded cross. On its various floors, this tower, though not more than fifteen feet square, provided the parlor, the community room and the Oratory. The Bishop claimed that the ground and the building cost him almost £2,000.

Anxious to begin their apostolate, the Sisters began visiting the sick the day after their arrival. However, because the classrooms were still under construction, they were not able to open their school until the first of March in the following year. When they did so, the increased demands the school made upon them caused them to be grateful for the entry into their midst of a new and highly talented candidate. This was Maria Nugent, sister of J. Valentine Nugent and sister-in-law of Sister M. Francis Creedon. Maria was a student of the Latin and Greek classics, was fluent in Italian and French, and an accomplished musician. Her life-story

was unusual. Born in Waterford in 1799, after an unsuccessful attempt to join the Ursuline Convent in that city, she
had come to Newfoundland with her family in 1833. Here
she tried her vocation with the Presentation Sisters but,
after twice making her novitiate, ill health again forced her
to retire. Now, becoming acquainted with the Mercy Sisters,
she became convinced that her true vocation lay with them.
She was received in early 1843 at the age of forty-four and
took the religious name of Sister M. Joseph. She was professed on March 25 of the same year, the first Mercy Sister
to be professed in North America.

Unfortunately, this profession became a source of
intense dissension within the small community. Unusually,
it took place without Sister M. Joseph having made the normal year's novitiate required by Canon Law. In accepting
her profession, Bishop Fleming probably considered that the
prolonged   novitiate   she   had   undergone   with   the
Presentation Sisters fulfilled the Canonical requirements.
Nevertheless, this irregularity added to the friction which
was developing between the Bishop and some of the community.

There seems to have been considerable confusion as to
who actually was the Superior of the convent. According to
the Baggot Street Annals, when the group left Ireland,
Sister M. Ursula held this position, but later Sister M. Rose
seems to have been appointed. Though about the same age
as Sister M. Rose, Sister M. Ursula was her senior in religion. Very apostolically minded, she was of an unusually
independent character, and seems to have objected to some
of Sister M. Rose's methods of procedure. She particularly
objected to the unorthodox reception of Sister M. Joseph.
Sister M. Rose was a great favourite of the new Superior of
Baggot Street, Mother M. de Pazzi, to whom she now con-
fided her unhappiness. Mother M. de Pazzi answered, con-
soling and encouraging her. Though apparently innocent
enough, this incident brought the confrontation between

the Bishop and Sister M. Rose to a head. It was the rule in Religious Orders that all incoming and outgoing mail had to pass through the hands of the Superior, but it is perhaps understandable that, given her temperament and the circumstances, Sister M. Ursula failed to follow this procedure when writing to Mother M. de Pazzi. When Bishop Fleming heard of this omission, he was furious and dashed off an impetuous letter to Archbishop Murray of Dublin accusing Mother M. de Pazzi of causing a breach of discipline in the convent by encouraging clandestine correspondence. Mother M. de Pazzi denied this accusation vigorously. When the Bishop received her reply through Sister M. Rose he was not amused. In a sharply worded letter, he informed the Reverend Mother that he knew "nothing more likely to loosen and render insecure the Holy Bond of Religious discipline in a Community of Nuns than thus to encourage the throwing off of all order and obedience in a Convent." He left her in no doubt as to who was in charge of the Convent: "I beg leave to intimate that the Convent of Mercy of Newfoundland is utterly and entirely independent of every Institution of the kind in any country whatever and owing obedience alone to the Vicar Apostolic of Newfoundland." We can only surmise that the Bishop must have already become disillusioned, for instead of attempting to ameliorate the situation, he went on to say that, if Mother M. de Pazzi now regretted having sent her Sisters "I shall be most happy at a moment's notice to resign them once more to your care and have them conducted under suitable attendance to their original domicile, reserving, of course, my own immediate subjects with whom I hope and expect with the Divine aid to be able to form a respectable and useful establishment."

Whether Mother M. de Pazzi accepted this invitation and withdrew Sisters M. Ursula and M. Rose, or whether Sister M. Ursula decided on her own that enough was enough (which apparently she was quite capable of doing, for in her later career in Australia she fought continual battles with various bishops), we do not know. But in any case, on November 18 of the same year, Sisters M. Rose and M. Ursula returned to Ireland leaving Sisters M. Francis and M. Joseph to carry on alone. Perhaps if Mother McAuley had been still alive and her health had permitted her to come to Newfoundland to begin the foundation, as it is reported she intended to do, or perhaps if Bishop Fleming had been less inflexible, the story might have unfolded differently.

It appears that for a while Bishop Fleming was undecided as to the future of the Order in Newfoundland. Given his strained relationship with Mother M. de Pazzi, he saw little hope of further help from her. Instead he decided to make a wider appeal and wrote to his friend, Doctor O'Connell, in Dublin, a series of letters which he asked him to publish. In one of these letters, he spoke of the great work the Sisters were doing but deplored the fact that "the community is now so small, and as they are engaged in teaching between the hours of ten and three, without a moment's relaxation, the necessary result of this is, that during that time the sick must be entirely neglected." He continued with an impassioned plea for assistance: "Would to God that the Spirit of the Holy Ghost would inspire some three or four daughters of the Island of Saints, gifted with an education and accomplishments suited to the fulfillment of the varied and important duties of such an institution, to embark upon a mission that promises so rich a harvest." But the appeal was to no avail. Meanwhile, Sister M. Francis' former companions both in Ireland and in the United States were pleading with her to join them, but she seemed to sense that she was called to establish the Mercy Sisters in Newfoundland and resisted all such appeals. So for four long years this heroic duo of Sister M. Francis and Sister M. Joseph struggled on, strictly maintaining their religious Rule and observances, teaching their classes, performing all the duties of their state until, in 1847, further tragedy was to strike.

If the Bishop was upset by his conflict with the Mercy Sisters, he was even more frustrated by the obstacles to making progress on his Cathedral. The impressive amount of stone which his curates had gathered while he was away, added to the several cargoes of stone he had ordered in Ireland, was still not sufficient to occupy the masons for even half a year. There was indeed sufficient stone ready on Kelly's Island but, in spite of his earnest pleas to the sealers to bring it to St. John's, continual storms prevented them from doing so. With the greatest reluctance, therefore, he was forced to abandon the work for the year even though two cargoes of cut stone arrived from Ireland as well as a great quantity of excellent sand from Trepassey.

However, he did not let 1843 pass by without making headway on another front. The erection of a convent and school for the Presentation Sisters had been a priority of his since the Sisters had first arrived in 1833 with the Bishop's assurance that he would provide a suitable convent and school for them. Various circumstances had up to the present prevented his fulfilling this promise, and the Sisters were still living in Archdeacon Wix's house on Nunnery Hill while teaching the children in the school house which the Bishop had built for them next door. By now, 1843, the Archdeacon's house was deteriorating and becoming unsafe to live in. Moreover, it was too small for the growing community which was being slowly but steadily augmented by additional recruits from both Ireland and Newfoundland. In any case, the lease could not be renewed.

In November 1842, before leaving for Europe, the Bishop had purchased from Benjamin Grier Garrett, at a cost of £300, a lot of about two acres on Long's Hill with the intention of building the convent there. Some time later, he bought from the Crown another smaller lot of twenty-two perches across the street from the first. On this second lot, he planned to build a school to be joined to the Convent by a "light metal bridge"—a surprisingly modern touch.

Now he put his project into effect. As usual, the people gave him enthusiastic support. During the winter, they brought out from the woods enough material to make a frame for the proposed convent. In the spring, as soon as weather permitted, they dug its foundations. So many people came to help in this that they had to be divided into groups working on alternative days and the work took only three days. The basement storey was then built of stone to a height of eleven feet. Above this was raised the wooden framework for the rest of the building. As conceived by the Bishop, the Convent rose as a tastefully designed edifice with its modest turrets in a commanding position above the town. One of its ingenious features was that the corridors were spacious enough for the Sisters to get exercise in winter without having to go outdoors. The Bishop proudly described it as the "principal embellishment of the town."

While the new Convent was under construction, on August 15, 1843, the Feast of the Assumption, the Bishop received two young ladies and a lay Sister into the Presentation Community. The young ladies were Catherine Phelan, who became Sister M. Ignatius Aloysius, and Amelia Shanley who now became Sister M. Antonio Magdalen. Shortly afterwards, on the last day of the month, he moved the Sisters temporarily to a house located at the rear of the Cathedral grounds which he had purchased from James McCabe. Since it had previously served as a handball alley, it could not have been very elegant, but the Bishop repaired it at a cost of some £300-400 and appealed to the people to build a school house beside it. Once more, the people rallied to his support and in one day erected a substantial school "capable of accommodating 500." There the Sisters lived until their new Convent was ready for occupancy. The Sisters were impatient to get started and, as soon as they possibly could, they moved into what they presumed would be their permanent abode. While waiting for their school to be completed, they immediately set up classes in the lower part of the Convent for some 800 children.

Meanwhile on the piece of ground opposite the convent, the Bishop was erecting a school house ninety feet long and forty-five feet wide—sufficient, he claimed, for upwards of 2000 children! His funds ran out before he could finish this project, but fortunately in the spring of 1844, the Legislature awarded a grant of £300 towards its construction and he was able to complete it.

The Sisters were delighted. Finally, eleven years after their arrival in St. John's, they were to have a permanent convent and school. They would have been shattered if they had known how short their occupancy in both was actually to be. Like gold, they were still to be tried in the fire.

CHAPTER TWENTY-SEVEN
EDUCATIONAL INFIGHTING

Education cannot be carried on without religion.

- Bishop Feild

he gift of £300 from the legislature towards the completion of the Presentation school house was not an isolated phenomenon for the Newfoundland Government was now beginning to take an active interest in the education of the children of the Island. In 1836, the country had been divided into nine educational districts and Boards of Education were appointed for each. However, it was the impact of the new democratic and liberal ideas on the upper class children who were going abroad for their advanced education that most concerned the political and religious leaders of Newfoundland. As far back as 1827, the Anglican Bishop Inglis, when concluding his visitation of the Island, had pointed out to Governor Cochrane the obvious need of a classical school in Newfoundland, which ought to be established in St. John's. His reason was that many children of the respectable inhabitants were being sent to England or Ireland or, even worse, to the United States of America for their education and were there imbibing the liberal ideas being disseminated in the schools. In 1830, Governor Cochrane wrote to the Colonial Office that some "adopt the perhaps still more pernicious system of sending them [*their sons*] to the United States of America there to imbibe republican principles with which to return and disseminate them in a monarchical government."

In 1843, just as the Mercy Sisters were about to begin their apostolate for the wealthier Catholic girls, an Act was introduced in the Assembly, to provide advanced education for the upper-class boys. The Act called for the establishment in St. John's, of "two Colleges, one for Protestant students and one for Roman Catholics." The Act provided for a Board of Directors for each College. In the case of the Protestant College, the seven Directors were to be Protestants with the Anglican Bishop among their number. The Board had the sole power to appoint the Principal and staff while the Principal had to be a graduate of Oxford, Cambridge or Trinity College, Dublin. For the Catholic College, the inclusion of the Catholic Bishop was not stipulated. Bishop Fleming promptly protested to both the Governor and the House of Assembly. While congratulating the Assembly on their initiatives in education, he pointed out that the Catholic Bishop was *de facto* and *de jure* superior of every Roman Catholic College within his jurisdiction. The Wesleyans, who were now quite a force in the Colony, also objected. They realized that, with the finances under the control of the Anglicans, they were not likely to play a role in proportion to their numbers in what promised to be a most important educational development. They presented petitions declaring that they had read the Bill "with sorrow and regret. . . .that the language. . .of the bill is powerfully calculated to awaken the jealousies, and call for the opposition of all those whom an uncourteous (*sic*) and untrue phraseology classes under the general designation of 'Dissenters.'" They then went on to suggest that "one Educational Institution totally free from all religious tests, and sectarian domination in Professors, would amply meet the exigencies of St. John's."

In view of these objections the Bill was shelved temporarily, but in 1844, Governor Harvey again urged the

Assembly to adopt some such measure. A flurry of activity ensued. Academies were approved for both Carbonear and Harbour Grace, both non-sectarian, and the question of a Grammar School in St. John's was reopened. A Bill was introduced which accepted the recommendation of the Wesleyans and provided for the establishment of a single non-denominational Academy for the town. This Bill, likewise, met with strong opposition. The Newfoundland School Society (Anglican) objected that they "feel bound to record their dissent from any system of Education which shall involve the neglect of the religious principles of any portion of the youth of the country." They demanded for their children "that early instruction in the faith and fear of the Lord . . . to which every child that is born in a Christian land has an undoubted right." Bishop Fleming objected to his having no say in the selection of teachers.

However, it was Bishop Feild, Bishop Spencer's successor, who was the most determined opponent of the proposal. When Bishop Spencer, finding the climate too severe for his health, left Newfoundland for Bermuda in 1844, he had declared that his successor would need:

> ...the strength of constitution to support him under a climate as rigorous as that of Iceland; a stomach insensible to the attacks of sea sickness; pedestrian powers beyond those of an Irish Gossoon, and an ability to rest occasionally on the bed of a fisherman or the hard boards of a woodman's tilt. With these physical capabilities he must combine a patient temper, an energetic spirit, a facility to adapt his speech to the lowest grade of intellect ... and a thorough preparation for controversy with the Romanist....

Bishop Feild, did indeed possess many of these qualities, though not, perhaps, the common touch. He was already a distinguished educator [*several schools in England are still named after him*], with a passion for educational reform. He was convinced that "education cannot be carried on without religion," and even before he left England to take up his new duties, he took steps to counteract the Assembly's intentions. He decided to open his own Grammar School in St. John's in opposition to that proposed by the Assembly and brought out with him the Rev. Charles D. Newman, M.A. Oxon., to be its first Principal. The ironies of sea travel at the time are illustrated by their separate passages. The Bishop traveled in his yacht *Hawk* which a wealthy friend had given him to assist his visitations around Newfoundland. Newman declined to accompany him, perhaps fearing to trust his life to such a small vessel on a trans-Atlantic voyage. Instead he travelled to Cork where he took passage for St. John's. Later Bishop Feild wrote smugly to a friend:

> Mr. Newman refused a passage by ye Hawk that he might make ye voyage more quickly and thought he had taken the best and most certain method, by crossing over to Cork from Plymouth. That passage occupied twenty-four hours, he was detained a week in Ireland, and was then three weeks in crossing from Cork to St. John's... My Hawk sailed almost from his own door in sixteen days.

Within a few weeks of the Bishop's arrival in St. John's on July 4, 1844, he opened his Academy, "The Classical School for Boys" on Forest Road. The following year he opened a similar school for girls on Military Road. Nevertheless, in spite of all this opposition, the Education Bill was passed and, on September 29, 1845, the St. John's Academy opened its doors with great fanfare and with full Government support. Temporarily it was located in rented quarters called "Castle Rennie" on Signal Hill Road. Bishop Feild must have been disgusted when the Rev. Newman "jumped ship" from the Bishop's school and moved over as Principal of the new Academy at a princely salary of £300 per annum. John Valentine Nugent was appointed Junior Master at a salary of £250. During the following year, Thomas Talbot was added to the staff as Writing Master.

Nevertheless, in spite of its impressive launching and the undoubted ability of its teachers, the Academy had very limited success. There were never more than sixteen pupils in attendance. The prediction of Bishop Feild in 1844 seems to have been fulfilled that "the proposed academy may very probably degenerate into anarchy; at once become an Institution of which the youth of the lower portion of the Community, viz. Roman Catholics & Dissenters may alone avail themselves, the members of the Established Church being self-excluded." When in 1849, the Government made an official inquiry into its problems, the most serious objection brought forward by the Principal, Mr. Newman, was the lack of all religious instruction, as a result of which, "discipline in a school of this kind can only be maintained by severity, and the fear of punishment, or hope of reward." Following this inquiry, the Academy was divided into three sections, Anglican, Catholic and Wesleyan.

For the ordinary schools, each denomination formed its own board. At the first meeting of the Catholic Board, Bishop Fleming was elected Chairman and Valentine Nugent offered to act as Secretary "gratuitously." We find other familiar names on the Board: Patrick Morris, John Kent, Laurence O'Brien, John Dillon, Richard Howley and (rather surprisingly) Patrick Kough. Apparently by now, the Bishop had patched up his differences with both Morris and Kough.

Although Bishop Fleming was not alive to see many of these developments, readers may still be interested in learning that, after the division of St. John's Academy in 1850,

Valentine Nugent took charge of the Catholic section—still at the salary of £250 a year. He conducted it very successfully, first from his home in Monkstown, and then in various other locations on Queen's Road. He closed it in 1856 when he was appointed the High Sheriff. Fortuitously, just at that time, the Bishop's residence on Henry Street became vacant because Bishop Mullock, Bishop Fleming's successor, had built a new clerical residence adjacent to the Cathedral. Bishop Mullock then took advantage of the opportunity to open his own Classical School-Seminary in the vacant building on December 1, 1855, while awaiting the completion of its permanent home on the grounds of the Cathedral. It was he who named it "St. Bonaventure's College" after the scene of his own theological studies in Seville, Spain. However, this has taken us far ahead of our story, and we must return to 1843 when all these educational developments were in their infancy.

Bishop Fleming may have been very pleased with the progress of the Convents for the Presentation and Mercy Sisters and he may have looked askance at the Government's educational initiatives, but he was undoubtedly frustrated at the hiatus in the building of his Cathedral. Consequently, on November 20, 1843, without even waiting for the Presentation Convent to be completed, he set out once more for Ireland on another winter voyage and another major effort to purchase stone. A few days previously, perhaps becoming aware of his waning physical powers (he was to die less than seven years later) and of the dangers that the passage might hold in store for him, he had hurriedly made his will which, incidentally, was never implemented since it was superceded by another made some years later.

After Fleming's arrival in Dublin, he set up his headquarters with his fellow Franciscans at the Church of St. Francis, Merchants' Quay. From here, the Bishop began to search far and wide for more stone for his Cathedral. In

Dublin itself, he purchased a large quantity of granite for moldings. Then in Galway, he found a source of black marble. By the summer of 1844, his wharf in St. John's was a hive of activity as a constant succession of large ships arrived bearing the results of his quest, and his helpers transported the stone to the building site. Besides all this, Bishop Fleming also purchased in Europe large supplies of chalices, monstrances, candlesticks, missals and vestments for the various churches under his charge.

Many people wondered where he got the money for all these purchases. One of these who questioned was his Anglican counterpart, Bishop Feild. The latter wrote to a friend in England shortly after his arrival in Newfoundland in July 1844: "Doctor Fleming, their bishop, is not here, but is expected shortly, and no doubt will come well supplied with money. Indeed he seems to command any sums for any purpose he pleases. His own estates near SJ are said to have cost many thousand pounds. One was purchased for him this week. The Cathedral will cost full £50,000 when completed and fitted up."

A major source of his income was the munificence of the sealers. Still in the possession of the Roman Catholic Archives in St. John's is a large, leather-bound ledger with the names of each sealing ship and its complement of men carefully entered. Opposite each man's name is the amount which he had contributed (usually one shilling) from the proceeds of the voyage.

The long delay and the consequent exposure to three Newfoundland winters had naturally caused considerable damage to both the walls and the scaffolding of Bishop Fleming's Cathedral. Bishop Feild commented in August, 1844, not, we suspect, without some satisfaction: "The two towers of ye RC Cathedral were poor because obliged to be taken down several feet this year at a loss, as it is said, of from 700 to 800 pounds." In February of 1845, the Rev. Charles Palairet, the Anglian rector, reported further deterioration: "I see a great deal more of ye walls of ye RC Cathedral must be taken down this spring."

Bishop Fleming arrived back in St. John's on September 7, 1844, determined, now that he had accumulated the needed materials, that 1845 would see the Cathedral finally completed. But now a new and different type of obstacle reared its head.

CHAPTER TWENTY-EIGHT
THE FINAL PUSH

I have just finished the main walls of my Cathedral and have roofed the Building.

- Bishop Fleming

By now, 1844, in the sixteenth year of his episcopacy and the fifty-third year of his age, Bishop Fleming was forced to accept that his health was deteriorating rapidly. As *The Patriot* reported: "the health of this admirable Prelate is so extremely dangerous that he has been advised by his medical attendants to quit these shores for a more temperate clime." He accepted his doctors' advice and on January 5, 1845, after only a three months' hectic stay in St. John's, he set sail again across the Atlantic on the *Herald*. He was accompanied once more by Father Charles Dalton who, besides hoping to improve his own health, was looking for cut stone for his own new church in Harbour Grace. Their destination was Oporto, Portugal.

Before leaving, the Bishop had various matters to attend to. These included arranging with his clergy for a major effort to finish the Cathedral in the coming year. They also included his administering in one three-day period the minor Orders and then the Sub-Diaconate, Diaconate and Priesthood on William Forristal, the younger brother of Father John Forristal, a curate at the Cathedral. During the same period, he petitioned the Colonial Office for an increase in his annual salary of £75, pointing out his service to the military for whose benefit he had built a special gallery in St. Mary's Church so that "they have been now for the last six years enjoying comparative comfort in attending their place of worship." Governor Harvey's remarks to the Colonial Office supporting this petition are noteworthy, so different was his attitude from that of his predecessors. He wrote: "It is further due to Doctor Fleming to add the expression of my conviction that to the agency and influence of Doctor Fleming & his clergy is mainly referable the peaceable, orderly, and moral conduct of the lower classes of Her Majesty's subjects of that persuasion throughout this community." Answering an Address from the Benevolent Irish Society regretting his departure for Europe, the Bishop replied that recently his health was improving rapidly and that he hoped to devote more time this coming year to roofing and covering the Cathedral.

Even as he left, active preparations were being made by his curates for the approaching summer's drive to obtain needed materials for the Cathedral. In late January, Father Kieran Walsh arranged for a major haul of wood to replace the scaffolding which had deteriorated over the past several years. The event was accompanied, as usual, by a band and festive celebrations. In the following month, there was a great haul of stone from Outer Cove, this time arranged by Father Waldron, another of his curates. It must have been quite a sight to see more than 150 horses and sleds constantly bringing in their loads all day long. Rather than being discouraged by the long delay, the people seem to have rallied to the work with increased zeal, for a local journal reported: "we believe that at no former time was such a call so enthusiastically obeyed." Indicative of the prosperity of the times was that this spring there were over 125 vessels engaged in the seal hunt.

By February 17, the Bishop and his companion had reached Oporto for a well-earned rest but one which didn't meet the approval of their perennial critic, Father Browne.

From Perugia where he had been forced to retire from Rome, the disgraced priest continued his attack on the Bishop, detailing to Propaganda Fide still more cases of alleged clerical abuses, and concluded his diatribe with this note: "Doctor Fleming last October has visited like a bird of passage the Colony . . . he obtained his money, abandoned his people, and flies off to a warmer clime accompanied by the Merchant Priest Dalton who goes to England to arrange his mercantile affairs with his partners."

In April, the Bishop, now well rested, was in London where he received word from Thomas Murphy of Waterford that 100 tons of the best limestone had been loaded on the vessel *John* which was waiting for a fair wind to set sail for Newfoundland. Father Dalton returned to Newfoundland on this vessel, but the Bishop remained in Europe to complete his business affairs. Altogether during the summer, he sent out to St. John's four cargoes of stone and gathered enough for two more. A newspaper reported that "three vessels have sailed from Galway freighted with cut stone . . . and there are now loading at Bangor two other vessels with slate [*for the roof*], and thirty-six crates of glass are being shipped from London for the same purpose." He continued to recruit more priests and, on July 30, Bishop Foran of Waterford ordained two more priests, Patrick Burke and Edward Condon, for the Newfoundland Mission.

On Wednesday, August 20, the Bishop set sail from Liverpool for St. John's on *The Britannica*. The destination of the vessel was Halifax, but so anxious was he to get back that, off the southeast coast of Newfoundland, he literally jumped ship. *The Britannica* encountered a fishing boat and the Bishop and a few other passengers seized the opportunity to have it take them directly to St. John's. They arrived on the night of Saturday, August 30, eleven days after leaving England. Responding to the customary Benevolent Irish Society Address on his return, he hoped that no further voyage would be necessary for many years to come. He claimed that his health was comparatively restored. This improvement, however, did not last, for he soon suffered a severe illness of whose nature we are not informed, but which was probably due to total exhaustion.

Still the work went on. By November the Bishop could report with joy: "I have just finished the main walls of my Cathedral and have roofed the Building in so that I shall be able, with God's blessing, to commence with renewed activity in the Spring to bring it towards completion. . . . The works up to the present time have cost me upwards of £21,000." An editorial in *The Patriot* of November 29 gave a glowing account of the entire project:

> The roofing of this magnificent edifice is proceeding rapidly, and as it proceeds it opens up the striking graces of this grand and tasteful piece of architecture. It is, indeed, a noble structure even in its yet unfinished state—what will it be when its interior decorations and altars shall have been completed? No Catholic can look upon that superb building without feelings of pride and exultation, and a hope will arise in his bosom that he shall live to put up his prayers in a temple so worthy of his Faith. And we know that if its self-denying, persevering Founder, Doctor FLEMING's means were equal to his zeal, the oldest of his devoted flock need not despair of a confirmation of his fondest aspirations.

The same account paid an equally eloquent tribute to the Bishop himself:

> The necessities of this Diocese are so numerous that it's a matter of deep astonishment that so much could have been accomplished in so short a time, looking at the Convents and Chapels erecting and completed at the same period. We say it

with the utmost sincerity and without a particle
of flattery, that there is not a second man on this
side the Atlantic, who would have surmounted
the difficulties which gathered in the Right Rev.
Prelate's way in regard to this erection, or who
would persevere with the disinterested, Christian
ardour which has marked Doctor FLEMING's
prelacy. It is marvellous how his Lordship has
proceeded, without receiving a single fraction
from the Government beyond the paltry £70
granted in the time of Bishop O'Donnell.

On Tuesday, December 9, the roofing was finally completed—it was to be slated in the spring, and the following
day the *Patriot* reported that the event "was celebrated by a
bonfire on top of the building"— a rather hazardous method
of celebration.

At about this time, he was disturbed by an incident
involving one of his clergy. In Placentia, a dispute between
Father James Walsh, the Parish Priest, and Patrick Hogan,
the agent for the Sweetman merchant firm there, developed
into actual fighting between their respective supporters and
took on the complexion of a full blown factional row between
the men of Wexford and those from Kilkenny. Hogan wrote
to Sweetman in Waterford: "All the county Wexford men are
to be driven out. The gang on the street publicly singing 'out
now the Yellow Bellys'. . . .Father Nowlan's[1] influence here
is nothing. They call him a good for nothing old Yellow Belly
. . . I dare not stay. A storm has been raised against me. My
life is sought in open day." Fifteen of Father Walsh's supporters were arrested and tried, but a partisan local jury
acquitted them. Angered by both sides, Bishop Fleming
decided to transfer Father Walsh to Merasheen. This decision sparked a riot and, when the leading heads of house-
holds refused to be enrolled as special constables, government troops were requested from St. John's. On November

28, an Address was presented to Father Walsh by the parishioners, in which they expressed the hope that he would appeal his transfer but wishing him well if he should leave. In replying three days later, Father Walsh assured the people that he had no choice in the matter but continued: "neither have I, nor much less have you, a right to question the wisdom of our Spiritual superior in arranging the difficult affairs of the Diocese, in which he is guided by the Omnipotent Spirit." He reminded them that they had always been distinguished by their respect for law and order and implored them "to let nothing induce you to do anything from this day forward that may have the effect of giving your district an irregular or turbulent character." A deputation went to St. John's to request Bishop Fleming either to restore Father Walsh or to provide them with another priest. The rumor was spread that Father Walsh had himself instigated this deputation and this caused great indignation among the people of Placentia who issued a disclaimer saying that Father Walsh had left for Merasheen a week before the petition was got up and, since all communication between Placentia and Merasheen had ceased for the winter, he could not have known of it. Eventually the situation was calmed when the Bishop appointed the recently ordained Father William Forristal to replace Father Walsh.

In the midst of such crises, ordinary business affairs still had to be attended to. The need for more teachers for the school he was building on Long's Hill was very much on the Bishop's mind. Sometime in the autumn of 1845, he wrote the new Bishop of Galway, Doctor O'Donnell, on the matter—Bishop Brown having died in the meantime. Simultaneously the Sisters in St. John's wrote to the home convent in Galway requesting assistance. It would appear, however, that his letter to Bishop O'Donnell never reached its destination for, when the Sisters in Galway answered their companions in Newfoundland, they made no mention of it. Several of them, including the Superior herself, the

Assistant Superior, and the Mistress of Novices, volunteered to answer the appeal of their missionary Sisters, but they could take no action without the approval of Bishop O'Donnell. Therefore, in March 1846, Bishop Fleming wrote again to the Bishop, telling him of the great need for additional Sisters, of the willingness of the Sisters to come to Newfoundland, and asking him to give his consent. This time his letter arrived safely, and Bishop O'Donnell gave his approval.

Even as this good news was received, Bishop Fleming's health had deteriorated to the extent that he was unable to attend the St. Patrick's Day dinner of the Benevolent Irish Society and Father John Forristal had to take his place. Nevertheless, to arrange for the travel of these new recruits, at the end of May the Bishop had to cross the high seas again. He hoped to persuade as many as four of the Sisters to come to his aid, but in this, he was only partially successful. Only two Sisters accompanied him back to St. John's. They were Sister Josephine (Catherine) French and Sister Francis de Sales Lovelock, both of whom were to give heroic service to Newfoundland in the years to come.

It would seem, then, that at long last, in spite of so many obstacles and at such tremendous cost to himself, he had finally achieved all his objectives as, on July 2, 1846, he wearily prepared to set sail for home with his precious boon of Presentation Sisters never, he hoped, to have to leave Newfoundland again. But such was not to be.

CHAPTER TWENTY-NINE
RAVISHED BY FIRE

(I) am still filled with the hope that even from this desolation will come peace and consolation.

- Bishop Fleming

uddenly on July 2, as Bishop Fleming waited in Liverpool for the boat that was to take him and the two Sisters to Newfoundland on the following day, all his hopes and plans were dashed. He received the horrifying news that, on the ninth of the previous month, a disastrous fire had destroyed two-thirds of St. John's. The new convent he had just built for the Presentation Community and the unfinished school adjoining had both been burned to the ground. He was stunned but his first thought was for the Sisters who were with him. Magnanimously, in view of this tragedy, he offered to release them from their engagement. Valiant women that they were, they refused his offer. They were determined to come to the assistance of their Sisters in Newfoundland no matter what might befall them. While the Bishop's spirits must have been uplifted somewhat by their continued commitment, still even this was an additional worry. How was he now to provide for them? Where was he to find accommodation not only for the Sisters already in Newfoundland but for this new contingent as well? What a heart-rending blow and what a test of his faith this disaster must have been. As he and the Sisters embarked on their Atlantic voyage, what thoughts must have occupied his mind? How great had the disaster really been? Had the reports been exaggerated? How were the Presentation Sisters in St. John's faring with their convent destroyed? What about his priests? The new Cathedral-to-be and St. Mary's Church and rectory had all been spared, but how were his clergy coping with this dreadful catastrophe without his being there to lead them? What about his Cathedral? How was he now to obtain the finances and manpower he needed to complete it from a people who had lost everything? Most of all, his thoughts were with his poor people themselves. How much were they suffering? Were they completely disheartened? What could he do to help them with his finances now utterly exhausted? The voyage must have seemed interminable as he ached to be back among his people as he had always been when calamities had struck. Still, he did not lose his trust in God. Writing to the Society of Lyons, a few months after the fire, he would say "...sad as the picture is that surrounds me and dismal as would appear the prospect before me, I cannot bring myself to believe that we are forsaken. I do, indeed, in all humility, accept the scourge as a favor from the Most High and am still filled with the hope that even from this desolation will come peace and consolation, and that He will in His goodness, in His own good time lead us thence in triumph." Even in the depths of his spiritual desolation, he could say like Job: "The Lord has given, the Lord has taken away.... Blessed be the name of the Lord."

It was probably during this passage that he came to face the fact that his health and strength were no longer equal to his overwhelming responsibilities and that he must look for a suitable successor. He had in mind Father J. Thomas Mullock, a fellow Franciscan, brilliant scholar and able administrator as well as a personal friend, whom, as far back as 1837, he had unsuccessfully recommended for the Bishopric of Jamaica.

What had caused the catastrophe in St. John's? On Tuesday, June 9, a very hot day with a strong wind, a glue

pot in a cabinet maker's shop in the west end of St. John's
had caught fire. Soon the building burst into flames. There
had been a prolonged drought in the area, and the wooden
buildings, being built "cheek by jowl," were soon exploding
like fire crackers. The fire spread in all directions but mainly to the east fueled by the increasing gale as the people of
the town tried in vain to contain it. At one point, Governor
Harvey, hoping to create a fire break, personally directed the
blowing up of a house. Unfortunately, the charge went off
prematurely, killing one artillery man and seriously wounding two others. It did nothing, however, to hinder the fire
which roared on, gathering momentum as it went. It was fed
by the oil vats in the merchants' premises which were filled
to the brim and burst into uncontrollable balls of flame. One
spectator compared the noise of the fire to the roaring of the
Niagara Falls. On both sides of the entrance to St. John's
harbour are high cliffs separated from the town by the
waters of the harbour. Yet so fierce was the blaze, that
shrubs on the top of both hills caught fire. When the conflagration, having run out of fuel, finally subsided at about 7
p.m. almost every business premises in the town had been
destroyed together with the Anglican Cathedral, the Court
House and other major buildings. Twelve thousand people
were left homeless and largely penniless. The value of the
property destroyed amounted to well over £1,000,000. That
night saw hundreds of desolate families, hungry and cold,
huddled around the burnt-out ruins of their homes, while
others crowded into tents provided by the military on the
grounds of Government House and on the Barrens near the
proposed Cathedral. *The Courier* described their pathetic
plight: "It was a sad sight to see shivering mothers endeav-
ouring to shelter their little babes, and hush them to sleep;
while the cries of the older ones for food had in many cases
to be answered by 'wait till daylight, and we shall try to get
some for you.'"

What had happened to the Convent? Because of its remote position on a hill outside the town and with the winds blowing away from it, the Convent had been thought to be out of danger. Therefore, when the fire started, many of the refugees hurried up the hill to deposit there what belongings they could carry. Among these belongings was a mattress which, unnoticed by its owner, was already smoldering. Eventually it burst into flames and quickly ignited the other goods among which it was stored. These in turn set fire to the building itself.

Before this occurred, the Bishop's residence being endangered, all its contents had been conveyed to the Convent for safety only to be utterly destroyed. Ironically, by heroic efforts, the townspeople succeeded in saving the rectory even though the only water available was from the rectory kitchen pump. But while they were doing this and unnoticed by them, the Convent with its unfinished school across the street were being destroyed. The Sisters fought valiantly but to no avail, barely escaping with their lives, their belongings almost all lost. Eventually, alerted to what was happening, the priests rushed up. One of them broke through the chapel window to rescue the Blessed Sacrament from the burning altar and was himself badly burned in the process. Colonel Law, the commandant of the garrison, also galloped up as soon as he perceived the flames but he too could do nothing.

As for the Sisters, what a sight was now before them. Describing the scene, one of them wrote back to Ireland: "Our convent, for whose establishment we had sighed so many years, and which was just at the point of flourishing—those schools which we used to look on with such pleasure, in hopes of being soon surrounded with our little flock—in a moment we were deprived of all." People came swarming to the scene to do what they could, lamenting the loss and, as one of the Sisters wrote, "the ruins of our convent were well watered with their tears." Both Catholics and Protestants offered the Sisters accommodation in such houses as had been spared. The Mercy Sisters arrived to comfort them, and, when their agitation had lessened somewhat, accompanied the eight desolate refugees to the Mercy Convent next to the Cathedral. Here they stayed until evening when they trudged to the Bishop's cottage on his farm at Carpasia and, in this cramped, unfurnished abode, set up their home, sleeping on the floor, four to a room. The people were still very concerned about them, fearing that, with the loss of all their provisions, they would have nothing to eat. Hence they hurried to share with the Sisters what little they had. The kindness of the people was a tremendous consolation to the Sisters. "If these people had but one loaf they would divide it with us," one of them wrote.

As news of the disaster in St. John's spread abroad, relief poured in from all over the English-speaking world. But before this could arrive, the people were forced to live in almost indescribable conditions. One vivid, if revolting, pen-picture of the situation was given by the Anglican Rector who appealed to the Assembly just a week after the fire for a grant to restore the fence around the Church property, which included the public cemetery. In his appeal he stated:

> Troops of starving dogs infesting the town have become dangerous as well to the living off the dead, and have commenced desecrating the tombs and may be seen gnawing the bones of those who have been buried in the said churchyard. Pigs and goats infest it in great numbers... and the gravestones and monuments of the deceased are daily violated.

The most immediate need was food and shelter. Providentially, when the danger was apparent, some of the merchants had transferred their goods to ships in the harbour and were thus able to come to the aid of their fellow cit-

izens. The traditional resilience of Newfoundlanders was well displayed when, the very next day after the fire, the town was already starting to be rebuilt. One of those present described the scene: "The very next morning some of the citizens were at work excavating amongst the ruins of their dwellings, and preparing to erect temporary sheds; thousands were ruined, but everywhere there was a hopeful, determined spirit that St. John's should rise again. . ."
Governor Harvey acted promptly and effectively. Laying an embargo on the exportation of provisions, he wrote to the heads of all the British colonies and to the British consuls in Boston and New York asking for help and they responded nobly. He chartered two vessels to bring provisions: one from Halifax, the other from New York. The English Government, in course of transition, sent immediately a sum of £5,000, and as soon as the new Government was established, a further £25,000. On the other hand, on August 24, with incredible insensitivity to the desperate needs of the people of St. John's, the British Government transferred Governor Harvey to Halifax as Governor of Nova Scotia. He had been sent to Newfoundland to pacify the situation, had succeeded admirably, and so his new appointment was his reward. Indeed, from the Governor's own point of view, he must have felt relieved. His family was unhappy in Newfoundland, one of his sons had just died, and another was causing him a great deal of grief in St. John's. When he left, Colonel Law took over the administration of the colony until Harvey's successor, Governor LeMarchant, arrived on April 22, 1847.

CHAPTER THIRTY
ONCE MORE INTO THE BREACH

I meet so many scenes of wretchedness that call to me for assistance
that now alas! must so sadly be omitted.

- Bishop Fleming

t was into this maelstrom of immense human misery confronted with equally defiant courage that Bishop Fleming stepped when he arrived in St. John's on August 9, exactly two months after the catastrophic fire. As he gazed with deep sadness at the scene which unfolded before him, how different must his sentiments have been from those of twenty-three years before when he had first seen St. John's. Then he had been in his prime, full of apostolic zeal and youthful vigour, sure of his ability to meet whatever challenges life held in store for him. Now he was prematurely old and sick, weakened by the incessant demands he had made on himself during the intervening years. What a contrast from the city he had left three months before was the one he now saw before him.

> When, in May last, I embarked on board the packet for England, I left a city whose streets were crowded by a wealthy, because industrious, a intelligent and thrifty, population, whose wharves manifested the rapid triumphs of trade, judiciously conducted; and whole harbour was filled with shipping destined to bear the most striking evidence of a place that promised at no distant day to

stand among the first commercial cities of the
West, and prosperity and happiness seemed to
light the countenances of all you met.

But Oh! when I landed on the morning of the
9th inst. from the same steamer, what a sad
reverse! I had often fancied, I had often hoped,
that the account I had seen had been over-
charged.... Alas! How vain the expectation! I left a
city rapidly rising in beauty and found it after an
absence of little more than two months, a heap of
unsightly ruins, a forest of blackened and crum-
bling chimnies [*chimneys*].

At first, the suffering of his people and the demands
their needs would make upon his depleted resources left him
mentally paralyzed. He could not even put a pen to paper.
But soon, with his amazing powers of recuperation, he had
aroused himself and was searching far and wide for aid, particularly to rebuild the convent. He wrote to the Irish people
appealing for help. He wrote the Society for the Propagation
of the Faith in Lyons, even to the French King Louis
Philippe, relying on the King's connection with St. Pierre.

But such assistance from afar, even when provided,
could not fully repair the material damages the Bishop had
suffered, nor the shattering effect of the catastrophe on his
health. The destruction of the beautiful Presentation
Convent involved the loss of everything of value that he personally possessed—all his furniture, his books and other
valuables. He had lost about £1,000 worth of vestments and
other liturgical garments, enough to provide for the entire
mission. A large quantity of household plate, most of which
had been handed down by his predecessors, and a considerable number of chalices, missals, ciboria, worth as much
more, had also been destroyed. He had lost his papers,
including his own manuscripts and correspondence as well

as numberless deeds, grants, and other legal documents, placed in his hands for security by their owners.

As he bemoaned his losses in a letter to his friend Father O'Connell, PP, Dublin, his discouragement was obvious, amounting almost to despair. He feared that, not only would the people be unable to help him rebuild the Convent, but that they would not even be able to contribute to his own support. Never had he felt the burden of poverty so much as when on every side he witnessed scenes of misery and found himself unable to alleviate them.

Yet one thing he had to do and that was to find some way to take care of the sorely tried Presentation Sisters. Only two Mercy Sisters now lived in the convent on Military Road, which had been built to accommodate six, and the Bishop took advantage of this to arrange for them to divide their convent with the Presentation Sisters. Still it must have been a tight squeeze when eventually, in November, the Presentation Sisters, now ten in number, came to live with them. Through the generosity of the Mercy Sisters, this arrangement continued until, after Bishop Fleming's death, his successor, Bishop Mullock built for the Presentation Sisters the fine stone convent in Cathedral Square which still serves as their Generalate.

As if the effects of the fire were not bad enough, the situation of the people was made even more desperate when one of the worst storms ever to visit Newfoundland hit the island on September 19, just ten days after the Bishop's arrival. The hurricane-force winds killed over one hundred people and destroyed such an immense amount of property on both land and sea that the storm was considered a greater calamity than the fire itself. All along the coast, fishing stages were destroyed together with the fruits of the summer's fishery. Houses were blown from their foundations and turned into rubble. Rivers rose to as much as ten feet above their normal level, destroying bridges and similar constructions along their route. Many of the newly built houses in St. John's were damaged. The wind was so high that St. Thomas Church was moved off its foundations. The large, unfinished Natives' Hall, which was giving shelter to several families, was destroyed and several of the occupants killed. The Natives' Society never recovered from this disaster. Many of the vessels in the harbour were damaged or sunk and one fishing boat, trying to find shelter from the gale, sank in the Narrows with the loss of the six or seven men on board.

There was one aspect of the fire's aftermath that made the Bishop very unhappy. This was the distribution of funds. There seems little doubt that much of the relief money was squandered on projects having little or nothing to do with the fire-sufferers. John Greene, in his *Between Damnation and Starvation*, claims that much of the money had been spent on public buildings or at the personal whim of Governor LeMarchant. But what infuriated Bishop Fleming most of all was that £14,000 had been allocated to the building of the Anglican Cathedral to replace the almost worthless St. Mary's Church which had been destroyed in the fire, while he could get no support at all for the rebuilding of the Presentation Convent and School.

Early in 1847, Bishop Fleming wrote to Earl Grey, now Secretary for the Colonies, pleading for assistance to rebuild the Presentation Convent and School. His request did not succeed, but the local Legislature granted the sum of £1,500 for this purpose. The Bishop's finances also received badly needed assistance when a wealthy parishioner, Mary Ann Bulger, died and left her estate in Ireland to him as well as £1,000 for the building of the Cathedral. In her will, she also remembered both the Presentation and the Mercy Sisters. Fortunately, this time there was no Judge Boulton to prevent her wishes from being fulfilled. It was possibly this bequest that enabled the Bishop to purchase the Belvedere property from Hugh Emerson. Emerson had bought this

estate as a family home, but his wife died and, no longer
wishing to live there, he had placed it on the market.

Physically and mentally exhausted and ill as he was, one
would expect that Bishop Fleming would now seek some
respite from his arduous activities until his successor would
arrive to take up the reins of office. Yet incredibly by May he
was on his way across the Atlantic again.

To understand why Bishop Fleming should undertake
this exhausting voyage when he was already suffering from
the ravages of terminal tuberculosis, one must recall an ear-
lier-mentioned group with whom the Bishop's relations
alternated between cordiality and distrust. This was the
Benevolent Irish Society (BIS). It will be remembered that
this Society was formed by a group of prominent Irishmen
in St. John's in 1806. The Society's purpose was to combat
the abysmal poverty confronting so many of their fellow
Irish men and women. With the passing of time, living conditions improved in St. John's to the extent that the Society
could turn its attention to other pressing needs. In 1823 the
BIS opened a school on land granted by the Governor at the
junction of Queen's Road and Garrison Hill. Originally, the
society had planned to open an orphanage and had actually
begun such an operation on a small scale. However it quickly discovered that such a project was beyond its capabilities
and decided instead to limit its sponsorship to the school
which was originally intended to be part of the orphanage.
Hence it received the name *The Orphan Asylum School* even
though no orphanage was ever attached to it. The BIS
always prided itself on being a civic society, open to all
creeds, rather than a denominational group. It will be
remembered that, when Bishop Fleming was still an assistant priest, he had been refused permission to give religious
instruction to the children—who were all Catholics—in the
BIS school, even after school hours. Some years later, the
Bishop of Harbour Grace attempted to take control of the

branch of the Society in that town, and his efforts led to open warfare between him and them.

Except for a short time at its beginning, its master had been a Mr. John Grace who gave exceptional service over the years. By 1847, however, his health was deteriorating and it was clear that he could not continue. The search for a suitable successor proved unsuccessful. The schools for girls under the Presentation and Mercy Sisters were flourishing and it seemed to the BIS that the introduction of a similar group of Religious men would be the logical solution for their problem.

So, on March 9, 1847, a deputation met with Bishop Fleming to discuss this possibility. The Bishop received them warmly, listened to their request and outlined his views. He explained that he had always been anxious to provide Religious Brothers for the school, but had refrained from acting because, when word got abroad of his intentions, it was rumored that he wanted to take control of the Society itself. For this reason, Bishop Fleming told the deputation, "I was literally paralyzed, and I dared not broach the subject of your school." Now that the Society had come to him with the problem, this objection was removed and he could state his convinced opinion that "it is only by engaging members of the Brotherhood of those schools of education in other countries to superintend the Orphan Asylum School you can hope to render that school worthy of yourselves and capable of accomplishing your wishes."

He promised them that, if the Society would agree to pay salaries equivalent to those now paid to the lay teachers, he would commit himself at once to establish a community of these Religious Brothers and, at his own expense, to erect for them a suitable monastery. On April 3, the Bishop wrote to Propaganda Fide saying that he was on the point of leaving for Ireland:

...principally for the purpose of obtaining a community of monks, perhaps brothers of the Christian Schools, for the education of the male poor, a work grievously wanted in our society and which I had long set my heart upon, for here our little boys at St. John's at the age of six years begin to earn for themselves 1s 6d to 2s per day attending to the curing of fish, turning and curing in the sun, and this tends so early, by rendering them independent, to estrange them from the authority of their parents that the effects of it are greatly calculated to alarm, and I know of no other means of counteracting the evil better than bestowing on them a sound Christian education and therefore it is that, though still feeble from protracted illness, I have resolved to brave the hazards of another voyage across the Atlantic.

Before leaving Newfoundland, however, he had another battle to fight. Bishop Walsh of Halifax proposed to establish an English-speaking Canadian seminary for eastern Canada. The British Government was prepared to subsidize such a venture much as they had done in Ireland with the establishment of Maynooth College, and for the same reason—they were anxious to remove prospective priests from the democratizing tendencies prevalent on the European continent and in the United States. All great men have their peculiarities, and Bishop Fleming was no exception. One of his was that he refused to accept local youth into the priesthood. He believed that such local priests inevitably become involved in partisan politics. Further, he was greatly opposed to the idea of governmental subsidies because of the influence it would give the Government over the institution. He wrote a strong letter against the proposal to Propaganda Fide, pointing out that most of the priests in Newfoundland came from Irish seminaries and finished their education in

Rome, and that a local seminary was unnecessary. Because of his opposition, the proposed seminary died still-born.

After an uneventful voyage across the Atlantic, he arrived in Dublin on June 15 and was greatly saddened to learn that his friend and protector, Daniel O'Connell, while making a pilgrimage to Rome, had died suddenly in Genoa a month before. He must also have been terribly distressed to see the effects of the great famine which was then ravaging the Irish peasantry as a result of the potato blight. The day after his arrival, he travelled with Father Mullock to Clongowes, the Jesuit academy in Kildare, and to Maynooth, the national seminary just south of Dublin, to see two young seminarians, John Mackin and Michael Kent. One suspects that he had already informed Father Mullock of his request to have him appointed his coadjutor.

In Dublin, however, his efforts to obtain a community of Christian Brothers were fruitless and he was forced to turn to Galway to his old friend Archbishop McHale who had succeeded to the See of Tuam in July 1834. The Archbishop had a group of Brothers of the Third Order of St. Francis in his Archdiocese. He held similar views to Bishop Fleming in educational matters, appreciated his predicament, and agreed to release one of the Brothers to him. The letter of the Archbishop confirming this, dated June 29 1847, read: "I therefore freely release from his obedience for a time, Brother John Hanlon, a young man of the most excellent character, well fitted to instruct youth and to mould their hearts to virtue, in order that he may place himself under your jurisdiction." Laurence O'Brien, the President of the Benevolent Irish Society, happened to be in England at the time and wrote home to the Vice-President, Patrick Kough, that "after considerable difficulty . . . he [the Bishop] at length succeeded in procuring four monks of superior qualifications, some of whom were selected to establish several schools in Ireland." Ominously, however, O'Brien mentioned that "hearing of his [the Bishop's] bad state of health," he went over to Dublin to see him. It should be noted also that Archbishop McHale in releasing Brother Hanlon, stated that he did so "for a time," and it may well be that he intended this to be but a temporary arrangement. If so, this may have had its effect on future developments. The other three Brothers were Brother Angelus as Superior, Brother Bernadine, and Brother Felix O'Mara[1]. We do not know from what particular community or communities the others came. Bishop Fleming must have been elated with his success as he prepared to return to Newfoundland with his prize.

The group travelled separately. On August 19, the Bishop took passage from Liverpool for Newfoundland via Halifax. The Brothers left Liverpool on the August 24 on the Brig *Mary*. Father Mullock remained with them until their departure and then returned to Dublin. In Halifax, the party must have been reunited because on September 7, they arrived together in St. John's on the steamer *Unicorn*. The monks took up residence in the Belvedere homestead which Bishop Fleming had purchased for that purpose. They attended Mass every morning in the Chapel on Henry Street, but this proved very inconvenient because of the distance and the terrain. Some years before, the BIS had set up an apartment on the east of their school as a home for Mr. Grace. This was now renovated and placed at the disposal of the monks. Meanwhile, the Bishop was happy to learn that during his absence, the British Government had voted an increase of his annual stipend from £75 to £300. In informing Governor LeMarchant of the increase, Lord Grey "expressed the sincere hope of Her Majesty's Government that he will use his best exertions to repress religious differences in Newfoundland, and promote the peace and contentment happily now subsisting among all classes in the Colony."

The hoped for improvement in the Orphan Society Schools occurred almost immediately. The records of the

Society state that "the effect on the school of the transfer of the management to the care of these Religious Brothers was prompt and beneficial. Before they were at work three months the attendance increased considerably, and both the upper and lower rooms of the buildings had to be used to accommodate the classes. The most excellent order pervaded the whole institution." The Society was very happy with the results—and so must have been Bishop Fleming, his long-held ambition finally accomplished—or so he thought!

CHAPTER THIRTY-ONE
THE CHANGING OF THE GUARD

*. . .so is my constitution weakened and my health broken
and my frame attenuated by my toils. . . .*

- Bishop Fleming

hile the Bishop was thus grappling with his problems at home and abroad, both good and bad news was emanating from Rome. The good news was that, in October, Rome had forwarded a Rescript to the Archbishop of Quebec raising the Vicariate of Newfoundland to a full-fledged Diocese, with Father Mullock as Bishop Fleming's coadjutor Bishop. The bad news—and this was why the Rescript had been sent to Quebec rather than directly to St. John's—was that Rome was placing Newfoundland under the jurisdiction of Quebec. As soon as he received this communication, Bishop Fleming wrote a strong protest to Cardinal Fransoni pointing out in his own dramatic fashion the difficulties this arrangement would cause. To reach Quebec from St. John's, he wrote, the traveller had a choice of two routes. One of these was by sea along the treacherous southern coast of Newfoundland and through the wild gulf of St. Lawrence, then up the St. Lawrence river to Quebec, a distance of at least a thousand miles of ocean. The other possible route, via Halifax and Boston, would more than double the distance while the risk would be still greater since the seven hundred mile voyage between St. John's and Halifax was through "the most boisterous ocean in the world." Perhaps his most telling argu-

ment against the proposed arrangement was that this journey would have to be made during the summer, since during
the winter the sea routes were usually closed by ice. But the
summer was the only time when his priests could come to
see him or when he himself could travel to see his own far-
flung people.

He admitted that his objections sounded strange coming
from one who seldom passed two years without crossing the
Atlantic to Europe, a distance nearly double that between
St. John's and Quebec. But, he noted there was weekly traf-
fic between Newfoundland and Europe, the maximum price
of a passage was £12 and sometimes he had been able to
make the journey free of charge. On the other hand, the
expense of visiting Quebec would be a heavy financial burden on an impoverished diocese. He claimed that his voyages
to Europe were essential for the advancement of his mission
and would therefore have to be continued no matter what
his other obligations might be. Moreover, his successor
would have to follow the same course for many years to
come.

This being the case, he pointed out, it would be unrea-
sonable to force him to add to this the risk and expense of a
dangerous voyage to and from Quebec. He concluded,
"Believe me, Your Eminence, the geographical position of
Newfoundland imperatively forbids its association with any
Province whatever . . . Canada alone is a continent equal in
extent to two thirds of Europe. Surely that is a jurisdiction
at least wide enough for an Archbishop without flinging an
arm a thousand miles across the sea to grasp a remote petty
fishing Island as an adjunct." In fact, he could see no profit
in joining Newfoundland to any other mission. Halifax,
Annapolis and Charlottetown, as well as the missions of
Upper Canada (Ontario) had been made dioceses without
any such condition.

He also took advantage of the situation to remind
Cardinal Fransoni of the hardships which his journeys had

imposed upon him. During his episcopacy, he claimed, he had visited Europe no less that twelve times, crossing thirty-six thousand miles of ocean. Yet, being subject to severe sea-sickness, he had never done this except when he considered it imperative. On his last two voyages, indeed, he had passed immediately from his sickbed to shipboard. He played on the heart strings of the Cardinal when he added a pathetic note:

> As for my part, the question cannot, I fear, during my sojourn in this life affect me for good or for evil, for so is my constitution weakened and my health broken and my frame attenuated by my toils that I fear I cannot hope at any time to meet that prelate for whom I entertain so high an esteem that it would be happiness indeed to embrace him before I pass away.

A few days earlier he had written in a similar vein to the Archbishop of Quebec.

Meanwhile Father Mullock had set out from Dublin to Rome to be ordained Bishop, arriving in the Holy City on September 17. Sending back to Bishop Fleming an account of his interview with Cardinal Fransoni, he wrote that he hoped to receive his letter of appointment almost immediately and to arrive in Newfoundland on November 4 or 5. However, Rome was still on holiday, and it was on December 7 before he received the official notice of his appointment—by coincidence, exactly twenty-two years to the day after he had entered the Franciscan Order. In a second interview, Cardinal Fransoni mentioned to him that Newfoundland was being made a diocese. Two weeks later, on December 21, he received the brief officially appointing him Bishop of Thyatira *in partibus*, and coadjutor to Bishop Fleming. On December 27, he was ordained Bishop in St. Isidore's by Cardinal Fransoni and wasted no time in assuming his responsibilities. On January 4, he wrote a lengthy letter to the Cardinal vigorously seconding Bishop Fleming's objections against Newfoundland being joined with Quebec. As a result of the representations of both bishops, the project of joining Newfoundland to Quebec was quietly abandoned.

Meanwhile, back in St. John's, Bishop Fleming, in spite of his rapidly declining health, was still attempting to finish his Cathedral and his other building projects. Shortly after his return from Europe, he requested financial aid from Governor LeMarchant for rebuilding the convent and school. The Governor offered him £1,000 but the Bishop rejected this as insufficient, claiming that he needed at least double that figure. Several interviews failed to resolve their differences. Turning elsewhere for assistance, he wrote, in June, to his old reliable source of funds, the Society for the Propagation of the Faith in Lyons, with what result we do not know.

He was still struggling with the actual construction of the Cathedral. On January 21, 1848, he wrote to Bishop Dollard, O.S.F., of New Brunswick: "I have now completed the structure of this beautiful edifice as to the externals. The walls, thereof, the towers are all finished, and I have only the interior now to struggle through."

His adamant determination to have the Cathedral finished before his death led him into several building indiscretions. He had engaged the firm of Conway and Sons to slate the roof. Conway advised him that the roof beams were not strong enough to support the weight of a slate roof, but the Bishop was so impatient to see the building completed that he insisted that the slating be done. The result was that, after his death, the roof had to be taken down and replaced by a sturdier one.

On April 23, 1848, Bishop Mullock left Greenock in Scotland for Newfoundland, arriving on May 6. Not knowing where he stood in the political scene and not wishing to be compromised in any way by Addresses and formal greetings, he shrewdly avoided the throng that was waiting for him on the wharves by getting in a small boat and landing privately with Chief Justice Brady who had succeeded Judge Bourne the previous year. Bishop Fleming put his new assistant Bishop to work almost immediately, sending him at the end of June on an extended visitation of the Island, starting at Cape Broyle on the East Coast and extending as far as Sandy Point on the West. On the West Coast, according to Bishop Mullock's diary, he was nearly lost, "saved by almost a miracle . . . when all human hope was lost." He was getting his first taste of the dangers of travel in Newfoundland waters. While he was away, Bishop Fleming, on August 22, sailed to Halifax with his old friend Father Dalton. We are not told why, but can surmise that he wanted to see Bishop Walsh in connection with the problems of the regional seminary and with the proposed affiliation with Quebec, as well as to arrange for timber for the Cathedral. They returned on September 28 on *The Unicorn.*

The rest of the year seems to have passed quietly enough. It seems to have been a time for reconciliation. Some two years before, the Bishop had come to terms with his long time adversary, Henry Winton. This touching incident is described by Pedley in his *History of Newfoundland.* One day, Mrs. Winton was sitting alone in her parlour when a knock came on the door. She was startled and thrown into a flutter to see Bishop Fleming entering the room. He came in, sat down in a chair opposite her and began to talk. To Mrs. Winton's amazement, the Prelate told her that his days were numbered and that he wished to die at peace with all his neighbors. As they took tea, he lamented the bitterness which had prevailed in the community. Revealing an unsuspected degree of humility, he said that, if he had given offence or done any wrong to Mr. Winton, he wished to be forgiven and reconciled to him. There were other parties with whom Bishop Fleming had been in a state of hostility who now received and accepted a like reconciliation. Among those was McLean Little, who had caused such trouble with Rome. Little was reconciled to the Church and published an abject apology in a local newspaper.

A touching instance of his continued concern for others is shown in a letter, dated July 8, 1848, which he wrote to Robert Parsons, the editor of *The Patriot*. It will be remembered that Parsons had been involved in a split in the ranks of the Liberal party and was thought to have deserted their ranks. The letter was a private one and was not published until 1851 after the Bishop's death. It reads as follows:

My Dear Mr. Parsons,

The moment your bill for my half-year's subscription to the Patriot had been placed in my hand, it instantly occurred to me, - from the fact of its being always, until now, furnished with my account annually - that you must be in some difficulties, and I am truly pained to think so, and particularly as I have it not in my power, should it be unfortunately to case, to assist you out of them as my heart desires. With this, however, I send you ___ pounds, which I pray you to accept as the small gift of a friend, and regret I could not send fifty instead, for be assured if I had it in my power, I would feel greater pleasure in sending it than the present trifle. Excuse me the liberty I take, and believe me to remain....

The poor state of the Bishop's health is revealed in his postscript to this letter:

P.S. Please just to say you have received this note. The tremor of my hand, from the great debility of constitution, renders me scarce able to hold my pen.

Still another instance of this solicitude for others concerns an indentured servant who came to Newfoundland in the 1830s. He was working on one of the wharves belonging to his employer when an overseer used a whip on him. The servant retaliated, was arrested and placed in irons. Bishop Fleming heard of this incident, used his influence to get him released from irons and arranged for him to work off his indentureship on a Government Farm. Later, this man was able to buy a small farm which he added to until it became a prosperous plantation. His name was Philip Stamp, and the street in St. John's called Stamp's Lane now perpetuates his memory.

With Governor LeMarchant, however, the Bishop was still at odds. Apparently the Bishop was now prepared to accept the grant of £1,000 which the Governor had previously offered, but the latter now withdrew his offer saying that conditions had changed. In the aftermath of the fire, aid had been so abundant and the people had prospered to such an extent that the chairman of the Charitable Committee for the Benevolent Irish Society could report that he had not had one applicant for relief since the fire. But, by the end of 1848, all that money had been spent and the people were feeling the full effects of the disaster. When the winter of 1848 set in, great poverty existed in the city and all available funds were needed for their relief. Hence the reluctance of the Governor to use the funds at his disposal for other purposes. The Bishop wrote to Lord Grey his usual lengthy letter, accusing the Governor of duplicity. However Grey defended the Governor and supported his decision.

It has been noted previously that, as part of the Assembly's program for the educational advancement of the people, school boards had been formally set up for each Denomination. The Bishop, as Chairman of the Roman Catholic School Board, was expected to send annual reports to the Governor. During December, the Bishop took advan-

tage of this responsibility to include a reference to the
Orphan Asylum School and the Presentation Sisters. In
speaking of the Orphan Asylum School, he reported that the
community consisted of five members (one being a lay-
Brother). A total of 600 boys were enrolled in the school,
although during the winter season this had dropped to 450.
If there was room to accommodate them, he claimed, 800
children would be immediately enrolled as pupils.

He wrote that since the fire, the Presentation Sisters
had been forced to live with the Sisters of Mercy in very
inadequate accommodations. The crowded conditions in the
convent, he claimed, were dangerous to their health and
already, he claimed, one Sister had died. Yet his means had
been so badly decimated by the fire that he was unable to do
anything to remedy the situation.

When reporting that one Sister had died, he was referring to Sister M. Joseph Nugent of the Mercy Community,
the sister of Valentine Nugent. In doing so, he was being less
than candid, for Sister M. Joseph's demise had little to do
with the crowded conditions in the convent. It will be
remembered that she had joined the community in 1843 and
that, when Sisters Rose Lynch and Ursula Frayne returned
to Ireland, she and Mother Francis Creedon, as a lonely duo,
continued to live their regular religious life until the
Presentation Sisters joined them after the fire in 1846. In
1847 an epidemic of typhus swept through St. John's and
the two Sisters were untiring in their care for the sick. (The
Presentation Sisters, being cloistered, could not join them.)
Finally on June 3, Sister M. Joseph herself caught the disease. After two weeks' intense suffering, this heroic Nun
died on the afternoon of June 24. Her death was considered
a public calamity. To her belongs the honour of being the
first woman to perform the duties of a nurse in
Newfoundland.

CHAPTER THIRTY-TWO
THE LAST DAYS

*I feel it necessary to withdraw myself, as far as it lies in my power...
in preparation for that awful account I shall soon be called upon
to render.*

- Bishop Fleming

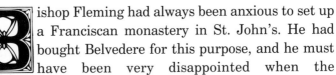 ishop Fleming had always been anxious to set up a Franciscan monastery in St. John's. He had bought Belvedere for this purpose, and he must have been very disappointed when the Franciscan Brothers decided to move their residence from Belvedere to the Orphan Asylum school. Still, this move presented him with another opportunity. He was now seriously ill and he determined to move to Belvedere himself and there to end his days. It would seem that Bishop Mullock joined him and thus they maintained a Franciscan presence there. They were cared for by two devoted elderly servants, Margaret Dellahunty and Elizabeth Walsh.

Even now he could not escape the cares of the Diocese. The two graveyards in the city, the Anglican one in their church grounds and the Catholic one at the foot of Long's Hill, were filled and had been closed. Although Bishop Fleming had opened another at Belvedere, it was his private property and people had to pay for grave sites. Some people objected to this and demanded that part of the Cathedral grounds be set aside as a graveyard as had been proposed in the original deed. The Bishop called a public meeting on July 9 to discuss the problem and, as Bishop Mullock noted in his diary: "A ruffian named Hogan excited the people to demand the Cathedral ground"—(Bishop Mullock probably did not know Hogan's previous history of opposition to Bishop Fleming). A heated discussion broke out, and the meeting eventually closed without coming to any decision. To solve the problem, Bishop Fleming bought some property near Quidi Vidi Lake with his own money and opened this as a public graveyard, now Mount Carmel Cemetery.

Bishop Fleming's condition grew steadily worse. On June 10, 1849, Bishop Mullock noted in his diary that he was very sick. Sadly, it would appear that his illness was now beginning to affect his judgement. The sculptor Carew had been commissioned to create much of the main altar for the Cathedral, including the massive sculpture of John the Baptist baptizing Christ. He was asked also to carve the statues of the Blessed Virgin and St. Francis for the side altars. Bishop Fleming became uneasy at the apparent lack of progress of this work and the failure of Carew to respond to his queries. Consequently, in spite of his condition, the Bishop insisted on getting up from his sick bed and setting out for Ireland yet again to find out what the problem was. Perhaps he who had so often forced his physical energies beyond their capacity thought that he could do so once more. While one has to conjecture what actually happened, it would seem that all Bishop Mullock's persuasive powers were unable to restrain him. Frustrated, Bishop Mullock noted in his diary, *"capo perduto,"* which, under the circumstances, could be translated as "He has lost his head!" In desperation, Bishop Mullock sent to Harbour Grace for Father Dalton, Bishop Fleming's close friend and companion on several voyages, hoping he could persuade the Bishop to change his mind. But Bishop Fleming was unmovable, and the only effect of these maneuvers was that Father Dalton accompanied Bishop Fleming when, on July 11, he sailed to Halifax. Having arrived there, the Bishop suffered a serious relapse, but revived and insisted on continuing his journey. He and Father Dalton then left Halifax on August 3 on the *Caledonian* for Liverpool. Arrived in England, he once more collapsed and was finally forced to concede defeat. He turned his back on Europe for the last time not having even met Carew though the latter was now living in London. He arrived back in St. John's at the beginning of October. Father Dalton returned separately a week earlier.

On his return to St. John's, Bishop Fleming became involved in still another dispute, this time with the Benevolent Irish Society. Clearly his prickliness remained with him to the end. What caused the controversy was a very minor affair. Towards the close of 1849, J. Valentine Nugent, then President of the Society, gave permission for a series of lectures to be given by a Mr. Mooney in one of the school rooms. After the first of these lectures, which were on the history of Ireland, it was reported to the Bishop that Mooney's approach to Irish history was unacceptable. Without inquiring further, the Bishop peremptorily ordered the Monks to close the rooms and to exclude Mr. Mooney from them. Mr. Nugent, whose temperament was as fiery as that of the Bishop, considered this a denial of his right as President of the Society to grant the use of the premises. When the ensuing debate within the Society did not support his position, he resigned. Irritated by the whole affair, Bishop Fleming also resigned as Vice-Patron. This action caused great regret to the Society particularly in view of the Bishop's state of health. After much communication back and forth, harmony was more or less restored, but the Bishop declined to resume the position of Vice Patron, citing his failing health and his inability to "sustain even the slightest excitement," but principally the fact that "as I feel I am upon the threshold of Eternity, I feel it necessary to withdraw myself, as far as it lies in my power, from every affair that may by possibility disturb, and every care that may distract me, in preparation for that awful account I shall soon be called upon to render to an all-seeing, but good and merciful God." The Society respected his wishes but

suggested that Bishop Mullock might be elected Second
Vice-Patron. However, in his reply the Bishop made no mention of this suggestion, while Bishop Mullock's attitude may
be gauged from his description of Nugent in his diary:
"furbo e furbissimo," which may be translated as "a very
wily fellow."

Bishop Fleming still insisted that Carew had to be confronted about the statues, so, possibly to pacify him, Bishop
Mullock left for England on October 18, just two weeks after
Bishop Fleming's return, to see what could be done.
Arriving in Liverpool on November 6, he went immediately
to London and, on the following day, challenged Carew. It
would appear that Bishop Mullock, too, was very dissatisfied
with Carew for in December he noted in his diary: "annoyed
at Carew's scheming and delays." From England he traveled
briefly to Ireland and arranged with James Murphy of
Limerick for the eight columns of polished granite which
still grace the high altar of the Cathedral.

While he was still away, there occurred in St. John's an
event which he must have found very frustrating to miss.
The Cathedral, though a mere shell, was now usable, and
Bishop Fleming, in spite of his condition and against all the
advice of his doctors and fellow priests, insisted on celebrating the first Mass there. On Sunday, January 6, 1850, the
Feast of the Epiphany, this solemn ceremony took place. It
would be difficult to imagine a more poignant event.

The day arrived, bitterly cold with drifting snow. The
Bishop rose early and was brought to the Cathedral. In spite
of a piercing draft within the church, he remained for an
hour absorbed in prayer, wrapped in his brown Franciscan
cloak, until the time came for the ceremonies to begin. A
reporter depicted the sad contrast between Bishop
Fleming's appearance on this occasion and on that of the
laying of the corner stone in 1841, nine years earlier:

The writer of this article well recollects the manly and energetic form, and the apostolic contour of features which characterized this untiring Missionary, when, clothed in his pontifical robes, on the 20th of May, 1841, he proceeded through this City preceded by an immense procession, to the site of the present Cathedral to lay its foundation stone, and he could not but be moved by the change which a little time had effected, when upon entering this massive structure, and straying along its extending aisles, he perceived at the foot of a temporary Altar, erected for the occasion, an attenuated and feeble figure, clothed in the habit of the Franciscan Order, and this was the prelate who in '41 was full of life and energy, entering with all the vigor of mind peculiar to himself, into this gigantic undertaking, the hope of completing which made skeptics of even those who knew the indomitable energy of his enlightened mind.

As one would expect, the Cathedral, in spite of its great size and the inclement weather, was packed to overflowing. Newspapers reported that there were no less that six thousand people in attendance including all the clergy from the neighbouring outports. Fittingly, in view of his long relationship with Bishop Fleming, Father Troy acted as Master of Ceremonies. The children from the schools also attended, the girls clad in white. Because it was thought that the Bishop could not possibly get through the ceremony, Father Condon, Parish Priest of Placentia, remained fasting so as to be ready to replace him if necessary. During the Mass, the Bishop twice weakened and had to sit down to recover. Yet at the end he rallied and—typical of the man—made still another superhuman effort. He rose and "preached an eloquent sermon . . . with a spirit and energy which surprised

but highly delighted all who had the satisfaction of witness-
ing." No wonder that he seemed quite exhausted at the end.
Bishop Mullock at the time of this first Mass was at St.
George's in London. He hurried back to Newfoundland. On
his arrival, he was delighted to find that Bishop Fleming,
with typical generosity, had presented him with a very fine
carriage "the most beautiful one on the Island." Now
Ordinary in all but name, he pushed forward the work of the
Cathedral and of the new Presentation Convent. This infor-
mal situation, however, did not last long, for, as he recorded
in his diary, on April 18, while at breakfast with Bishop
Fleming, the latter formally resigned the care of the Diocese
into his hands and, in this casual manner, he became the
Fifth Bishop of Newfoundland.

On June 26, two months later, Bishop Fleming, feeling
his end approaching, asked Bishop Mullock whether he was
in danger of death. When informed that this was indeed the
case, he asked Bishop Mullock to anoint him on the following morning. He lingered on for another two weeks, attended by the fervent prayers of all his people until, on Sunday,
July 14, at 10:20 p.m., having received all the sacraments of
the Church, he departed this life.

Next morning, the bell of St. Mary's Church tolled the
sad news continuously from 6-8 a.m. As word spread, the
whole town went into mourning. The merchants' establishments were closed and flags flown at half-mast on all the
main buildings as well as on all the ships in the harbour, no
matter what the nationality of the owners. The Prelate's
body was laid out in Belvedere Monastery and thousands of
people came to pay their respects throughout the day and
until a late hour of the night. Crowds just as numerous
packed the Cathedral to pray for the repose of his soul.

At 11 p.m. that night his body was placed in a coffin and
removed from the Monastery to the Cathedral accompanied
by hundreds of people. There, on Tuesday and Wednesday,
the body lay in state while almost the entire population of

the town came to pay their respects. Masses were offered each day for his eternal repose.

On Thursday morning, Bishop Mullock, assisted by fifteen priests, presided over the funeral ceremonies in a packed Cathedral. The solemn Office for the Dead was chanted and then High Mass offered. The entire ceremonies took almost three hours to complete. At 2 p.m., the funeral procession was formed and wended its way through the town. It was undoubtedly the greatest procession ever seen in St. John's, numbers being estimated at 10,000, in spite of the absence of the fishermen, as the whole town vied with one another to give due recognition to one "in whom they had seen, when in life, a public benefactor—the guardian of the poor—the disseminator of morality—a missionary of civilization, and a promoter of the education of his people." Having circled the town, the procession returned to the Cathedral where, after some concluding prayers, the coffin was enclosed in an oaken shell lined with lead and interred in the vault under the main altar where it rests to this day together with the remains of his predecessor, Bishop Scallan, and his successors, Bishops Mullock, Power, and Roche.

Shortly afterwards, his will was published. In it he regretted "that I cannot in justice to the Church leave any portion of my property to my sister Johanna,[1] as I feel myself in conscience bound to bequeath the same for charitable and religious purposes." He made provision for the support of the Sisters of Mercy and the Presentation Sisters. To the Mercy Sisters, he also left provision for the erection and support of an Orphan Asylum for destitute girls. He left an annuity of £20 to each of his aged servants, Margaret Dellahunty and Elizabeth Walsh, £10 to his widowed sister in Ireland, and enough funds to obtain an interest of £7 for an annual High Mass for the repose of the soul of Mary Bulger who had been a great benefactor of the Church, and £200 for an annual High Mass for the repose of his own soul and for that of his parents. He left £700 towards the completion of the Cathedral, £300 towards the erection of the Presentation Convent, £600 for a sculpture *The Dead Christ* for the main altar of the Cathedral to be made by Hogan, and £200 for a monument to be erected to the memory of the late Bishop Scallan[2]. The properties and monies which he had acquired in his capacity of Bishop, he left to his successor in office.

The last acts of kindness by the Church for Bishop Fleming were performed on Thursday, August 22, with the customary Month's Mind[3] during which the Divine Office was sung and High Mass celebrated for the repose of his soul. Bishop Mullock officiated at the Mass, assisted by many priests from outlying areas who had been prevented from being present at the burial because of time and distance. Father Condon gave an eloquent sermon, lasting for an hour and ten minutes—not an unusual length in those days, on the Bishop's life. The very next day Bishop Mullock laid the corner stone for the new Presentation Convent, an event which would have delighted the deceased Prelate.

At the end of woe, suddenly our eyes shall be opened,
and in clearness of light our sight shall be full.
- Mother Julian of Norwich

EPILOGUE

The year was 1855, the day the 9th of September. His heart overflowing with gratitude, Bishop Thomas Mullock waited patiently in the square before the Presentation Convent in the shadow of the Cathedral which he was about to consecrate. He thought of the joy it would have given Bishop Fleming to see this beautiful stone Convent which he had struggled so many years to provide for his beloved Sisters, and which it had been his own privilege to erect. He surveyed the Cathedral grounds now beautifully adorned. One hundred flags placed throughout the grounds waved in the breeze and adorned as well the triumphal arch which graced the entry. Over the cross on the centre of the facade was erected the Episcopal flag of Bishop Mullock. On the twin towers on either side of it billowed a Papal flag and the flag of St. Francis, each flag more than twelve feet square.

During the previous week, people from many parts of the Island had poured into St. John's for this historic occasion. On Friday and Saturday, the streets were literally thronged by what seemed to be the entire Catholic population of the Island, and on Sunday itself, everywhere one looked, crowds of people in their best attire were hastening to the Cathedral grounds with an air of eager expectation.

Now, as the ceremonies began, Bishop Mullock watched the colourful procession before him as it wound its ponderous way towards the massive Cathedral through the excited crowd of spectators. Immediately in front of the exultant prelate, now in his fifth year as Bishop of St. John's, walked a group of visiting church dignitaries: John Hughes, Archbishop of New York, Armand-Francois de Charbonnel, Bishop of Toronto, Thomas Connolly, Bishop of New Brunswick, and Colin MacKinnon, Bishop of Arichat [now the diocese of Antigonish], all robed in their richest liturgi-

cal vestments. They had come long distances to assist him in the consecration of his Cathedral, voyages which the recently-introduced steam-driven vessels had made possible. As he gazed at them, Bishop Mullock cast his mind back to their arrival a week before. A flag raised on Signal Hill just after nightfall had announced their appearance and, as the steamer came into sight, the whole town and outskirts seemed to be in motion, every space along their route to the Cathedral and every window and doorway crowded with enthusiastic spectators. After landing, the prelates mounted open carriages, with Bishop Mullock and Archbishop Hughes in the lead, and proceeded to the Cathedral through the cheering crowd which had never before seen such an assembly of episcopal dignitaries. The church bells rang out their triumphant peal, guns fired, bands blared. All this with the glow of the lighted candles in the windows of the buildings made the scene a fairyland of colour and sound. How wonderful it would have been, mused Bishop Mullock, if Bishop Fleming had still been alive to partake in this spectacle.

The Bishop brought his mind back to the present and to the lengthy procession of priests walking before him, twenty-one of whom were from the diocese of St. John's itself and many of whom had made great sacrifices to be present for the occasion. What a difference from the beginning of Bishop Fleming's episcopacy when he had found only three active priests to assist him in the whole Vicariate. Now, twenty years later, there were ten times as many, due, under God, to Bishop Fleming's burning desire to spread the Gospel of Christ.

The procession entered the Cathedral and viewed its rich interior adorned with beautiful flowers and glittering with lights on its nine altars and illuminating its walls. The throng rushed in after them, filling every inch of the church. The Cathedral presented a very different spectacle from the bare shell of a building which had sheltered the dying Bishop Fleming when, on a bleak January morning five years before, he had celebrated the first Mass there on a temporary altar amid masses of debris and a clutter of scaffolding, the flooring unfinished, the unplastered walls bare of adornment, the seating non-existent. It had taken Bishop Mullock five years of unceasing effort and over £8,000 to achieve this transformation. Bishop Fleming was hardly in his tomb before Bishop Mullock issued his first pastoral letter telling his people that it would be his "constant endeavor, with the Divine assistance, to carry out his [Bishop Fleming's] pious intentions." He listed these intentions as finishing of the Cathedral, building the Presentation Convent and erecting a residence for the Bishop and Clergy.

Now, five years later, all these objectives had been accomplished. The great main altar had been erected in 1851. The fine stone Presentation Convent and school from which the procession had started, the corner stone of which had been laid just a month after Bishop Fleming's death, had been completed in 1853, the episcopal residence in the following year. Now as the Bishop entered the Cathedral, he could survey the culmination of his efforts: a Church of grace and beauty, with a spacious sanctuary dominated by the high altar, which he once described as "the finest specimen of art in the whole western world." Above the altar was the large sculpture, representing the baptism of Christ by John the Baptist, created by the noted Irish sculptor Carew, and which had caused both him and Bishop Fleming so much trouble. On the altar also was a bronze crucifix which had previously adorned the high altar in the Cathedral of Ypres. Under the high altar lay "The Dead Christ," a life-size marble masterpiece of the great Irish sculptor Hogan. Around the walls were beautifully carved Stations of the Cross and other magnificent sculptures and paintings. Conspicuous among them, on either side of the nave, were the exceptionally beautiful high-reliefs by Hogan, one commemorating Bishop Scallan, and the other, Bishop Fleming. Even the ceiling had been beautifully embellished. As the procession moved up the cen-

tre aisle, the Cathedral resounded to the melodious pealing of the mighty bells which Bishop Mullock had ordered from Ireland, and to the soaring harmonies of the majestic organ which he had donated to the Cathedral and which he had described as "by far the finest ever erected on this side of the Atlantic, and among the greatest instruments of the world." To have an organist worthy of this instrument, he had persuaded his brother Thomas to come to Newfoundland to play it and to act as choir master.

As he viewed this magnificent public display of Catholicism, he must have reflected on the extraordinary change Bishop Fleming had wrought from the time when, as a youthful curate, he had been refused permission by Bishop Scallan to parade the school girls through the streets for their First Communion for fear that their Protestant neighbours might be offended. What a transformation had taken place in the morals of the people. Early in his episcopacy, Bishop Fleming had described them as "a wild and hardy race . . . reckless of every consequence when their passions are excited . . . little removed from a savage State." Yet, in 1842, an impartial observer, Sir Richard Bonnycastle, could observe: "It is universally admitted that there is no country in the civilized world where greater simplicity of manners or less crime exists, than in Newfoundland," and in 1850, Bishop Mullock could note in his diary that there was "not a prisoner in the whole island except for debt."

As the ceremonies of the Mass began, Bishop Mullock must have reflected also how fitting it was, in the light of Bishop Fleming's close relations with Rome, that the magnificent gilt chalice he would be using was a gift of Pope Pius IX,[1] who was also to suffer so much from the civil authorities.

The elaborate ceremonies, the culmination of Bishop Fleming's endeavours, lasted several hours. It was accompanied by sonorous music and the soaring polyphony of the Cathedral choir especially formed for the occasion. When the

Cathedral had been dedicated and the various altars conse-crated, the age-old solemn rite of High Pontifical Mass began. These lengthy preliminary ceremonies had so taxed Bishop Mullock's endurance that he asked Bishop Connolly to act as main celebrant. Bishop Mullock and the other Bishops sat on thrones on either side of the main altar while six priests assisted the celebrant in various capacities. The Benevolent Irish Society which, accompanied by a fine band, had walked in procession to the Cathedral, was given a spe-cial place of honour behind the main altar.

The high point of the Mass was the eloquent and lengthy sermon preached by Archbishop Hughes. He took as his theme: "Faith is the substance of the things to be hoped for." Elaborating on this topic, he pointed to the Cathedral itself as a supreme example of Christian faith. He claimed that, though it was erected by the contributions of the impover-ished fishermen of Newfoundland, it was a Cathedral of which any city in Europe or the world might be proud. For richness of material and perfection of design, its altar was unrivaled on the Western side of the Atlantic ocean. He reminded the congregation of the day on which Bishop Fleming had laid the corner stone of this edifice with but the blessing of heaven and the support of his impoverished peo-ple to rely upon. He suggested that if Bishop Fleming had lived to see this day, he would have considered it sufficient earthly recompense for all the toil, the anxieties, and care which he underwent, and to which he sacrificed his health, and perhaps his life. Archbishop Hughes brought out the greatness of Bishop Fleming's achievement in building the Cathedral when he asserted: "Considering the means by which it has been erected, this monument of Catholic faith has not been surpassed, nor perhaps equalled, by anything to be found in the annals of the Christian Church." The Mass concluded with a resounding Te Deum and then, as the con-gregation left the Cathedral, the clergy and the BIS processed back to the Presentation Convent where much appreciated refreshment awaited them.

That evening was the occasion for spectacular celebrations. As darkness set in, the sound of the Cathedral bell gave the signal for the Catholic houses to be illuminated. One by one, these homes were lit up by ingenious arrangements until every part of the city became flooded with light of all colours and descriptions. The Cathedral, the Convents, the Bishop's Palace, the Orphanage, the BIS building, the Triumphal Arch were all beautifully decorated. At various cross roads, tar barrels and torches blazed to add to the festivities. At about eight o'clock, the people all began to stream out of their homes and the streets became alive with a rejoicing multitude. Every man who owned a sealing gun brought it forth, countless skyrockets shot forth their streams of fire, all adding to the jubilation as did every available musical instrument. Eventually even the hardiest reveler became exhausted, all retired to their homes, basking in the common glory, and a peaceful quiet descended.

Nine months earlier, on December 8 of the previous year, Pope Pius IX had proclaimed the Dogma of the Immaculate Conception, and the Cathedral in St. John's was probably the first church in the world to be dedicated to her honour after that event. Fittingly therefore, the next three days after the consecration of the Cathedral were devoted to a solemn triduum in honour of the Immaculate Conception. Each morning, Solemn Pontifical Mass was celebrated, Benediction of the Blessed Sacrament imparted and a sermon preached. A different Prelate celebrated and another preached each day. At its conclusion, the BIS hosted a magnificent banquet accompanied by numerous speeches. Interestingly, Bishop Mullock, during his speech, referred particularly to Father Kieran Walsh, who had become Bishop Fleming's right-hand man in the construction of the Cathedral, and Father Vereker, who each summer, had gone to Labrador attending to the needs of the fishermen and collecting for the Cathedral.

On Wednesday, September 12, the Bishops paid a visit to Harbour Grace where they were again most enthusiastically welcomed. They returned to St. John's via Brigus and Portugal Cove. There, on Sunday morning, the final ceremonies marking the consecration took place. On the following Wednesday, the Prelates left for their various dioceses, the steamer on which they travelled being festooned with colourful flags. Their departure was attended, as had been their arrival, by the ringing of bells, the firing of sealing guns and the cheers of the appreciative people.

With their exodus, we ring down the curtain on the final act of the life of "that incendiary priest," Michael Anthony Fleming, O.F.M. His was a life of profound faith, of total devotion to the love and service of God and his neighbour. Like the Good Shepherd, he literally gave his life for the spiritual and material welfare of the people of his adopted country. His monument exists not only in the fabric of his majestic Cathedral but also in the countless numbers of people whom his self-sacrificing labours have enriched, materially, culturally, and, above all, spiritually, down to the present day.

Surely his life and achievements—as we have tried to show—are the stuff of greatness, and his heroic virtues bear the indelible mark of sanctity. No wonder, then, that the author considers him one of the great personalities of the nineteenth century, a man the calibre of whose life marks him as a fit candidate to be raised to the altars of the Church. That the book may make Bishop Fleming better known and may contribute to the advancement of his Cause is the author's ardent hope and fervent prayer.

PRINCIPAL CHARACTERS

Boulton, Judge Henry J. (1790-1870). Born in Kensington, England, he practiced law in Toronto where his father was Solicitor General for Upper Canada. In 1830, he became Attorney General but was dismissed in 1833 for resisting attempts at reform. He was then appointed Chief Justice of Newfoundland. He was dismissed from his position in 1838 and returned to Toronto to practice law. He was replaced by John G. Bourne.

Browne, Reverend Timothy, O.S.A. (1755-1855). Born in Wexford, Browne became an Augustinian priest and came to Newfoundland in 1812. His main parish was Ferryland. In 1841, he was dismissed from his post by Bishop Fleming. He returned to Ireland where he died in 1855.

Capaccini, Monsignor (later Cardinal) Francesco. (1784-1845). In 1828, he was appointed internuncio to the Low Countries (Belgium and Holland). From October 26, 1831, until the end of 1844 he was a member of the Secretariat of State. Made a Cardinal in 1844, he died the year following. He was considered one of the best papal diplomats of the nineteenth century.

Bishop of Carpasia. When a priest is ordained Bishop without a diocese to govern, he is assigned some diocese which is no longer in existence. Carpasia, once the diocese of Cyprus, was suppressed in 1222.

Carson, Doctor William. (1770-1843). Born in Kircudbright, Scotland, and obtained his MD at the University of Edinburgh. He arrived in St. John's in 1808 and served first as physician to the garrison and then as director of a general hospital which he helped to found. He continually urged the improvement of the social conditions, the development of agriculture and the establishment of representative government. He became a member of the Assembly in 1833 and Speaker of the House in 1837. A free thinker, he belonged to no religious organization.

Cochrane, Governor Thomas J. (1789-1872). Governor of Newfoundland from 1824 to 1834. He encouraged the development of road-building and agriculture in Newfoundland but opposed representative government. Very unpopular, he was recalled suddenly to England and his carriage was pelted with mud as he left. Bishop Fleming, in spite of several disagreements with him, considered him an outstanding governor.

Crowdy, James. (1794-1867). Born in Bristol, England, Crowdy came to Newfoundland in 1831, having been appointed Colonial Secretary to the Governor. He became Speaker of the amalgamated Council in 1841. In 1855, he resigned in opposition to the granting of Responsible Government and returned to England.

Fransoni, Cardinal Filippo. Prefect, i.e., was the head of the Vatican Department for the Propagation of the Faith (Propaganda Fide) while Bishop Fleming was bishop.

Glenelg, Lord Charles. (1778-1866). Secretary for the Colonies from April 18, 1835, to February 1839 under the Whig (i.e., Liberal) Government. He was friendly towards Bishop Fleming but his administration was considered too weak by the other members of his party and he was replaced.

Hogan, Timothy. One of the groups of dissident Catholics who opposed Bishop Fleming politically. He was a member of the Committee which ran the Catholic Church during the time of Bishop Scallan.

Kent, John. (1805-1872). Born in Waterford, John was a brother of James. He came to Newfoundland in 1820 as a clerk to his uncle, Patrick Morris. He became a commission agent, married Bishop Fleming's sister Johanna. His candidacy for the first Assembly caused a major split between Bishop Fleming and the establishment. From 1852 to 1861 he was Prime Minister of Newfoundland.

Kough, Patrick. (1786-1863). From Wexford, came to Newfoundland in 1804, established himself as a builder and was responsible for many prominent public buildings including St. Thomas Church, the Colonial Building, and the Presentation Convent in Cathedral Square. Like Hogan, he was a member of the Church Committee and opposed Bishop Fleming politically. He was elected to the first Assembly. He established a large farm which he called Ken Mount on the edge of the city.

Lambruschini, Cardinal Luigi. (1776-1854). Born in Italy, he became a member of the Barnabite Religious Order. In 1814, he joined the Roman Curia, became Nuncio to France in 1816. Created a Cardinal in 1831, Pope Gregory XVI appointed him Secretary of State in 1836 which position he held until the death of the Pontiff in 1846.

Little, Michael McLean. A shop-keeper in St. John's, he opposed Bishop Fleming politically and was ostracized by the Catholic community. However he was patronized by the merchants. Eventually, he re-established relations with the Bishop and the Church.

Palmerston, Lord Henry J. (1784-1865). An aristocrat, liberal in sentiment but entirely opposed to democracy. He was Secretary for Foreign Affairs from 1830 to 1841 and from 1846 to 1885. His independent actions created a climate of distrust between England and the rest of Europe. In 1855 he became Prime Minister of England which post he held, with one short exception, until his death.

Prescott, Governor Henry. (1783-1874). Born in England, he became a naval officer. Succeeded Cochrane as Governor on November 3, 1834. His resignation was accepted in 1841.

Presentation Sisters are a congregation of Religious women founded in 1775 by Nano Nagle for the education of poor girls. At the time of our story, they had already spread throughout Ireland. Newfoundland, where they established themselves in 1833, was their first foundation outside Ireland. They are now world-wide.

Propaganda Fide or the congregation for the propagation of the faith, will be met frequently in this narrative. It is the department of the Vatican which is responsible for overseeing the Church in missionary countries. Newfoundland fell under its jurisdiction until early in the twentieth century. Its head is called the Prefect. At the time of Bishop Fleming, the Prefect was Cardinal Fransoni and its secretary was Cardinal Mai.

Rice, Spring Hon. J. Succeeded Lord Stanley as Colonial Secretary in June 1834 but lasted only until December 20 of that year when he was succeeded by Lord Aberdeen.

Select Committee of the British Parliament. In 1839, much disturbed by the political unrest in Newfoundland, the British parliament set up a committee of its members to investigate the situation. This committee held hearings in the spring of 1841.

Stanley, Lord Edward (Earl of Derby). Secretary for Ireland in 1830, was moved to the Colonial Office in 1833 because of his antipathy for Daniel O'Connell. He had little sympathy for the Irish Cause but was otherwise liberal in his thinking, favoring the abolition of slavery. He resigned in 1834 in protest of the reduction of the property of the Irish Anglican Church. He was succeeded by Mr. Spring Rice.

Secretary of State for the Colonies:

1830 - 1833	Lord Goderich
March 1833 - June 1834	Lord John Stanley
June - December 1834	Hon. J. Spring Rice
December 1834 - April 1835	Lord Aberdeen
April 1835 - February 1839	Lord Glenelg (Hon. Charles Grant)
September 1839 - September 1841	Lord John Russell
September 1841 - 1846	Lord John Stanley
1846 - 1852	Lord Henry Grey

Stephen, Sir James. Undersecretary for the Colonies and was the grandfather of writer Virginia Woolf.

Winton, Henry. Born in England, Winton came to St. John's in 1818 and there founded the *Public Ledger* which became known for its independent stance on political issues and its often virulent editorial denunciation of opponents. He was the victim of the infamous "earcropping" incident described in this volume.

Wix, Archdeacon Edward. Head of the Anglican Church in Newfoundland where he arrived in 1820. He was strongly anti-Catholic. He made a sudden departure from the Island in October 1838 partly because of financial problems associated with the building of St. Thomas' Church.

FOOTNOTES

PROLOGUE

[1] There are three steps in the development of a bishopric. First a priest, called a Prefect Apostolic, is made responsible for the area, a Prefecture Apostolic, under the close supervision of Rome. Next the priest (or a successor) is ordained a bishop, the area becomes known as a Vicariate Apostolic, and the bishop acquires considerably more authority. Finally, the area is made a bishopric and the bishop acquires the normal authority over it.

CHAPTER 2

[1] At that time, to attend the services of another denomination was not just an act of brotherly solidarity as it is today, but rather a statement that one accepted the tenets of that denomination.

[2] However, he was careful to respect the secular nature of the Institute itself, and not to claim any control over it. It was the failure of Bishop Carfagnini in Harbour Grace to maintain the same respect which led to a great schism in that diocese, the excommunication of many excellent Catholics and, finally, the transfer of the Bishop from the Diocese.

[3] He was buried in the grounds of St. Mary's Chapel, but when the Cathedral of St. John the Baptist was completed, his remains were exhumed and interred in the vault under the high altar.

CHAPTER 3

[1] The six who came out first were Father Edward Troy, Father Pelagius Nowlan, Father Charles Dalton, O.S.F., Father Keilly (who shortly afterwards returned to Ireland), and two seminarians, Edward Murphy and Michael Berney, both of whom Bishop Fleming ordained on November 1, 1831.

CHAPTER 7

[1] It is worth noting that this expression was commonly claimed to have been hurled by Church authorities against those who opposed them, most notably Bishop Carfagnini in Harbour Grace. That those concerned actually used such expressions is very doubtful.

^{2} Perhaps he did not want the events to be related to the day in Manchester in 1819 when a vast crowd assembed on St. Peter's Fields to demand parliamentary reform. The magistrates panicked and ordered the soldiers to charge, killing dozens and seriously injuring hundreds more. The event was called *Peterloo* because it seemed to cancel the nation's debt of gratitude to Wellington who was Prime Minister at the time.

CHAPTER 10

^{1} "Ranger" in this connection was meant one who would provide sexual services.

^{2} The reference is to Judge Jeffreys (c.1648-1689) who, by his actions in the aftermath of Monmouth rebellion in England (1685) made his name "a synonym for a monster of bloodthirsty cruelty, blasphemous rage, and brutish intemperance," *Encyclopedia Britannica,* 1896, Vol. XIII, p.618.

CHAPTER 11

^{1} It is difficult to refrain from noting the poetic beauty of this description by one whom successive governors described as "vulgar and illiterate!"

CHAPTER 12

^{1} A *Relatio* is a formal report (usually presented every six years) submitted to Rome by a Bishop relating the affairs of his diocese since the last report.

CHAPTER 14

^{1} In law, a 'rout' is a group of three or more people assembled to perform an illegal act.

^{2} In a recent exhumation, his body was found to be incorrupt.

CHAPTER 15

^{1} The Catholic cemetery was located at the foot of Long's Hill. It was so crowded as to be a danger to public health. His plan to make a new cemetery was to cause him considerable difficulty with some of his flock in his later years.

[2] This land was bounded on the south by New Gower Street, and on the north by what is now LeMarchant Road.

[3] Every bishop, when making a formal visit to Rome, is expected to give a detailed report of his diocese, called a *Relatio annularis,* to the Holy Father. This report is then summarized by Vatican officials and forms the basis of the Pope's discussion with the bishop during his audience. It was the lack of this report which was the obstacle to Bishop Fleming's participation in the Easter services at St. Peter's.

CHAPTER 20

[1] This model was unfortunately destroyed when the Bishop's residence was burned in 1921.

[2] He was paying an annual stipend of £60 sterling for her support and that of another Sister, possibly his niece, Sister Justina Fleming.

CHAPTER 22

[1] John Dalton, (1819-1869) was born at Thurles, Tipperary. He was ordained in 1847, became assistant to his uncle at Harbour Grace, and in 1856 became the first bishop of the newly erected Harbour Grace diocese.

[2] On the eve of the elections, Father Walsh was peremptorily moved to Placentia, thus giving rise to the claim the Bishop had moved him for political reasons. But some years later, an incident there caused Father Walsh to be "banished" to Merasheen because of his conflict with the local agent. He seems to have been an independent, prickly character.

[3] Emphasis added.

[4] Mr. Tobin was the sole Catholic member of the Chamber of Commerce.

CHAPTER 23

[1] In Ireland, a National System of Education had been introduced in 1831 whose avowed aim, according to the Rev. Doctor Whatley, its main proponent, was to "Wean the Irish from the abuses of Popery."

CHAPTER 24

[1] These memorabilia included a parchment signed by all the priests present, a current newspaper, coins, etc.

CHAPTER 25

[1] He often confused the Mercy Sisters with the Sisters of Charity who had recently (1815) been founded in Ireland by M. Mary Aikenhead, and whose main apostolate was the care of the sick in hospitals.

CHAPTER 28

[1] Father Pelagius Nowlan was the Parish Priest of the nearby settlement, Little Placentia, now called Argentia.

CHAPTER 30

[1] There is considerable confusion over both the number and the names of those Brothers. It has usually been assumed that there were four: John Hanlon, Bernadine, Angelus and Francis Grace. But Bishop Fleming mentioned a fifth - a lay Brother, and on October 11, 1853, a notice in *The Patriot* stated: "On Monday last - Feast of St. Francis, the profession of Brother Felix O'Mara who came to Newfoundland in 1847 - Third Order Franciscan. Brother Francis Grace and Brother Foley of NF received the religious habit. The most likely scenario is that the original four from Ireland were Brothers Hanlon, Bernadine, Angelus and Felix, and that Brothers Francis Grace and Lahey joined them after their arrival in Newfoundland. Brother Lahey was probably the lay Brother in question since Brother Francis taught in the school.

CHAPTER 32

[1] It will be remembered that Johanna was married to John Kent, and was not in need.

[2] The *Dead Christ* is the artistic glory of the Cathedral and still rests under the High Altar. The monument to Bishop Scallan is on the left wall (as one faces the altar) opposite the monument to Bishop Fleming himself.

[3] It was customary to have a remembrance service a month after the death.

EPILOGUE

[1] This chalice is now on display in the Basilica museum.

BIBLIOGRAPHY

Anspach, Lewis Amadeus, *History of the Island of Newfoundland,* c.1818, Marchant, England.

BIS, Benevolent Irish Society, Minutes of Meetings, 1822-1979, MG 612, PANL.

Bonnycastle, Sir Richard Henry, Knt., *Newfoundland in 1842*, Vol. 2, London, 1842.

Bright, J. F., *History of England, Vol. 3, Constitutional Monarchy, 1689-1837,* London, 1880.

Byrne, Cyril J., ed., *Gentlemen Bishops and Faction Fighters,* St. John's, 1984.

Burke, Vincent P., "Education in Newfoundland, *The Book of Newfoundland,* Vol. 1, 1937.

Cahill, Thomas, *How the Irish Saved Civilization*, Doubleday, Toronto.

Carlyle, Thomas, "Jesuitism", *Latter-day Pamphlets, The Works of Thomas Carlyle, Vol. 6, ed. Peter Fenelon, Collier, NY, 1897.*

Centenary Volume, Benevolent Irish Society, St. John's, Newfoundland, 1906.

Chadwick, Owen, *Catholicism and History, The Opening of the Vatican Archives, The Herbert Hensley Henson Lectures in the University of Oxford, 1976,* Cambridge University Press, 1978.

Christian Brother, *Edmund Ignatius Rice and the Christian Brothers,* Benziger, NY, 1926.

Cormack, W. E., *A Journey Across the Island of Newfoundland in 1822,* ed. F.A. Bruton, centenary issue, Longman, Green, London, 1928.

Cornwallis, Lord, "Letter to the Duke of Portland, *The History of Ireland, Ancient and Modern,* Martin Haverty, Dublin, 1865.

Crowley, Walter, O.F.M., *The Story of the Church and Friary, Carrickbeg,* Carrickbeg, 1987.

Cusack, M.F., Sister. *Life of Daniel O'Connell,* Sadlier, NY, 1872.

D'Alberti Transcipts, 1748-52, 26 December, 1759.

Encyclopedia of Newfoundland and Labrador, 5 volumes, 1967.

FitzGerald, John E., *Conflict and Culture in Irish-Newfoundland Roman Catholicism, 1829-1850*, unpublished doctoral thesis, University of Ottawa, 1997.

Fitzhugh, Lynne D., *The Labradorians*, Breakwater Books, St. John's, NF, 1999.

Fleming, Most Rev. Michael A, O.F.M., various letters, reports & speeches, CBASJ.

Garvin, Tom, "Daniel O'Connell and the Making of Irish Political Culture."

Green, John Richard, *A Short History of the English People*, NY, 1893.

Gunn, Gertrude E., *The Political History of Newfoundland, 1832-1864*, Toronto, 1969.

Hanington, J. Brian, *Every Popish Person*, Halifax, 1984.

Hann, Emily, *Fractured Emerald: Ireland*, Doubleday, Garden City, NY, 1971.

Hatton, Joseph & Harvey, Rev. M., *Newfoundland, Its History, Its Present Condition, and Its Prospects in the Future*, Boston, 1883.

Haverty, Martin, *The History of Ireland, Ancient and Modern*, Dublin, 1865.

Hogan, Sister M. Williamina, *Pathways of Mercy, History of the Foundation of the Sisters of Mercy in Newfoundland 1842-1984*, Harry Cuff Publications, St. John's, 1986.

Howley, Most Rev. M. F., *Ecclesiastical History of Newfoundland*, Boston, 1888.

Johnson, Paul, *The Birth of the Modern World Society, 1815-1830*, Weidenfeld & Nicolson, Ltd, London, 1991.

Joyce, P. W., *A Concise History of Ireland from the Earliest Times to 1908*, Longmans, Green, London, 1920.

Jukes, J. B., *Excursions in and about Newfoundland during the years 1839 and 1840*, Murray, London, 1842.

Keneally, Thomas, *The Great Shame, and the Triumph of the Irish in the English-Speaking World*. Doubleday, NewYork, 1998.

Keogh, Dáire, *The French Disease*, Four Courts Press, Dublin.

Kurlansky, Mark, *Cod, a Biography of the Fish that Changed the World,* Toronto, 1984.

Lahey, Most Rev. Raymond,

————- , "The Building of a Cathedral, 1838-55", *The Basilica-Cathedral of St. John the Baptist, 1855-1980,* ed. Wallis, Walsh, et. al.

————-, *James Louis O'Donnell in Newfoundland,1784-1807,* Monogram, NF Historical Society. St. John's, 1984.

———— "Duffy, Father" *DCB,* Vol. VIII, 1851-1860, Univ. of Toronto Press, 1989.

———— "Fleming", *DCB,* Vol. VII, Univ. of Toronto Press, 1988.

Le Fanu, W. R., *Seventy Years of Irish Life,* 3rd edition, Arnold, London, 1894.

Maguire, Francis, M.P., *The Irish in America,* N.Y., 1868.

Minutes of Evidence taken before the SELECT COMMITTEE appointed to inquire into the State of the Colony of NEWFOUND-LAND, 1841, CBASJ.

Newmann, Sister M. Ignatia, R.S.M., Ed. *Letters of Catherine McAuley 1827-1841,* Helicon Press, Baltimore, 1969.

O'Callaghan, Sister M. Rosaria, P.B.V.M., *Flame of Love, a Biography of Nano Nagle, Foundress of the Presentation Order,* Aberdeen, South Dakota, 1961.

O'Flaherty, Patrick, *Old Newfoundland, a History to 1843,* Long Beach Press, St. John's, 1999.

O'Neill, Paul, *The Story of St. John's, Newfoundland, Vol. I, The Oldest City,* Toronto, 1975, *Vol. II, A Seaport Legend,* Toronto, 1976.

Ó Tuathaigh, Georóid, *Ireland before the Famine, 1798-1848,* Gill & MacMillan, Dublin, 1972.

Power, Dr. Patrick C. , *Carrick-on-Suir and its people,* Anna Livia Books, Carrick, 1976.

Prowse, D. W., Q.C., *A History of Newfoundland from the English, Colonial, and Foreign Records,* MacMillan, London, 1895.

Reeves, John, Esq., *History of the Government of the Island of Newfoundland,* London, 1793.

Rollman, Hans, *Journal of the Canadian Church Historical Society,* Vol. XXX, No. 1, April, 1988, "Additional letters."

Rowe, Frederick W., *A History of Newfoundland and Labrador,* McGraw-Hill, Toronto, 1980.

—————————-, *The Development of Education in Newfoundland,* Ryerson Press, Toronto, 1964.

Smallwood, Joseph R., *Doctor William Carson, The Great Newfoundland Reformer, His life, Letters and Speeches,* Newfoundland Book Publishers (1967) Ltd., St. John's, 1978.

Toque, Rev. Philip, A.M., *Newfoundland, as it was, and as it is in 1877,* Toronto, 1878.

"The Irish Famine", *New Oxford Review,* July-August, 1996. (author not given.)

Trevelyan, G. M., *History of England,* Longman, Green & Col Ltd., London, 1928.

Vanier, Jean, *Becoming Human,* Anansi Press, Toronto,1998.

Walsh, T. J., *Nano Nagle and the Presentation Sisters,* Gill & Co., Ltd., Dublin, 1959.

Wexford History and Society, ed. Kevin Whelan & W. Nolan, Geography Publications, Dublin, 1987.

Whateley, Jane, *Life and Correspondence of Richard Whately,* London, 1866, Vol. 2.

ARCHIVES

AASJ- Anglical Archives, St. John's, Newfoundland and Labrador.

APF - Archives of Propaganda Fide, Rome.

CNS - Centre for Newfoundland Studies, Memorial University, St. John's, Newfoundland and Labrador.

CBASJ - Christian Brothers Archives, St. John's, Newfoundland and Labrador.

EB - Encyclopaedia Britannica, 1988.

ENC - Encyclopedia of Newfoundland of Labrador, St. John's, 1988, various articles.

FLK - Franciscan Library, Killiney, Ireland.

PANL - Provincial Archives of Newfoundland and Labrador.

RCASJ - Roman Catholic Archives, St. John's, Newfoundland and Labrador.